MYTH AND MEMORY IN THE MEDITERRANEAN

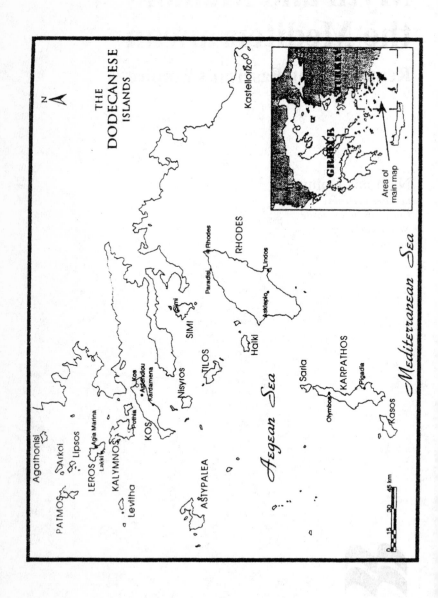

Myth and Memory in the Mediterranean

Remembering Fascism's Empire

Nicholas Doumanis
Lecturer in History
University of Newcastle
New South Wales
Australia

First published in Great Britain 1997 by
MACMILLAN PRESS LTD
Houndmills, Basingstoke, Hampshire RG21 6XS and London
Companies and representatives throughout the world

A catalogue record for this book is available from the British Library.

ISBN 0–333–68232–7

First published in the United States of America 1997 by
ST. MARTIN'S PRESS, INC.,
Scholarly and Reference Division,
175 Fifth Avenue, New York, N.Y. 10010

ISBN 0–312–17243–5

Library of Congress Cataloging-in-Publication Data
Doumanis, Nicholas, 1964–
Myth and memory in the Mediterranean : remembering fascism's
empire / Nicholas Doumanis.
p.   cm.
Includes bibliographical references and index.
ISBN 0–312–17243–5 (cloth)
1. Italians—Greece—Dōdekanēsos—History—20th century.
2. Fascism—Greece—Dōdekanēsos.   3. Dōdekanēsos (Greece)—History.
4. Italy—Politics and government—1922–1945.   5. World War,
1939–1945—Campaigns—Greece—Dōdekanēsos.   I. Title.
DF901.D6D68   1997
325'.3145'094958709041—dc20   96–44829
                                                            CIP

This book is printed on paper suitable for recycling and made from fully managed and
sustained forest sources.

10   9   8   7   6   5   4   3   2   1
06   05   04   03   02   01   00   99   98   97

Printed in Great Britain by
The Ipswich Book Company Ltd
Ipswich, Suffolk

Contents

Acknowledgements

Luisa Passerini, Richard Bosworth, Max Harcourt and Michael Herzfeld encouraged me to pursue this project during its various stages, and each, in different ways, has been an enormous source of inspiration. Denis Mack Smith generously offered material from his vast personal library, while Robert Aldrich, Richard Janus, Frank Alafaci and Eleni Amvrazi kindly gave me the benefit of their expertise. Much was gained from lively and uncensored discussions in the staffroom of the School of History at the University of New South Wales. I am particularly indebted to Martyn Lyons, an ideal PhD supervisor, a stern but kindly critic, who read every page. So too did fellow *macchiato* drinkers Damien McCoy and Milan Voykovic, and Mark Rolfe, an *espresso* drinker and 'non-historian'. None of them are responsible for any errors. Nick Pappas, David Sutton, the late Bill Edmonds, the 'Locality' mafia, 'the Globalists', the people of Caffè Ciao, and my colleagues at the University of Newcastle also made the whole experience of writing this book a happy one. I should also register my gratitude to the Faculty of Arts and Social Sciences at the University of New South Wales for a travel grant and a Commonwealth Postgraduate Scholarship.

All my interviewees deserve special thanks, as do the Koulouras, Kougioumzoglou, Lambros, Tsounias, Kastrounis and Paschalis families for the hospitality. The same goes for uncle Manolis, A. S. Korakis, I. Alahiotis, friends in Asfendiou and the Fikos Bar, T. Diakomanolis, V. Hatsivasiliou, M. Mastroyannis, T. Sapounaki of the Anagnostirion, M. Koulianos, M. Isihos, and Nick and Alex Procopiadis. I must also add Gary Messider of Watford, all the Duguids, Tony and Natalie Wrench of Thane, Mark and Cedric of Dartmouth Park, and Philip O'Mahony of Cork and David Jones.

I met Helen when this project began, and in the end she married me regardless. Her patience and love could never be adequately repaid. Thanks also to Sylvia, Adam, Chloe, Danise, Aphro, Chris, Kelly and Giagiá, and to the Tirekidis, Kallias and Dimitriadis families. Finally, I could not have even contemplated embarking on this project without counting on the loving support of my parents. This book is dedicated to them.

List of Abbreviations

AAI   *Annuario dell'Africa Italiana ed Isole dell'Egeo*

AD   *Avgí Dodekanisakí*

AKPL   *Anagnostirion* (Kalymnian Public Library)

APO   Apostolou Mitropolitou Rodou, *Apomnimonévmata, ítoi chronografikí istoría tis Ekklhsiastikís Eparchías Ródou epí Italo-Germano-Agglokratías*, Vol. A (Athens, 1947).

CIP   Apostolou Mitropolitou Karpathou-Kasou, *Tó chronikón tis Italokratías tis Ródou* (Athens, 1973)

DHA   Dodecanesian Historical Archive (Rhodes)

DI   *I Dodekanisiakí*

MR   *Il Messaggero Di Rodi*

OT   Oral Testimony

NOTE ON GREEK TRANSLATIONS AND TRANSLITERATIONS

In transliterating Greek words into English, I have followed the example set by many historians of ancient Greece by avoiding Latin translations of place names. Thus 'Kos' instead of 'Cos'. Better known place names like 'Rhodes' have been retained.

I have not always used standard demotic Greek in citing the interviews I transcribed. As an alternative, I have employed spelling which accords with local idioms, thus 'min kous' instead of 'min akoús', and 'prámata' instead of 'prágmata'.

Glossary

attendismo	waiting for the occupiers to leave, and remaining unobtrusive in the interim
árchontes	notables, community leaders
campanilismo	parochial loyalty
carabiniere [-i]	Italian policeman
çiflik	Ottoman feudal estate
demarchía [-íes]	local government [town]
demogerontía [-íes]	council of elders
finanza (Guardia di Finanza)	inspectors of customs and excise
katohí [-és]	foreign occupation
koinotitá [ités]	local government [village]
laós	'the people'
Mahtoú	colloquial name for Dodecanesian privileges in the Ottoman imperial system
maresciallo	warrant officer
mísos	hatred
morphoménos [-oi]	an educated person, or a 'learned-one'
patrída	fatherland
podestà	appointed mayors
oréa prámata	beautiful things

Introduction

The archipelago of Aegean islands known as the Dodecanese has played a passive, but significant role in the history of the Mediterranean in the early twentieth century. It has been used as a pawn in Great Power diplomacy, cherished as a jewel in Italy's imperial crown, and coveted by an expansionist modern Greek state. Occupied in turn by the Ottomans, Italians, Germans and the British, it remains a privileged site for the study of relations between occupiers and the occupied. This study will focus on the nature of such relations during the Italian Occupation, which began in 1912 and ended during the Second World War (1943).

The particular task I have undertaken is to analyse the Italian Occupation of the Dodecanese as experienced by the occupied, and to account for the different ways in which these indigenous experiences have been represented in contemporary social discourses. Popular memory holds a central place in this study, especially as this rich historical source can evoke the kinds of conditions and choices faced by ordinary people under foreign rule. Some scholars have asserted that 'consent' and 'dissent' do not adequately account for the range of attitudes and practices associated with life under foreign domination or domestic political oppression, yet such univocal categories have dominated historiography.[1] Dodecanesian oral tradition on the Italian period conveys the complexities which characterise occupier–occupied relations, including the ways in which these relations were played out in their quotidian contexts. This is not a monograph on the Dodecanese in international politics, for which some work has been done, nor is it an analysis of colonial administration in the Dodecanese, which is in need of scholarly attention.[2] Rather, this is an appraisal of everyday life under foreign rule, an examination of the attitudes and life strategies of ordinary people during three decades of political oppression.

This is also a case study of how ordinary people responded to, interpreted and remembered the various policies and measures implemented by their overlords. Attention will be given to those areas of Dodecanesian culture and *mentalités* which had implications for issues of wider significance, such as Greek nationalism and Italian colonialism. The Dodecanese formed a very small part of a short-lived Italian empire, but developments among the islands tell us much

1

about the peculiarities of Italian colonialism in general. The Second
World War completely exposed Italy's weaknesses on the
international stage, as revealed by the dominance of her Axis
partner, and by the rapid collapse of her colonial empire, which had
included Ethiopia, Eritrea, southern Somalia and Libya. Most
students of Italian colonialism have largely been interested in
showing how the empire reflected Italy's weaknesses as a world
power, or have used the colonies to list the corruption and
brutalities of Fascism. However, Dodecanesians tend to remember
Italian domination in more variegated terms, and characterise the
occupation in ways which bear a limited resemblance to portraits
given by historians. The intention here is to account for this
discrepancy, and to outline the possible implications of popular
memory for the historiography on Italian colonialism.

Indeed, one of the most intriguing features of contemporary
Dodecanesian life is the highly ambiguous reputation of their former
Italian occupiers in popular memory. When I visited the islands in
1990 to conduct my research nearly fifty years had elapsed since the
end of Italian control, but memories of the occupation remained fresh
in peoples' minds. The islanders continued to feel bitter about certain
abuses committed by the occupiers, but more often they spoke of their
Italian legacy in appreciative terms, and affectionately referred to
ordinary Italians as people who were very much like themselves, as
'una faccia, una razza'.

The implications of this ambiguity, however, have never been
appreciated by Greek historians, whose portraits of the Italian
Occupation have been guided by strict patriotic principles. As the
great majority of the Dodecanese islanders were ethnically Greek,
historians and other patriotically-minded Greeks have always
regarded the Italian Occupation as a moral injustice, and have
insisted that the occupation was an oppressive experience for which
nothing redeemable could be said. Writing the history of the period
has therefore involved recounting Italian misdeeds, both alleged and
real. Thus the occupiers were said to have gaoled thousands of
islanders, taken their land, closed their schools, wilfully starved
them, and threatened their language and religion. The following
excerpt from a recent publication is a typical example of how Italian
rule has been portrayed:

It was an autocratic regime, with laws to destroy the local culture,
and an administrative system designed for the annihilation of the

islanders. As appointed governors, trusted exponents of Fascist ideas, and who would try to completely Italianise the islanders, Mario Lago and Cesare Maria de Vecchi crushed the economy, the Church and Greek education, and debased the public and local institutions.[3]

While Greek historians have insisted on the severity and bleakness of the occupation, they have been equally concerned with highlighting manifestations of local resistance, largely in order to offset suspicions that locals may have been demoralised and cowed by their foreign adversary. The islanders, historians claim, were inspired by an undying love for 'Mother Greece' (Mitéra Ellás), and despite threats of violent retaliation, their opposition to Italian rule was loud and vigorous. The islanders voted against Italian rule in plebiscites, sent petitions to the Great Powers, and occasionally held open protests. For Greek historians, oppression and resistance are the only themes worth considering, and the Italian Occupation must be remembered as a test of the resilience of the Greek people, their patriotism and moral worth.

Writers of fiction, poetry and other genres have also portrayed Italian rule in terms of foreign oppression and patriotic resistance, and this undifferentiated understanding of the occupation, which has monopolised the print media, has never really been challenged by any writer. Greek nationalism has set the rules for what can be written about the past, and because of the moral weight of nationalism in contemporary Dodecanesian life, local historians have dutifully avoided critical analysis and debate which might undermine the nationalist line. Despite the overwhelming dominance of Greek nationalism, however, other social discourses on the past do exist, though not in printed form. Extensive interviews with ordinary Dodecanesians regarding the Italian Occupation revealed powerful 'counter-memories' which contradicted the official line and opened many new lines of investigation. Many locals described the occupation as a time of progress and development, when there was plenty of work and the cost of living was low, while others characterised the period as an uneventful and quiet time in their lives, a much welcomed respite. Individual Italians were generally described as civilised people, exemplars of manners, courtesy and European culture. Overall, ordinary Dodecanesians remembered life under Italian rule in much more appreciative terms than Greek writers, which raises an important question: why do Dodecanesian oral sources provide us with such a radically different picture? How does one account for the distance between the written and oral traditions?

My interest in this project began when I noted the discrepancies between these two traditions, and accounting for these differences has given me a deeper appreciation of the social function of history. Following the lead set by several oral historians and the ever growing number of students of memory, I have been less interested in categorising the oral and written sources according to their 'factual' reliability, and found it more fruitful to present them as two different ways of seeing the past. As Luisa Passerini has suggested, the historian has much to gain by turning 'two apparently static and opposed positions...(into) an exchange and two-way flow between them'.[4] Comparisons expose the political and social functions of each tradition, and by the same token, reveal some of the issues and themes on which each tradition is silent. As Passerini's own studies on the Turin working class under Fascism have shown, the juxtaposition of oral tradition and historiography on the Fascist period has revealed the extent to which historians have ignored the history of culture and *mentalités*, and how historiography has failed to recognise the possibility of cultural resistance to Fascist rule. As a consequence, Passerini has provided a compelling case for exploring the cultural factors influencing relations between the dominant and the dominated.[5]

Oral sources are employed in this study in order to understand how Italian colonialism was experienced by the occupied, and to appreciate the complexities which are usually associated with occupier–occupied relations. While Greek historians have been unable to provide a balanced portrait of the occupation because of their patriotic beliefs, the oral sources have been much less inhibited. While the oral sources were certainly no less subjective than their written counterparts, they perform a function in everyday life which is less politically prescribed.

ITALIAN COLONIALISM 'FROM BELOW': SOME IMPLICATIONS

As mentioned earlier, I intend to show how the view 'from below' has considerable implications for the historiography of the Italian Dodecanese and Italian Colonialism in general. In some ways the Dodecanese was a unique part of Italy's colonial empire. The islands enjoyed a favoured status in the empire, officially regarded as a 'possession' rather than a 'colony'.[6] The islanders were also spared the violence and destruction which came with the conquest and brutal subjugation of Libya or Ethiopia. There were also many similarities. As in the African colonies, the Dodecanese was subjected to Italian colonisation, massive development projects, and ill-conceived cultural engineering programmes. The Italians built modern towns, constructed roads and buildings, opened factories and plantations, and introduced modern technology such as automobiles and aircraft. The occupiers sought to transform the islands into monuments of Italian modernity in order to show the world how Italy was as worthy of ruling other peoples as Britain and France. Consequently, the impact of Italian colonialism on the Dodecanese was as profound as it was in East Africa and Libya.

The imperative to build and invest in the colonies reflected the empire's enormous symbolic importance in Italian public life, yet the empire has not loomed large in the writings of contemporary historians. Angelo Del Boca has produced a series of important works on Italian colonial history, but the company he keeps in this field remains quite small.[7] Textbook accounts of modern Italy tend to give the colonies a fleeting mention, while works that afford greater space to the colonies normally do so in order to illustrate the crimes and follies of the Fascists in power. This trend is exemplified by Denis Mack Smith's *Mussolini's Roman Empire*, which presents the empire as a paradigm of Fascist corruption, incompetence and barbarity, and while Mack Smith's approach might be viewed as idiosyncratic, most Anglo-American scholars have written of the empire in similar terms.[8] As Haile Larebo has noted, this highly critical literature has done much to vanquish popularly held Italian myths that the Italians were uniquely humane colonisers, but as Larebo further points out, in emphasising Italian crimes and follies, scholars have restricted the terms according to which the colonial experience can be studied.[9] All colonial empires left an appalling record of atrocities and sustained exploitation, yet Italian colonialism, due in part to the Fascist connection, has somehow been singled out as uniquely wicked. Among other things, a more differentiated analysis of Italy's colonial record would no doubt offer fresh insight into the social and cultural history of Italians and their African subjects, particularly in the area of popular identities and mentalities. The colonial regime in Ethiopia sought to impose racial segregation in order to uphold the racial supremacy of the colonisers, but authorities found it difficult to break down the sense of 'familiarità' which had developed among

Italians and Ethiopians.[10] Surely a close examination of attitudes among ordinary Italians in East Africa would shed light on popular conceptions of ethnicity and Italian identity, and what empire meant at this social level. Oral sources point us in that direction.[11]

While the islanders always regarded the Italian presence as illegitimate, they would remember the occupation as a mixture of things 'good and bad', and interviewees often stated that they would cover both good and bad features (ta kalá ke ta kaká). The islanders resented many aspects of Italian rule, such as the forced closure of Greek schools in the late 1930s, but they have also remembered the occupation as a time of high employment, civic order and economic development. They claimed they disliked some Italians, especially the Fascists, but they regarded most Italians as 'good people' (kalí ánthropi), whom they stereotyped as good-natured, warm and humane. They also employed catchphrases which simply threatened official discourse on Italian rule, as interviewees and others would often claim that under the Italians they 'lived well' (pernoúsame kalá). I am less concerned about the veracity of local myths than I am about the reasons *why* the islanders held such views. Whilst popular memory is a highly subjective source which must be used critically, it is a source which obliges the historian to look afresh at standard historical themes and issues, to question the credibility of established discourses, and explore exciting, though neglected, dimensions of social history.

This has certainly been shown by Luisa Passerini's path-breaking *Fascism in Popular Memory*, which provides compelling reasons for reappraising many standard ideas about Fascist Italy. Practitioners of the 'history of everyday life' approach (*Alltagsgeschichte*) in Germany have had an indelible impact in such highly contentious and mainstream debates as the relationship between German society and the Nazi regime.[12] As Geoff Eley puts it, scholars have tried to draw 'the elusive connection between the political and cultural realms', and to maintain that it is in the context of everyday life, such as the family, on the factory floor, and in the neighbourhood, 'where the possibilities for either are ultimately made'.[13] One could also say that 'grass roots' history can contribute to themes other than 'conformity or resistance'. Thus islander memories of Italian rule say much about the symbolic significance of 'Europe' and conceptions of modernity in Greek life, for the occupation prompted locals to question their own identity, and ask if they, like the Italians, were 'Europeans'. As with other cultures on the continent's periphery, the Greeks have held an ambivalent attitude towards 'Europe', and have questioned their propinquity to a 'modern', 'progressive' West, and their 'backward', 'oriental' or Ottoman legacy.[14] The oral sources show that the Italians were considered both familiar and 'other'. The islanders remembered the Italians as people very similar to themselves in terms of culture and mental outlook ('una faccia, una razza'), yet they would also concede that the occupiers were more 'advanced' than themselves, which seemed to be confirmed by innovations in, among other things, town planning, technology and administration. In many ways, Italian 'civilisation' seemed to represent the way forward, a model which the Greeks of the Dodecanese regarded as worthy of emulation. Attitudes towards the occupiers reflected considerably upon Dodecanesian self-perceptions, their place in the world, and their thoughts about their own future directions.

Oral sources therefore provide useful insights into the social and cultural history of modern Greece, but until very recent times most Greek scholars did not consider social and cultural themes as 'serious' history.[15] The social and cultural history of modern Greece is very much in its infancy, which means that new researchers will need to draw inspiration from historiography and debates outsides of Greece. Fortunately, Greece has attracted an able stream of ethnographers, particularly cultural anthropologists whose interests have frequently intersected with those of social and cultural historians. Among these interests are perceptions of gender, civic culture, community, progress, social memory, questions of identity, the symbolic meanings of language and practices, and ethnicity and nationalism.[16]

ORAL SOURCES

There are, of course, significant problems in analysing popular memory in a society scattered over a large archipelago. These include the selection of interviewees and how far the sample is representative of Dodecanesian society; securing 'inside' information and perspectives, which are not always granted to 'outsiders'; and the factual reliability of things remembered over forty years after the occupation.

This study is based on the recorded interviews of 46 Dodecanesians. Preference was given to candidates who lived through the height of the occupation (1923 to 1943), hence most interviewees were born in the first two decades of this century. As far as possible I sought to interview people from many different islands, though I did concentrate on five of the Dodecanese group; Kastellorizo, Kos, Kalymnos, Rhodes and Leros. Admittedly, this choice was partly determined by the fact that personal connections on these islands made it easier to find willing and suitable interviewees.[17] Another reason was that Italian economic development policies and military interests were focused on Rhodes, Kos and Leros, and this inevitably influenced the way in which the Italians were remembered. Kalymnos and Kastellorizo were representative of the rest, where the Italians conducted far fewer public works programmes and where locals consequently felt neglected. It was among these islands that the occupiers faced their most vociferous popular opposition.

Whilst 46 people from seven islands are hardly representative of the Dodecanese, their descriptions of the Italian period showed a significant convergence of views. Despite the distances between the islands, and the differing impact of Italian rule on each, most Dodecanesians have characterised the occupation in very similar terms. The people I interviewed drew on a common repository of images and stereotypes, which they invoked by employing similar words and phrases. Interviewees were encouraged to relate their individual experiences of the occupation, and to offer their personal opinions on various themes, but their testimonies showed the significant extent to which memory was socially informed. Regardless of whether interviews were conducted in private sessions or in public spaces, such as in cafés, where other patrons assisted in answering my questions, the result was the same; the islanders would convey their impressions of the Italian period through a commonly held oral tradition. The recurrence of images and ideas in the oral testimonies is reminiscent of Durkheim's notion of collective representations reflecting a 'composite of individual minds which are in perpetual interaction through the interchange of symbols'.[18] Durkheim's rather provisional ideas on *l'esprit collectif* were used by Passerini in her work, where she showed how oral autobiographies of Torinese workers showed a predominance of beliefs and representations which were of a social, rather than individual, character.[19]

While Dodecanesian oral tradition provides a very different picture of the Italian Occupation from that given by Greek writers, the recollections of some interviewees did accord quite closely with the Greek historiography. What distinguished this group from the rest was their social status and educational backgrounds. Interviewees with a high level of literacy and extensive schooling had been thoroughly socialised in nationalist ideology, and consciously ascribed to official readings of Greek history. However, as I was primarily interested in the oral tradition, I consciously sought interviewees who were illiterate or semi-literate, and who were therefore less 'nationalised'. Unlike educated interviewees, whose recollections of the period were refashioned by patriotic concerns like 'Fascist' oppression and patriotic resistance, and whose testimonies were full of nationalistic catchphrases and allusions, illiterate and semi-literate interviewees selected different themes and even ascribed to a different chronology.

Oral historians have been encouraged to take a reflexive approach to their subject matter, and as mentioned earlier, this includes a recognition of the 'otherness' of interviewees. To be sure, interviewees can also regard the oral historian as 'other', and often employ evasive techniques to resist unwelcome questions. After all, social memory is fundamental to any group identity, and certain memories are not told to outsiders because they might reflect adversely on the group's image. The difficulty in extracting 'inside' information is a problem which most anthropologists and oral historians have to face. Fortunately, I began this project with a distinct advantage in that I was born into an expatriate Dodecanesian family in Sydney, and grew up listening to family and other elderly Dodecanesian expatriates talking about the peculiarities of Italian rule. Thus I was privy to 'inside' information and viewpoints well before I took upon the threatening status of prying interviewer. I had been long acquainted with the oral tradition before I had ever read about the occupation, and hence I was better placed to identify subject matter on which interviewees were silent during the course of research. This is especially true of the theme of intermarriage during the occupation. Marriages between Greek women and Italian men were not uncommon, but interviewees avoided the subject because they feared people outside the Dodecanese might interpret intermarriage as a form of collaboration, or as a negative reflection on the virtue of local women. As I had already been familiar with the subject, I could note their silence and try to question them more forcefully on the topic.

My background, however, did not automatically make me an 'insider', and I was still required to learn techniques for getting 'inside' information. Some interviewees were not completely sure that I was not from the taxation department, and some remembered times when loose talk meant the loss of one's livelihood. I met some male interviewees by simply waiting in village cafés and by opening conversations with other patrons, but more often I was referred to them by their friends, family members or local officials. Of the 46 interviewed, I had only known six personally, yet even they were reticent on a number of subjects, as they knew that whatever they related to me could be read by outsiders. For example, few would divulge the names of collaborators, and would only do so if these people were dead. Thus my position as either 'insider' or 'outsider' was contingent on many factors, though most of the time I found myself challenged by the difficulties faced by researchers in the latter category.

Another problem associated with using social memory as an historical source is the fact that memory is not immutable. As James Fentress and Chris Wickham point out, memory, unlike texts, evolves in thought and speech through time.[20] If memories are usually invoked in order to make sense of the present, this inevitably means that memories are re-negotiated and distorted. In the Dodecanese, people often reflect upon the incompetence of the Greek bureaucracy and apparent 'disorder' in contemporary Greek life by invoking memories of Italian administrative practices and policing, which supposedly operated in an ideal fashion. Their nostalgic reminiscences are employed to impart critical commentaries on present circumstances, which raises questions about how far their memories have been distorted. While some interviewees were prone to attributing too much credit to the Italians, one of the purposes of this book is to show how Dodecanesian nostalgia for Italian rule was mainly acquired from experience, from impressions gained during the occupation period itself. Besides, ten of the people interviewed for this project had been living in Sydney since the mid-1950s, and conditions in postwar Australian society would hardly have fostered any nostalgia for Italian administration and development. These interviewees did speak of many aspects of Italian rule in glowing terms, but did so without using these memories to criticise contemporary Australia.

The interviewees presented their oral version of the Italian period as objective knowledge. Their claim that the Italians were well mannered and excellent administrators was regarded as 'true', and most Dodecanesians would accept these as well known 'facts'. As Ronald Fraser claimed in his oral history of the Spanish Civil War, we cannot always know what really happened, but his interviewees gave him their 'truth' on the matter. 'And what people thought', he adds,

'– or what they thought they thought... constitutes an historical fact.'[21] Wherever possible, I have tried to verify such facts with other primary and secondary sources. Greek sources, especially newspapers, provided information for a general picture of objective conditions of the Italian Occupation, as did Italian language source material, especially the *Messaggero di Rodi*, the colonial regime's mouthpiece. Italian journals like *Critica Fascista* and *Orientale* are important sources for official views on Italy's place in the world, and of the 'funzione' of the Dodecanese in her imperial destiny. Excellent publications like the *Rassegna Economica Coloniale* provided statistical information on agricultural yields, trade and finance. These were supplemented by records from the Greek Church archives in Kos, which were useful for such matters as inter-marriage and education. The Dodecanesian Historical Archives in Rhodes Town, where most of the colonial regime's records are kept, covered the most comprehensive range of topics. Unfortunately, archivists had only just started to catalogue the Italian collection, and only a small fraction of the material was available for inspection.

HISTORY, PATRIOTISM AND GREECE

This book is concerned with establishing the importance of counter-memories when representing the past. It is therefore essential to understand the basis of officially acceptable memory, and recognise its merits and many drawbacks. Locally produced literature is an excellent source for nationalist mentalities, for while academic historians in Greece have, to some degree, absorbed international historiographical trends, local historians and other writers have held firm to essentialist ideas about the nature of history and its function. To be sure, these amateur writers have produced a modest collection of secondary sources which deal with such things as population figures, trade, religious matters and local government affairs, and which are crucial for constructing a picture of objective conditions.[22] But their representations of Italian rule are compromised by patriotic assumptions about the role of history, assumptions which enjoy common currency in contemporary Greek society.

Official conceptions of Greek identity are underpinned by an undisputed belief in the direct lineage between the Greeks of today and those of antiquity. This assumed 'blood' link has formed the basis of Greek chauvinism and claims to being an exceptional people. As

Greek school textbooks have long claimed, the ancient Greeks invented the arts and sciences, and therefore 'gave light' (dósame fos) to an uncivilised world. They 'created' Western Civilisation and invented Europe. Furthermore, modern Greeks of all social levels are aware to some degree that their ancestors were empire builders, significant actors on the world stage.[23] History has therefore taught every child that Greeks are an exceptionally gifted 'race', that they have enterprise, inventiveness, guile and boldness in their blood. The obvious problem with this widely accepted myth is accounting for Greece's modest place in the world today: why, unlike their ancient forebears, are modern Greeks not 'great'? How could the sons of Pericles and Alexander have been subjected to the domination of 'backward' Turks for so long? While modern Greeks have proved unable to emulate the glorious achievements of Periclean Athens, they have compensated by jealously guarding their historical heritage. The function of this heritage has been to remind modern Greeks of what they are supposed to be capable, and who they 'really' are. This partly explains why the current dispute over the name 'Macedonia' has inspired such heated emotions. The Greeks often complain that foreigners, especially western scholars, always try to 'take their history away' from them (théloune na paroun tin istoría mas), which is tantamount to stealing their identity. Along with a wealth of archaeological remains and relics, memory of a glorious antiquity is all that is left of Greek claims to exceptionalism.

The task of Greek historians has been to reaffirm the connection between Greeks ancient and modern. This role has also been performed by folklorists. In order to highlight the 'Greekness' of the peasantry, who might otherwise be construed as 'backward' and 'oriental', folklorists have tried to prove that many peasant customs and practices have an ancient pedigree.[24] The function of local history is similar. Its purpose has been to show how each locality has had a continuous history stretching back to ancient times, and how each has contributed to Greece's glorious heritage. Parochial chauvinism has served to foster this enterprise, hence such futile disputes as to whether the ancient poet Philitas was Koan or Kalymnian.[25]

The tendency of historians to write the history of the Italian Dodecanese only in terms of 'oppression' and 'resistance' is closely related to nationalist concerns. While the ancient Greeks 'created' Western Civilisation and forged empires, later Greeks seemed to spend most of their time fighting against, or living under, foreign domination. Thus historians assume that the greatness of the

Greeks, their ability to 'give light to the world', had been suppressed by a long line of foreign adversaries, from Darius's Persians to the Ottoman Turks. That Greece emerged from the War of Independence in a very 'backward' condition has been blamed on the 'barbarous' Turks, who for almost four hundred years (1453–1821) did everything they could to destroy Hellenism and impose their own 'regressive' culture. Officially prescribed textbooks have characterised the Ottoman period in the following manner; the Turks suppressed Greek education, imposed punitive taxation, instituted a cruel levy on first-born males, and committed occasional massacres to quench Turkish blood-lust. In response, the Greek people stoutly resisted by taking to the mountains and becoming warrior bandits, and saved their language and culture by sending their children to secret evening classes.[26] The Turks have therefore served as a convenient scapegoat for explaining Greece's 'backwardness' in modern times, while the emphasis on 'oppression' and 'resistance' have reflected her vulnerability in the face of, and her refusal to submit to, more powerful adversaries.

Such has been the symbolic power of 'four-hundred years' of Turkish domination that Greek historians have written of the Italian Dodecanese in almost identical terms (and many interviewees felt obliged to describe the Italians as 'Turks', at least initially). By concentrating on the themes of oppression and resistance, which were the hallmarks of the 'four-hundred years', historians have made the Italian Occupation a credible addition to the canons of Greece's national history, and a period from which patriotic lessons could be taken. Patriotic imperatives have ensured that the occupation could not be written in any other way. The oral sources are employed in this study to thoroughly revise the standard picture, to show how focusing on oppression and resistance is a wholly inadequate way to understand the nature of a foreign occupation. Existing historiography has almost nothing to say on the nature and development of nationalist consciousness, the meanings of 'resistance' and 'collaboration', and the extent to which the occupation tested popular beliefs and values. To a significant degree, these deficiencies in nationalist historiography can be vastly improved through closer reference to oral tradition.

1 The Dodecanese in 1912: The Physical, Social and Historical Setting

Communities select and maintain particular memories in order to construct and reaffirm collective self-images.[1] For the Greeks of the Dodecanese, memories of the Italian Occupation have been particularly important in upholding their unique identity within contemporary Greece. This chapter will deal with features of the physical, social and historical environment which influenced the nature of conceptions of local identity, and how background factors also shaped the ways in which the islanders remembered the Italian period. The dominant theme of Dodecanesian history was scarcity; scarcity of arable land, water and other necessary preconditions for population expansion. Italian rule had a profound impact on the islands because many of the constraints on local progress were removed. The new occupiers promoted economic development and brought high employment, much of which was subsidised by the Italian state. As later chapters will show, the islanders were forced to reconcile the political unpopularity of the occupiers with the many benefits which the occupiers brought with them. In general, interviewees remembered Italian rule as a positive experience because it brought progress and abundance, and represented a contrast to the scarcity and limited prospects which characterised island life before 1912.

GEOGRAPHY AND POPULATION

The Dodecanese Islands are located in the south-eastern corner of the Aegean Sea, distributed along the south-western littoral of Anatolia, stretching as far north as Agathonisi, which lies south of Samos, to Kastellorizo on the approach to the Gulf of Antalya. Between them lie Patmos, Lipsos, Leros, Kalymnos, Kos, Nisyros, Tilos, Halki, Simi and Rhodes. Two other major islands, Kasos and Karpathos, are situated between Rhodes and the north-eastern corner of Crete.

Another isolated member of island group is Astypalea, which is located west of the main body of the Dodecanese, and lies closer to the Cyclades group. The largest island is Rhodes (1412 sq. km), which constitutes over half the combined area of the Dodecanese (2681 sq. km), followed by Karpathos (306) and Kos (288). The average size of the other inhabited islands is sixty square kilometres, with Kastellorizo the smallest at eleven square kilometres.[2] There are also hundreds of smaller outcrops which are seasonally inhabited or completely uninhabited.

The term 'Dodecanese' is a misnomer. It literally means 'twelve islands', but there have always been more than twelve inhabited islands under that name. During the Ottoman period, they were better known as the 'Privileged Islands', for in 1521, all except Rhodes and Kos submitted to the conquering Suleiman II without resistance, and were granted significant tax and political concessions.[3] In the nineteenth century, island leaders struggled to defend these privileges, and did so on behalf of 'the Dodecanese'.[4] The Italians conquered the area in 1912 and eventually settled on a quite different name, '*Le Isole Italiane dell'Egeo*', which expressed Italy's belief in her rightful place in the Aegean. Outside of Italy, however, 'the Dodecanese Islands' remained the standard name. Other variations have included 'Rhodes and the Dodecanese' and 'the Southern Sporades'.[5]

The physical geography of the Dodecanese, which is equally complex, is closely related to south-western Anatolia, which is a mixture of rugged mountain terrain, fertile crevices and barren limestone coastlines. The islands are essentially an extension of the Anatolian continental shelf, as their terrain is hilly, valleys are divided by steep ridges, and the coastlines are often rough and jagged.[6] They also share the adjacent mainland's complex geological topography. The islands are characterised by four basic rock types: schists and marble, which produce evergreen shrub and some forestation; hard limestone which yields very little soil and is only amenable to scant vegetation; volcanic rock which can render rich soil, though this is in limited supply; and, as the chief basis for cultivation, a broad range of tertiary rock which provides soil of variable quality.[7] The distribution of these rock types is rather uneven. At one extreme are Kalymnos, Simi and Kastellorizo, which for the most part are characterised by bare limestone, and at the other extreme are Rhodes and Kos, which possess the bulk of the archipelago's fertile soil, and which far outstrip the other islands in agricultural production. The rest of the

Dodecanese share enough arable land to support very small peasant communities, but with limited scope for market production. Unlike Rhodes and Kos, which enjoy a comparatively plentiful water supply, the other islands suffer more from the effects of rainless summers and uncertain rainfall in colder months. The Dodecanese have virtually no rainfall for half the year, roughly from mid-May to mid-October. During the colder months, they share the disruptive winds which all the Aegean islands receive from adjacent mainlands, but as they lie on the south-eastern margins of the Aegean, and are closer to the dryer eastern Mediterranean climatic zone, the Dodecanese are not as certain as other Aegean islands of rainfall in the lead-up to December.[8]

The Dodecanese are therefore poor in natural resources, and this is reflected in demographic statistics which show the islands have always been thinly populated. In 1821, there were just over 87 000 inhabitants, reaching a peak of 147 000 in 1910, after which numbers declined to 115 000 by 1947. Population density amounted to an average of 55 persons per square kilometre in 1910.[9] Rhodes has always been by far the most populous, with some 45 000 inhabitants in 1910, reaching 61 567 in 1941. When the Italians arrived in 1912, the island had forty-seven villages, while Rhodes Town was by far the largest centre.[10] Kos had some 14 000 people in 1912, which gradually increased to 18 231 in 1941. About half of the islanders lived in the main centre, Kos Town, and the rest were settled in five large villages. Due to a flourishing sponge trade and merchant marine, much higher population density was to be found on Kalymnos, Simi and Kastellorizo. In 1910, for example, the people of Kastellorizo numbered 9000, averaging 782.6 people per square kilometre. The rest of the Dodecanese was very sparsely populated. In 1912, the large island of Karpathos supported just over 8000 permanent inhabitants, Leros had 6000, and the rest averaged under 2000.[11] With each successive generation, these islanders were forced to shed their excess population and spawned a large diaspora.

In his magisterial study of the Mediterranean and its geography, Fernand Braudel characterised its islands as 'lands of hunger', constantly threatened by famine because of their limited natural resources. Braudel had the larger islands of the Mediterranean in mind, like Sicily, Sardinia, Crete and Cyprus, but his characterisation would hold true even more for the Dodecanese. The 'Privileged Islands' had a far lower threshold for population growth than say Sardinia or Crete, and they looked even more to the sea for sustenance. As will be shown below, Rhodes and Kos were also potential 'lands of hunger' due to backward farming techniques and an inequitable distribution of land. In different ways, scarcity characterised all the Dodecanese Islands, but the distinct geographical environments of Rhodes and Kos on the one hand, and the 'Privileged Islands' on the other, provided the basis for divergent historical development. Italian rule was to have its most extensive and enduring impact on Rhodes and Kos because these islands were targeted by investors for their economic potential. With the exception of Leros, which became Italy's chief military base in the eastern Mediterranean, the other island communities were to complain that they had missed out on Italian investment, and that they had not progressed as Rhodes, Kos and Leros did.

ECONOMIC LIFE: THE 'PRIVILEGED ISLANDS'

Braudel also claimed that whilst domestic life was 'precarious, restricted and threatened...', the wider historical importance of Mediterranean islands far exceeded 'what might be expected from such poor territories'.[12] He pointed out that among other things, islands served as landfalls on busy trade routes and as linkages for the dissemination of crops.[13] While the sea left the Dodecanese vulnerable to marauding privateers and trading powers like Genoa and Venice, it also offered the islanders economic opportunities which were not available to land-locked communities. By the nineteenth century, some of the more barren islands had been transformed into thriving trading centres, and this was particularly true of Kalymnos, Simi, Kastellorizo and Halki, where the main impetus for economic growth was sponge fishing and merchandising.

Sponge fishing had been a traditional occupation among these islanders for centuries, though it was not until the second half of the nineteenth century that sponges became a lucrative business. According to legend, while the Turks were besieging Rhodes Town, the people of Simi offered Suleiman II fresh bread and sponges, and in return, the grateful sultan granted Simian sponge fishermen the right to exploit all his territorial waters.[14] Similar kinds of privileges were granted to most of the other Dodecanese islands which had followed Simi's example. The men of Simi and Kalymnos were renowned for their ability to dive to the most extraordinary depths for lengthy periods of time.[15] In 1687, an English traveller wrote that, 'they will dive 15 fathom under water being brought up to this profession from their childhood, they reckon those the best of men, who can longest keep under water'. He also noted that Simian divers travelled throughout the eastern Mediterranean, and their merchandise found its way to all corners of Europe.[16] International demand for sponges had risen significantly by the mid-nineteenth century, and the islanders made the most of this boom by trying to control all aspects of the trade, from diving and processing, to transportation and retail. Kalymnian and Simian merchants had established an international network, basing themselves in cities like St. Petersburg, Bordeaux, Trieste, and London.[17]

Buoyancy was reflected in radical population growth rates, which were due to a combination of natural increase and immigration. Between 1821 and 1910, the population of Kalymnos rose by 300 per cent, Kastellorizo 260 per cent, Simi 212 per cent and Halki 150 per cent.[18] A recent study of surnames at Halki confirmed the diverse regional origins of many of Halki's inhabitants, with such names as 'Karpáthios' (of Karpathos), 'Kasiótis' (of Kasos), 'Sfakianós' (of Sfakia, Crete), and 'Sifounianós' (of Sifnos, Cyclades).[19] Immigrants from surrounding islands were drawn by prospects of employment in sponge diving, sponge processing, sea transportation and merchandising. Sponge diving was especially popular; given the primitive nature of underwater fishing technology, diving was an exceptionally dangerous activity and hence commanded quite attractive pay. The sponge trade also fostered the growth of other small industries, as shown by an official Ottoman survey taken in 1886, which recorded 150 workshops on Simi, about 100 on Kastellorizo and twenty on Halki.[20] Cargo transportation and trafficking were also quite popular, especially in Kastellorizo and Kasos. These islanders specialised in building caiques which could transport cargo through the narrow straits of the Aegean and along the shores of the Levant. Kastellorizo gradually abandoned sponges and concentrated in transporting goods between Egypt and the southern coast of Anatolia.[21] Imperial monopolies made contraband activities a lucrative enterprise. The 'Privileged Islands' were exempt from the tobacco monopoly, and Kalymnian merchants in particular made small fortunes by smuggling tobacco to Kos and the Ottoman mainland.[22] In 1922, there were thirty workshops involved in tobacco processing, with each workshop employing between ten and 400 people.[23]

Such intense economic activity, however, based on fortuitous international conditions, was to be short-lived. Kalymnos, Simi, Kastellorizo and Halki reached their apogee on the eve of the Italian invasion, but serious economic misfortunes were to set in soon after, as sponge prices fell and were never to recover. As will be shown below, local historians have tried, with limited success, to establish a direct causal link between Italian rule and the decline of these islands. What is certain, however, is that Italian rule was perceived by locals as having ended their *belle époque*. This was to affect local popular memory of Italian rule, especially in Kalymnos, where the Italians seem to have left a bad impression.

As for the rest of the 'Privileged Islands' (i.e. Karpathos, Leros, Nisyros, Tilos, Lipsos, Astypalea and Patmos), each had just enough arable land to offset the need for such hazardous and risky pursuits as sponge diving. Tilos and Astypalea, for example, were more or less self-contained communities, based on subsistence farming, grazing and small cottage industries. Each could barely sustain more than 2000 permanent inhabitants. Similar conditions prevailed on Patmos, but as this island was an important monastic and pilgrimage centre, peasants could rely on steady demand for their agricultural products and handicrafts.[24] The local economies of Karpathos, Leros and Nisyros were also characterised by subsistence farming, though these islands also found alternative sustenance through emigration. For example, Karpathian tradesmen and merchants could be found all over western Anatolia and mainland Greece.[25] Nisyrian merchants set up shops and emporiums in Constantinople and Smyrna, and Lerians did much the same in Alexandria and Cairo.[26] Karpathos, Nisyros and Leros created large expatriate communities in centres like Piraeus, Athens, Odessa and New York, and as far off as South Africa, and each diasporan community maintained strong links with their beloved island by forming voluntary associations, which not only bound expatriates together, but regularly sent home generous public donations.[27] The islanders also benefited from private remittances to families, as well as from the beneficence of wealthy expatriates, who endowed their 'fatherland' or *patrída* with schools, clinics and other public utilities. Rich expatriates also liked to spend their summer vacations in their *patrída*. Wealthy Lerians in Egypt, for example, built neo-classical villas along the scenic shores of Leros, and indulged in modern water-sports like yachting.[28]

Wealthy Dodecanesian and common folk alike loved their *patrída*, but they recognised that economic opportunities and individual progress had to be sought elsewhere. As will be shown in Chapters 5 and 6, Italian public works programmes and other projects gave many Dodecanesians the chance to progress without having to emigrate. As the oral sources will show, Italian rule was remembered as having improved the employment opportunities and living conditions of most Dodecanesians, and these memories have served as the basis of positive collective impressions of the Italian Occupation.

ECONOMIC LIFE: RHODES AND KOS

Overall, geographical preconditions had oriented the islanders towards the world beyond their shores, and since the 'Privileged Islands' were endowed with very limited resources, maritime activities and emigration were the cornerstone of their existence. There was much greater scope for sustained economic growth and expansion on Rhodes and Kos, which shared the best fresh water resources and 85 per cent of Dodecanesian arable land.[29] The great majority of the inhabitants of both islands was engaged in agriculture, though Rhodes Town and Kos Town did have sizeable merchant communities. Both islands were situated conveniently on busy trade routes which connected Constantinople and Smyrna with Egypt. Rhodes was also a convenient landfall for shipping from the Adriatic *en route* to the Levant. As the Near East was increasingly enveloped into the international economy, Rhodian and Koan agriculture found a ready market for cash crops, especially Egypt, which enjoyed exceptional economic growth in the decades leading up to the First World War.[30] After the war, in an effort to have their colonies pay for themselves, the Italians would seek to exploit the full potential of Rhodian and Koan agriculture with heavy public and private investment. Local peasants generally benefited from these developments in direct and indirect ways, and these wholesale changes could not but leave a positive impression on local minds.

Rhodian and Koan peasants dealt primarily in viticulture, and during the last decades of Ottoman rule, raw currants were exported to Alexandria, Trieste, Constantinople and Crete.[31] Kos exported olives, olive oil, melons and citrus fruits, principally to Egypt, and Kos was also famous for her lettuce.[32] Rhodes exported a similar series of cash crops, though on a larger scale. Peasants favoured crops which could endure the long summer period, such as currants, olives, almonds, carob and citrus fruits. Bread was the staple

diet in the Dodecanese, but neither Rhodes nor Kos was self-
sufficient in cereals, especially wheat, and each was highly dependent
on wheat imports.[33]

Rhodes has enjoyed an image of fertility and greenery since
antiquity. For Virgil, the word 'Rhodes' was synonymous with
'orchard', while Suetonius claimed Tiberius loved the island because
it was 'beautiful and healthy'.[34] The Frenchman Victor Guérin
claimed that Rhodes was lush and fertile, one of few Aegean islands
suitable for large scale farming, but he also observed that the island's
productive potential was not fully realised.[35] In a detailed study of
mid-nineteenth-century Rhodes, Guérin wrote that agriculture was
retarded by the diminutive size of average landholdings, backward
farming techniques, heavy taxation, and labour shortages. Despite
images of abundance and fertility, the peasantry which Guérin
described lived in a wretched state.[36] The chief problem for the
people of Rhodes and Kos was the inequitable distribution of land.
Property was dominated by landed elites who resided in Rhodes Town
and Kos Town, and a small number of wealthy peasants who lived in
the villages. The majority of peasants worked either as tenant farmers,
who were usually paid in kind, or as labourers on landed estates, or
'tsiflíkia'.[37] The size of an average peasant plot, whether freehold or
rented, was under three acres.[38] Dependent and independent peasants
could not rely on their individual plots for survival, and were forced
to diversify their economic activities. They found supplementary
income as hired labour on landed estates, or in mining, handicrafts,
grazing, and selling home-made goods like cheese.[39] The villagers of
Asfendiou, Kos, virtually destroyed their woodlands in order to make
charcoal. As one villager claimed in his oral testimony, selling
charcoal was one of the few ways of getting extra income:

> We had poverty. We had a lot of poverty. Great poverty. Out of
> 365 days a year, you could not count on getting more than 100
> days worth of income. How could we live on that? How did we
> live? We'd go up to the mountain and make charcoal, we'd chop
> down wood and we ended up leaving nothing behind. There was
> nothing left. . . .[40]

Landed proprietors did their utmost to squeeze the peasants and
inflict more misery, and this was shown in the terms of tenancy leases.
Rhodian and Koan agriculture adhered to a 'two-field' system, with
land left fallow every alternate year.[41] Some proprietors therefore
favoured two year leases, during which they expected to receive the

same rent and share of produce for each year, even though production in the second year was expected to be significantly lower.[42] Local elites were also notorious usurers. They preyed especially on independent peasants, to whom they gave loans at extortionate rates, and whose property they seized on default of payment.[43] For peasants who sought to augment their holdings or were in desperate need of finance, there was no other choice but to approach these money-lenders, whom the peasants liked to call 'interest-suckers' (tokoglíftes).[44]

The suzerains offered very little assistance to peasant farmers. The Ottomans essentially practised minimal government, and the function of provincial administrations was mainly to supervise taxation.[45] Little was was done to develop the empire's economic infrastructure, especially in such relatively unimportant territories as Rhodes and Kos. In 1912, neither island had viable roadworks, and port facilities in the main towns remained antiquated and run-down. Public amenities were left in the hands of local communities, which were generally too poor to finance and develop these amenities on their own. Little help was forthcoming from Rhodian and Koan elites, who, unlike their 'Privileged Island' counterparts, were not known for their charity and philanthropy. Some wealthy Rhodians did endow their main town with schools and clinics, but the elites of Kos were notorious for their meanness, and some modern writers have blamed them for the persistence of Koan illiteracy and backwardness.[46]

Italian rule was to alleviate the plight of many Rhodian and Koan peasants by offering them alternative sources of employment and finance, and more stable prices for their primary produce. It was therefore quite difficult for these locals to resist the feeling that the Italians were benevolent colonisers, and that on balance their impact on island life was beneficial. Little wonder that locals would recall this period with some sense of nostalgia.

SOCIETY: CLASS AND *MILLET*

Until the nineteenth century, piracy had been the scourge of island life. Of Karpathos, one seventeenth-century traveller observed the inhabitants were 'very poor, and seldom free from visits from privateers', and at Patmos, piracy 'brought them (the inhabitants) so low that they are now as miserable as any'.[47] In one of Jules Verne's lesser-known novels, *L'Archipel en Feu*, which is set in the early nineteenth century, pirates continue to terrorise the Aegean,[48] but by then European naval forces had started to clear the Mediterranean of the scourge. By the mid-1800s, conditions were safe enough to attract more tourists from northern Europe.[49] The impact of piracy on Aegean demography was indelible, as it had forced inhabitants to live in fortified coastal centres like Rhodes Town, or to huddle in villages straddling mountain tops and steep ridges. Through the nineteenth century, villagers gradually felt secure enough to settle closer to their fields, and eventually many had relocated along the shoreline. The main town of Kalymnos, for example, was originally situated on a hill top, high up in the island's interior. By the middle of the nineteenth century, almost all the inhabitants had moved down to the base of that hill (Hora), and by 1900 the majority of Kalymnians had relocated again, this time to the island's main harbour (Pothia).[50] Such generational demographic shifts were repeated everywhere else in the Dodecanese and the Aegean. With the privateers gone, market agriculture gained impetus, land acquired greater value, and the seas became safer for sponge fishing and trading. In these settled conditions, new social structures began to take shape.

The nineteenth century saw the formation of new Dodecanesian elites, men who had acquired large tracts of land on Rhodes and Kos, and entrepreneurs who controlled sponge fishing and the merchant marine. Much of Rhodes and Kos had been dominated by Ottoman feudal estates (çifliks), but in the nineteenth century these estates had gradually been purchased by wealthy Greeks from the Dodecanese and Anatolia.[51] These elites were known as 'árchontes' or 'proúhontes'. Both terms denoted them as people of the premier class, though for the poor these terms would acquire a pejorative meaning. The rich were also known as 'tsiflikades', or '*çiflik* owners', which implied that the *árchontes* were no different to their former Turkish feudal lords.

Wealthy 'Privileged Islanders' also bought up land in Rhodes and Kos, and as will be shown further below, some of the wealth generated by these elites was invested in civic enterprises.[52] The legacy of the sponge trade is evident to anyone sailing into the main harbours of Simi or Kalymnos today, where the quays are dominated by rows of two- and three-storey homes with neo-classical facades, often painted in bright colours which distinguished them from smaller white-washed cottages of the common folk. In general, island elites resided in main towns and congregated in the same exclusive neighbourhoods. Here, the so-called 'good families' of the *árchontes* inter-married and formed a distinct social class. The *árchontes* were characterised by their receptiveness to modern bourgeois culture, their western attire and a more educated and less parochial Greek accent. They were also distinguished by a higher level of education; the sons of *árchontes* were sent to secondary schools and universities in Smyrna, Constantinople and Greece, with medicine and law as the preferred fields of study. Indeed it was the *árchontes*, through their greater contact with the wider Greek world and their access to higher education, who did most to disseminate Greek nationalist ideas in the Dodecanese during the nineteenth century. They were to lead the call for unification with Greece during the first decade of Italian rule, and would acquire a reputation as being 'great patriots'.

Overall, the *árchontes* considered themselves a distinct entity, defined by wealth, higher culture and by familial connection. Though an exclusive social class, the *árchontes* maintained their ties with the wider community through benefaction. A typical example was the Lerian merchant Panagiotis Trakkas, who gave the people of Leros 120 000 gold drachma in order to build a primary school and a pharmacy.[53] Another was the Rhodian merchant Minas Venetoklis, who built a secondary school and bequeathed an enormous sum to help establish a sporting club ('Diagoras').[54] Most Dodecanesian secondary schools and other significant institutions were endowed by, and named after, such local notables.[55] Benefaction was a source of prestige for these *árchontes*, for not only did it convey a sense of civic consciousness, but symbolised their personal success.

Lower down the social scale were petty merchants, artisans and shopkeepers, while each village had their 'kulaks' or wealthier peasants. Unlike the common folk, these middling classes could usually afford to pay for their childrens' education to secondary school level. They could also provide proper dowries for their daughters, which normally included a fully furnished home and a farming plot.

The peasantry was by far the largest class in the Dodecanese. They were dependent peasants in the main, most of whom struggled for subsistence and lived constantly in fear of destitution. The plight of the average Dodecanesian peasant was no different from that of Mediterranean peasants in general. Each had common adversaries; the state, landlords, harsh physical environments, lack of capital, primitive farming techniques, and plots which were too small. Unlike peasants among the 'Privileged Islands', Rhodians and

Koans had to pay regular taxes to the Sublime Porte. Most peasants were illiterate, though an increasing number of their children did manage to have one or two years of a functional education.[56] As one Rhodian peasant told Guérin, after paying off debts and taxes, there was little left for anything else:

> From father to son, all of us are condemned to live and die poor and uneducated.... Even with our total incomes, that of our wives and our children, we still only manage, with great difficulty, to earn what we can, to pay the many taxes with which we are burdened....[57]

In Dodecanesian oral tradition, peasant life is characterised as a hopeless struggle to make ends meet, as encapsulated in the popular phrase, 'the black life' (i mávri zoí). However, if Rhodian and Koan peasants did not regret the passing of Ottoman rule, the lower classes from the sponge trading islands did. Here the Ottoman period was associated with economic activity and high employment, and this prosperity was partly attributed to the fact that these communities were only required to pay the Sublime Porte a token annual tribute. This tribute was known locally as the 'Mahtoú', a term which symbolised times of plenty. As Nikolaos Poulas of Kalymnos claimed, the days of the *Mahtoú* were the best of times, which were then spoiled when the 'Fascist' Italians came:

> I'll tell you... we lived quite well. Then things went sour when the Fascists came. But back then, we had the Turks, we had the so-called 'Mahtoú'. We had privileges, and they brought fruit, they brought meat from the coast [Asia Minor], from the east. These Turks were good people.... And costs were low....[58]

The sponge islands gained much from the leadership and benefaction of local elites. Their civic consciousness was not only reflected in generous private benefactions, but also in their active involvement in local government. Public utilities, health and sanitation were some of the areas to which local government revenues and creative energies were channelled. University scholarships were granted to poor children with high scholastic potential, and on Simi, returning medical graduates were required to serve in a public clinic for two year stints. Simi also had a public pharmacy which imported high quality pharmaceuticals from companies like Em. Genevix et Cie of Paris, and sold them to the Simian public at subsidised prices.[59] Similar services were offered in

Kastellorizo. For Basil Galettis, Kastellorizo had 'socialism' before Marx ever thought of it, and as his characterisation of the *Mahtoú* period suggests, locals took much pride in the island's civic achievements:

> Kastellorizo had socialism before any other place in Europe. Before Karl Marx! Of course! We had free doctors, free pharmaceuticals, free education...all these things were happening in Kastellorizo before, many years before Karl Marx thought of it. Socialism was implemented way before. We had no poor. And every so often we passed around free clothing, the local government that is. For free! Free books too!...Socialism was implemented one hundred years before Karl Marx![60]

These island communities were well aware, however, that their success came at a very high cost. Sponge diving was so hazardous an occupation that by the time the Italians had arrived, only desperate poor folk were prepared to take the risk. In Kalymnos, diving was stigmatised as a 'bad job' (paliodouliá), work suitable for poor wretches and reckless ruffians.[61] In Simi, sponge diving was called 'The Tyranny', and as the British writer William Travis noted, it threatened the life of every able-bodied man, as 'year after year the drain continued until...one out of three men of Simi was either dead of it or crippled or marked for death before reaching marriageable age'.[62] By 1912 Simians had developed a growing social aversion to sponge diving, and a great many would prefer to emigrate and find safer employment elsewhere.

Apart from class differences, ethnicity was another important criterion in Dodecanesian social segmentation. This study will concentrate on Greek Dodecanesians and their experience of Italian rule, but Rhodes and Kos had significant ethnic minorities which would also share that experience. In the Ottoman imperial system, Muslims, Jews and Christians were organised into separate *millets*, headed by religious leaders in Constantinople. The Dodecanese was home to all three peoples of 'The Book', each of whom had different leaders, judicial systems and laws. In the 1880s, about 86 per cent of the Dodecanesian population was Christian, with just over 10 per cent Muslim, and under 4 per cent Jewish.[63] The Jewish community resided exclusively in Rhodes Town and Kos Town, as did the majority of Muslim Turks. In 1922, the population of Rhodes Town was 16 150, of which Muslim Turks constituted 40 per cent (6500), Greeks 33 per cent (5200) and Jews 25 per cent (3000).[64] Rhodes also had five Muslim villages, of which four were large enough to have a primary school. Of the 7495 people of Kos Town, 3717 were Turks, 3681 were Greek and 66 were Jewish, and there were also two Turkish hamlets called Kermete and Koniario.[65] The autonomous 'Privileged Islands' were not colonised by the Turks, though by the late nineteenth century, the Ottomans did establish small garrisons on each of these islands, and an official survey of 1886 recorded one mosque in Kastellorizo.[66] For most of the Ottoman period, the 'Privileged Islands' generally remained exclusively Greek. For Kalymnians like Sevasti Kortesi, ethnic homogeneity was thought to be a 'privilege', but there is little doubt that neither Muslims nor Jews saw anything to gain in settling among such barren outcrops. The following chauvinistic characterisation of Kalymnian homogeneity, however, is more a comment of inter-island *campanilismo* than ethnic prejudice:

> We had only seven Turks here in Kalymnos; one was an 'Arapi' [African] who was a judge. We got along well. They never bothered us. We in Kalymnos had the legendary *Mahtoú*. We were independent in the Dodecanese. They never conscripted us for the army, nothing...[the *Mahtoú*] was a promise... which made the Dodecanese independent. We were neither Italian, nor Turkish, and we were all Greeks. In Kos there were many Turks, so too in Rhodes, but not here in Kalymnos. We didn't have a bastardised community, we were all Greeks here. We didn't want them, only Kalymnians.[67]

The presence of large Turkish communities helped the Greeks define their own ethnic identity and, especially among the educated, their national allegiances. The Turks of Rhodes and Kos had settled after the Ottoman conquest in 1522, when vast tracts of land were turned into *çifliks*. Rhodes Town was protected by high walls built by the Hospitallers in the late middle ages, and when Guérin visited in the 1850s, he found that only Turks and Jews were allowed to reside within the walls, while the Greeks could conduct their daily business within these walls between sunrise and sunset.[68] The majority of Dodecanesian Turks were town dwellers who worked mainly in handicrafts and agriculture, and specialised in garden vegetables and horse breeding. Included in the Muslim *millet* were refugees who fled from Crete in 1908 after a Greek nationalist insurrection. These were Greek converts to Islam who spoke a Greek dialect and rarely mixed socially with the established Turkish community. Rhodes and Kos also had a small number of African Muslims who were descendants of imported slaves. Most of them worked as domestic servants and labourers.[69]

Conquering powers often look to minority groups to support their new regime. The Italians found their most ardent supporters among the 'Franco-Levantines' or eastern Catholics, who were often of Italian descent.[70] The Jewish community also seemed to favour Italian rule, partly because they were not Greek and did not share any of the enthusiasm for unification with Greece. The Jewish *millet* of Rhodes and Kos were part of a large diaspora of Sephardis who were welcomed into the Ottoman Empire after their expulsion from Spain in 1492. During the Italian Occupation they continued to speak a Spanish dialect (Ladino), and as with other *millets*, did not mix socially with other ethnic groups. Jews were mainly involved in shop keeping, food processing and textile manufacturing, and were particularly noted in trade, money-lending and banking – the Alhadeff dynasty of Rhodes Town was the premier Dodecanesian banking family. Tragically, the community was destroyed in 1944, when the Germans deported almost all of its members to death camps in central Europe.[71]

POLITICAL STRUCTURES AND LEADERSHIP

The Dodecanese Islands formed part of a province or *vilayet* which included all Ottoman controlled Aegean Islands. This province was subdivided into departments, in which the northern Dodecanese, from Patmos down to Nisyros came under the authority of a governor in Chios, while the rest of the Dodecanese were administered by a *pasha* in Rhodes Town. On paper, the *pasha* at Rhodes seemed to have a comprehensive administrative apparatus at his disposal. He was advised by a council which included the *millet* leaders, and he had small departments dealing with agriculture, finance, statistics, postage, trade and customs. He also had a modest sized *gendarmerie*. Furthermore, the *pasha* presided over sub-departments centred around the villages of Lindos and Kastelou, and in Simi, Kastellorizo, Karpathos and Kasos. The governor in Chios was responsible for sub-departments centred in Kos, Leros and Kalymnos.[72]

In reality, Ottoman officials had limited power over the 'Privileged Islands'. The Porte did attempt to abrogate their special rights in

1867, 1869, 1872, 1897 and 1908, but on each occasion it faced stout local resistance and, more importantly, Great Power intervention.[73] The anomalous standing of the 'Privileged Islands' within the *vilayet* was not a unique problem in Ottoman provincial administration. As Malcolm Yapp points out, provincial government in the empire consisted 'of various groups whose relationship to each other was like that of pieces in a mosaic', and, where 'different groups had different rights and interests and required to be governed in different ways'.[74] In an attempt to modernise the empire, the Ottomans unsuccessfully tried to streamline all the anomalies and turn the empire into an efficient and rationalised state.[75]

In the meantime, the *millets* had strengthened their influence in Ottoman political life, and were increasingly seen as an alternative source of authority.[76] In the Dodecanese, Greek bishops were widely recognised as natural leaders of the Greek community, and as *millet* heads they enjoyed considerable power in such fields as education and justice, particularly in civil cases.[77] The Greek Church also commanded quite a comprehensive ecclesiastical structure. The Dodecanese was divided into four bishoprics; the Diocese of Rhodes, (Rhodes, Simi, Kastellorizo, Tilos and Halki), the Diocese of Kos, which included Nisyros, that of Karpathos and Kasos, and the Diocese of Kalymnos, which included Leros and Astypalea. Patmos was a separate ecclesiastical unit governed by the abbot of the Monastery of St John. The Bishop of Rhodes carried greater prestige than the other hierarchs, but each bishop acknowledged the supremacy of, and was appointed by, the Patriarch of Constantinople. The Church's influence could therefore extend far and wide, into every town neighbourhood and village community, and thus prelates were in a good position to influence public opinion.

While Ottoman provincial reform had failed, local government continued to perform useful functions, and as shown in the case of Kalymnos and Simi, these institutions could be quite enterprising. The most common name for this institution was 'koinótita', which was derived from the Greek word for 'community', and was usually applied to village local government. In the main towns, the term most commonly used was 'demogerontía' which meant 'community elders', but by 1912 this was gradually supplanted by the more democratic 'demarchía', which connoted 'popular' leadership. In inter-island politics and representations, leadership was deferred by the village *koinótites* to the *demarchies*. *Demarchies* and *koinótites* were, however, separate administrative entities; each formulated its own constitutions and traditions. Each held regular elections, and appointed a council and a president. The *demarchies* were dominated by local elites, and the *koinótites* by literate and wealthy peasants. Water supply, grazing rights, roads, education and many other public concerns were the responsibility of these institutions, and, as shown earlier, local government in wealthier communities could draw on enough private resources to provide health and other welfare services.[78]

Local government, in concert with the Church, also served as the basis for the spread of Greek nationalist ideas and consciousness. The Dodecanese was one of many Greek-speaking territories which had rebelled against Ottoman rule in the Greek War of Independence, and which throughout the nineteenth century continued to identify with the Greek state.[79] Literate Dodecanesians remained receptive to currents in Greek nationalist ideas and discourses, particularly the ideological underpinnings of Greek irredentism. As Greece committed herself to a programme of recovering former Byzantine territories, driven by the popular expansionist ideology called the 'Great Idea' or 'Megali Idea', the *demarchies* and *koinótites* in the Dodecanese increasingly saw themselves as provisional administrations, waiting for 'Mother Hellas' (Mitéra Ellás) to 'redeem' them.

The *demarchies* and *koinótites* of the Dodecanese therefore likened themselves to patriotic cells within enemy territory, and their self-appointed task was to mobilise public opinion to support the interests of 'Mother Hellas'. The Young Turk revolt in 1908 exposed the nationalist proclivities of many of the empire's ethnic institutions. The new regime offered the empire its most energetic plan for imperial reform and revitalisation, which included granting all minorities equal rights and civil status. The reforms also involved the introduction of a parliament which represented all the empire's ethnic groups, but these political reforms were vigorously opposed by most of the empire's Greek subjects. The 'Privileged Islands' did not want to lose their privileges, none of the islanders wanted universal male conscription (only Muslims had hitherto been eligible), and few Greeks shared the Young Turks' desire to strengthen the ailing empire. (Indeed, Greeks throughout the empire were notorious for cheering on the empire's military reverses.)[80] Nevertheless, most Dodecanesian *demarchies* were advised by the Greek government to accept the Young Turk reforms, for ethnic Greek representatives in the new parliament could surreptitiously serve the national interests of

Greece, or at least do their patriotic duty and destabilise the parliament.[81]

Greek nationalist sentiments were expressed openly when the Italians seized the Dodecanese in April 1912. Italy had invaded Ottoman Libya the previous year, but the Italians found Turkish and local resistance hard to break. In order to induce the Ottomans into withdrawing completely from Libya, Italy planned an invasion of Anatolia, but settled instead on the Dodecanese, which was a far easier option. Astypalea was seized first on 22 April, and by the middle of May, all the Dodecanese except Kastellorizo had been secured. The Italians faced almost no resistance, save for a minor skirmish near the Rhodian village of Psinthos. The victorious general of the campaign was Giovanni Ameglio, veteran of Eritrea and the Boxer Rebellion, who, on entering the town of Rhodes on 5 May, received a hero's welcome from the Greek community.[82] Church leaders and the *demarchies* expressed their enthusiasm with speeches and gifts, and Ameglio and his lieutenants reciprocated with promises of full autonomy. All the Dodecanese Islands had welcomed the Italians as liberators, but Italy's failure to keep promises of autonomy would become an enduring grievance among locals. Initially, however, the general mood was one of jubiliation, except in Kastellorizo, where community leaders felt rather aggrieved that they too were not 'liberated'. They pleaded with Ameglio to liberate them, but he insisted that Kastellorizo was too far from the main body of the archipelago.[83]

Dodecanesian popular support for the occupation was conditional on the granting of autonomy, after which they expected to unite with Greece. In the ensuing months, however, there was little sign that the Italians were prepared to fulfil their promises, and local patience wore increasingly thin. The *demarchies* of the Dodecanese began to organise themselves and sent formal protestations to Ameglio and Great Power leaders.[84] In July, delegates from all *demarchies* met on Patmos to discuss the nature of an autonomous 'Aegean state', including its possible flag (a white cross against a dark blue background), its official emblem (Apollo), and its legal code. The meeting confirmed inter-island solidarity and offered local leaders a chance to air their disquiet regarding the occupation. The meeting was meant to be secret – many Patmians were initially hostile because they thought the delegates were Young Turk conspirators.[85] The Italians had been informed of the meeting, however, and the delegates were promptly arrested and taken to Rhodes for questioning.

Clear evidence of Italian duplicity surfaced in October, when island leaders were informed of the Treaty of Lausanne at Ouchy, in which Italy promised to return the islands to the Ottomans if Turkish troops were completely removed from Libya.[86] Horrified by the prospect of being delivered back to the 'barbarous' Turks, local governments responded by drawing up petitions of protest in every town and village during the winter months of 1912–13, and copies were sent to all the Great Powers.[87] There were also attempts at open protest. On 6 January 1913, the *demarchía* of Rhodes Town tried to turn a traditional religious festival into a patriotic rally. The occasion was the annual commemoration of the beheading of John the Baptist, which involved a procession from one of the main churches to the harbour (Mandraki). The Italians, however, got wind of the plan and surrounded the church with troops. The rally was foiled, but this Italian action had seriously disturbed the Rhodian faithful. 'Not even the Turks', exclaimed one Greek writer, 'intervened in our religious matters.'[88] The occasion fuelled growing antipathy towards the Italians, and many more protests were to follow until the fate of the islands was finally settled a decade later during the Paris Peace Conferences.

Modern Greek writers have generally worked on the assumption that Ottoman rule was the epitome of tyranny and cruelty, a regime committed to the destruction of Greek civilisation. At a popular level, however, many who remembered Ottoman rule would concede that the Turks were not particularly oppressive, nor were Turkish people 'barbaric' by nature.[89] In the Dodecanese, memories of Ottoman rule are contradictory, especially in Kalymnos and Simi where some old folk can still remember the golden days of the *Mahtoú*, and yet, due to the influence of Greek nationalism, also refer to it as a time of 'slavery' (*sklaviá*).[90] Ottoman rule was not as 'barbaric' as has been maintained, but there were sound reasons why the islanders welcomed the Italians as liberators. The rise of the Young Turks had fuelled growing inter-ethnic tension throughout the Ottoman world, and Dodecanesians often heard rumours of pogroms carried out against Greek communities in Anatolia. The threat of universal conscription and loss of privileges had also fostered Dodecanesian anxieties. The Italian invasion in 1912 therefore seemed timely.

The islanders realised, however, that rather than having been liberated, they now had a new occupier. Why did the Italians want to stay? The Dodecanese Islands, after all, had little economic value, yet Italian statesmen and diplomats fought tenaciously to keep them within their nascent colonial empire. Italy would later invest much time and energy in transforming the Dodecanese into a modern and 'Italianised' outpost of the metropolis, but in the final analysis, the Italians were to gain next to nothing from their efforts. As the following chapter will show, the Dodecanese, along with a number of large African territories, was valued much more for its symbolic value, as Italy sought 'Great Power' status by creating an empire. The nature of Italian rule in the Dodecanese was strongly influenced by Italy's desire to earn distinction on the international stage.

2 Italy's Aegean Possession: The Dodecanese Islands, 1912–47

The Great Powers did not approve of Italy's latest territorial acquisition. Britain and France in particular feared the consequences of the Dodecanese falling into the hands of Germany, Italy's powerful ally.[1] Close to both the Dardenelles and the Suez Canal, and within sight of Asia Minor, the Dodecanese were widely recognised as having much strategic significance, and many believed that Italy's foothold in the region would be a destabilising influence in the Near East. But as Richard Bosworth has shown in his works on Italian foreign policy before the First World War, Italy was largely able to keep the islands due to the duplicity and remarkable skill of her diplomats. They exploited the precarious condition of the Concert of Europe in the period leading up to 1914, during which one international crisis followed another, and when few of the Great Powers were prepared to alienate potential allies like Italy.[2] Her 'patron' in international affairs, Britain, actively opposed the occupation of the Dodecanese, but Britain stopped short of exerting real pressure, preferring to accept Italian undertakings that the occupation was temporary. In the meantime, the Italians sought to trade the islands to secure other interests, such as political influence in southern Albania, and economic concessions in Asia Minor. Yet as Bosworth has shown, the Italians tried to make, and often succeeded in making such gains while retaining their bargaining chip. In the Treaty of Lausanne of 1912, for instance, the Italians seemed to be offering an undertaking to exchange the Dodecanese for full control of Libya. Italy would return the islands provided that all Ottoman troops were withdrawn, but as the Italians had failed to quell Libya's desert tribesmen, and were not likely to do so in the foreseeable future, the diplomats at the Palazzo della Consulta in Rome could always complain of a continuing 'Ottoman' presence on Libyan territory. As Sir Edward Grey complained at the time, the Italians effectively won a '999-year lease' on the Dodecanese.[3]

In truth, the Italians wanted to keep the islands, and they managed to hold the Great Powers at bay with carefully worded assurances which seemed to suggest otherwise.[4] For Italy's wily diplomats, when it came to the Dodecanese, 'the general state of the Concert was everything; phrases of treaties or diplomatic parleying...were nothing'.[5] Unscrupulous diplomacy was necessary, for Italy's imperial ambitions far exceeded the realities of her power.[6] Italian public opinion, or rather, 'politically minded gentlemen',[7] believed their nation had to have an empire to support her Great Power status. A new Roman empire was envisaged in the eastern Mediterranean, even though Italy lacked the requisite economic, military and human resources to fulfil such imperial dreams. The mere fact that she could only deliberate over small pickings such as Libya and the Dodecanese reflected her weaknesses, and without Great Power approval, especially British, her occupation of the Dodecanese could only be classified as 'temporary'.[8]

Nevertheless, those who ruled Italy believed that making her a Great Power was a moral imperative. Empire building was a quest to construct an identity which would locate Italy among the major nation-states. Her eligibility for such high status also depended on the way she ruled her empire. In this age of empires it was important for ruling nations to be seen as highly civilised, as cultures worthy of ruling other peoples. The colonies would therefore need to evoke the high standards of Italian civilisation, as Italy's imperial record would substantiate her worthiness as a ruling culture. This chapter, which provides a general overview of the occupation, shows how the related concerns of foreign policy and cultural prestige were reflected in colonial governance.

The occupation can be divided into five distinct phases. The first phase covers the years 1912 to 1923, during which the Italians interfered relatively little in local affairs given that the occupation was ostensibly 'temporary'. Dodecanesians were to experience the full impact of Italian rule in the next phase, which covered the period 1923 to 1936. The Dodecanese enjoyed significant economic development and high employment, hence most of the islanders remembered the occupation as a time of progress. Though the Fascists had been in power since 1922, the islanders only began to talk of a 'Fascist' occupation after 1936, when the new governor, Count Cesare Maria de Vecchi, inaugurated a highly repressive third phase of Italian rule (1937–43). Worse was to come in the following phase (1943–45), when the Dodecanese were occupied by German troops, and when the Italians ruled in name only. As locals experienced the horrors and desperation of wartime, this phase had the far greatest impact on popular memory. From 1945 to 1947, the islands were placed under temporary British administration, after which they were ceded to Greece. To a significant degree, these five phases of the occupation served to underpin popular memory. While this overview is essentially a history of the Italian Occupation 'from above', it will serve to contextualise the rest of this study, which details the history of the Italian Occupation as seen 'from below'.

'TEMPORARY' RULE 1912–24

Between 1912 and 1920, the islands were governed by a military administration, with General Ameglio as the first governor.[9] Ameglio had established the character of this administration from the outset, promising to allow local institutions, traditions and customs to continue to operate undisturbed.[10] The *millet* system remained largely intact, and the Church was free to exercise its power and influence over the Greek community, much as it had done for centuries. The task of the military administration was quite limited; to fill the vacuum left by the Ottoman state, that is, to collect taxes and maintain law and order. In practice the new administration did, to a small degree, surpass its predecessors in its civic and social responsibilities. Kos Town's water supply, for example, was greatly improved by an aqueduct,[11] and when the islands were threatened with famine in latter stages of the First World War, the government made adequate provisions for food relief and rationing.[12] Much of the military's attention, however, went to monitoring and suppressing Greek irredentism. Between 1912 and 1923, many local activists were gaoled and expelled, and some of the more powerful and politically active institutions were closed down, like the *demarchia* of Rhodes Town in February 1913.[13] Throughout this first phase, the islanders remained wary of Italy's intentions in the Dodecanese. Suspicion also persisted abroad, as French and British critics questioned, for example, the necessity of economic development plans when the occupation was supposed to be temporary.[14] The establishment in 1914 of an Italian archaeological school in Rhodes was a more ominous sign.[15] Italian enthusiasm for local antiquities usually had a political subtext, as new findings were meant to confirm historical connections with Italy, supposedly legitimating her presence in the area.[16]

Many Dodecanesians, however, did regard Italian rule as a welcome change. According to the leading historian of Rhodes, Christos Papachristodoulou, 'the people no longer had the Turks as masters, but now had civilised Christians'. Unhindered by Ottoman authorities, Papachristodoulou claimed that Rhodians were now free to raise the standard of Greek education and establish many more schools.[17] The Greeks of the Dodecanese also felt quite safe from inter-ethnic conflict which began to erupt throughout Anatolia. An increasing number of Ottoman Greek refugees had begun to arrive during the first phase of Italian rule, spreading stories of victimisation and Turkish atrocities. Even the most ardent of Greek Dodecanesian nationalists believed Italian rule to be a far lesser evil than Turkish rule.

For some of the former 'Privileged Islands', however, which had long been accustomed to autonomy and exemption from taxation, any new regime was bound to be unpopular. In contrast to Papachristodoulou, the Kalymnian historian, Ippokratis Frangopoulos, argued that Italian rule in this first period was excessively interventionist. He claimed, with considerable exaggeration, that the Dodecanese now suffered heavy taxation and a loss of privileges, both of which destroyed the local economy and led to mass emigration.[18] To be sure, Italian rule did have its disadvantages for the 'Privileged Islanders'. As Italy and the Ottomans had been belligerents since 1911, and through the First World War, the islanders had found themselves cut off from important markets along the Anatolian coast, as well as from crucial resources; without access to Anatolian timber, for instance, the Simian boat building trade was devastated. Dodecanesian sponge divers were no longer allowed to exploit Libyan waters for military reasons, presumably to monitor movements between the empire and Libya. (Italian sponge vessels were allowed to fish in these waters.)[19]

Greek historians tend to blame the Italians for local decline, even though decline had been in the making before the invasion. Kastellorizo and Kasos had already suffered significant population decreases before the Italians arrived; between 1910 and 1912, over half the people of Kastellorizo had emigrated to Egypt and Australia.[20] With the steady penetration of motorised shipping into the local transportation market, the caiques of Kasos and Kastellorizo were eventually rendered obsolete. Meanwhile, Simi and Kalymnos

were deeply affected by the vicissitudes of the sponge trade. The
introduction of light diving suits and new fishing techniques
('Fernez'), which made sponge fishing more efficient and less
expensive, led to an over-supply of sponges just when demand in
Europe had been falling.[21] The First World War itself added further
misery to community life, disrupting maritime trade and causing
significant food shortages.[22] Between 1912 and 1922, the population
of Simi plummeted from 22 450 to about 7000 people, while that of
Kalymnos dropped from 23 000 to just over 15 000.[23]

The varying fortunes of the Dodecanese Islands between 1912 and
1923 left mixed impressions in popular memory. For the once
prosperous sponge trading islands, the first period of Italian rule
had brought an end to their golden age. And as Kalymnos, Simi,
Halki and Kastellorizo were not to benefit from much capital
investment and infrastructural development after 1923, they had less
reason than other islanders to be grateful for the Italian presence. The
Kalymnians especially were to develop an anti-Italian ideology
which came to define their own identity *vis-à-vis* the other islanders.
Kalymnian interviewees were less concerned than others in providing
a balanced portrait of Italian rule, largely because being Kalymnian
came to mean being anti-Italian. For other islanders, however, the
years 1923 to 1936 were times of prosperity and high employment,
and as will be shown later, Italian rule was in many ways their *belle
époque*.

No political protests against Italian rule were recorded during the
First World War. The islanders were unaware that the Dodecanese
was among many territories offered to Italy to entice her into joining
the Entente Cordiale. The secrecy surrounding the details of the
Treaty of London in April 1915 was effective, and nor did the
islanders know of another agreement at St Jean de Maurienne in
April 1917, where the Italians were promised even more territorial
spoils.[24] Failure to secure these agreements once the war had ended,
however, left Italy in the same position as before she entered the
war.[25] The future of the Dodecanese was again open to negotiation,
and Italian statesmen and diplomats were forced to use the same
diplomatic skills and guile they had exemplified before the war.

In the meantime, Dodecanesian leaders felt by 1919 that it was time
to resume their agitation for unification with Greece. Wealthy
expatriates in Athens and Alexandria, for example, fought hard to
lobby the support of Great Power leaders, who were meeting in Paris
for the Peace Conferences. Propaganda on the demise of the sponge

islands, which was presented as evidence of Italian 'oppression', was their chief weapon. The most prominent Dodecanesian agitator, Skevos Zervos, a Kalymnian doctor based in Athens, sent numerous works of propaganda to Paris, alleging that the Italians were committing genocide, that Dodecanesians were being wilfully starved and forced to emigrate.[26] Such attempts to influence international diplomacy 'from below' were common in the history of the so-called Eastern Question. Ottoman minorities had been conscious of the weaknesses of the empire, and actively sought the patronage and support of powers like Russia and Britain. Minority leaders were aware that reports of Ottoman atrocities, often greatly exaggerated, could sometimes sway European public opinion and statesmen. Interest groups like the Greeks of the Dodecanese, which were otherwise powerless, found the only way to have an influence in their own political destiny was through propaganda, plebiscites and petitions, in the hope that these would entice the major nations of Europe to act on their behalf. As the following example shows, the real impact of lobbying is difficult to estimate.

In early 1919, rumour spread that Italian delegates were misrepresenting Dodecanesian opinion at the Paris Peace Conferences, claiming the islanders wanted Italian rule to become permanent. To support their case, Italian delegates claimed to have declarations signed by seventeen prominent Dodecanesians.[27] Incensed by this Italian ploy, Dodecanesian leaders responded by organising a general plebiscite to re-confirm to the world, and to themselves, their unequivocal desire for unification with Greece. The plebiscite was orchestrated by the Church, which was headed by an energetic and politically active young bishop named Apostolos Trifonos. Apostolos organised the plebiscite for 20 April, Easter Monday, and as expected, the result was unanimous in favour of unification.[28] The celebrations which ensued throughout the Dodecanese were kept under control, but in the village of Paradisi, Rhodes, ill-disciplined Italian troops opened fired on a crowd, killing a local priest and a young woman.[29] The incident was to be remembered as 'The Bloody Easter of 1919' ('To Emateró Páscha tou 1919'). The dead, 'Papa Loukas' and 'Anthoula', were immediately consecrated as martyrs of modern Hellenism, and today the main square of Paradisi is dominated by statues of the two martyrs.[30] 'Bloody Easter', which had more propaganda value than the plebiscites, was used to some effect by the Greek Prime Minister, Eleftherios Venizelos, who was in Paris staking territorial claims for

Greece. He found a sympathetic ear in Lloyd George, who, along with Clemenceau, had been disturbed by Italian military operations in south-western Anatolia in the wake of the Ottoman collapse, and both leaders were keen for an excuse to curb further Italian expansion.[31] In July 1919, the Tittoni-Venizelos Accord was signed, in which most of the Dodecanese Islands were to be ceded to Greece, though the fate of Rhodes was to be decided in a plebiscite after five years. In August 1920, the Treaty of Sèvres extended the period to fifteen years.[32] Bishop Apostolos and other Dodecanesian leaders had come to believe that the Accord was a response to the plebiscite and 'Bloody Easter', but Wilsonian principles of national self-determination, and British and French resolve to take the islands out of Italian hands, were probably more telling factors.[33]

The Tittoni-Venizelos Accord and the Treaty of Sèvres were causes for celebration in the Dodecanese.[34] The islanders thought their fate had finally been resolved, that soon they were to be united with 'Mother Greece'. But before Sèvres could be officially ratified, international power relations were to change; the position of Britain and Greece would weaken significantly, allowing Italy to renege on old deals. Greek troops had occupied Smyrna and its environs in 1919, and then proceeded into the Anatolian interior, where they were checked and then driven back by Turkish nationalists under Kemal Mustafa Atatürk. By the middle of 1921, the resurgent Turks had begun to threaten positions in Anatolia held by British, French and Italian forces. Like the French, who had come to terms with Atatürk in October 1921, the Italians were unwilling to defend their new territorial gains and settled on economic concessions. The British came to terms with Atatürk rather belatedly in October 1922, but not before a tense stand-off at Chanak. The Treaty of Sèvres now had to be completely revised, and with the Greeks severely weakened after their crushing military defeat, the Italians felt they no longer needed to fulfil their part of the Treaty regarding the Dodecanese.[35] Outraged island leaders responded by drawing up more petitions, hoping their desire for unification might move Italian and Great Power leaders, but to no avail. Nationalist agitation continued; many local Greek leaders were dismissed from local government positions, while Bishop Apostolos and his colleague, Bishop Germanos of Karpathos and Kasos, were sent into exile.[36]

With Britain's position in the eastern Mediterranean weakened after the Chanak Crisis, Italy again felt confident enough to make deals, to trade the islands for new concessions. This time her eyes were set on Jubaland, a large territory on the southern border of Italian Somalia. On 24 July 1923, the islands were transferred 'temporarily' to Italian control under the Treaty of Lausanne. Britain continued to insist that the Dodecanese be given to the Greeks, but the Italians were only prepared to agree in return for Jubaland. Like many of his predecessors, the British foreign secretary, Lord Curzon, was determined not to allow the Italians to get their way, but the following year saw a change of government in London which finally left the door open for full Italian sovereignty. Ramsay MacDonald's new Labour government was eager to resolve international problems with 'strenuous action and good-will'.[37] On 6 August, the Treaty of Lausanne was ratified, giving Italy both the Dodecanese *and* Jubaland.[38] As Richard Bosworth has pointed out, the Italians showed that even after twelve years of uncertain 'temporary' rule, possession was shown to be 'nine-tenths of the law'.[39]

LE ISOLE ITALIANE DELL'EGEO: ADMINISTRATION

The Italians rarely referred to the islands as 'the Dodecanese'. Initially they employed the simple phrase 'Le Isole dell'Egeo', but after Lausanne had been ratified, the name was altered to 'Le Isole Italiane dell'Egeo'.[40] The change in name, from 'the Aegean Islands' to 'Italy's Aegean Islands', also augured a change in the nature of governance. The Italians had envisaged far-reaching changes to what had been an Ottoman provincial backwater. The architectural landscape was to be transformed, new industries were to be introduced, and a modern economic infrastructure established. The most ambitious and radical project was to make Dodecanesians into Italians. To implement modernisation and cultural assimilation policies, the regime itself had to be quite modern. Mere possession of empire was not enough to uphold the esteemed international status which Italy sought. After all, the Ottomans had a large empire, but the Sultans of Constantinople were regarded as 'Oriental Despots' who presided over backwardness, contended with endemic rebellion, and tolerated mass atrocities.[41] Empire could just as well show how 'uncivilised' a power was, for the way in which colonial territories were ruled reflected upon the nations which ruled them. Colonial territories were not merely testing grounds of European mettle, but also of their moral worth, their ability to tame and civilise, and to raise indigenous peoples out of their 'backward' condition.[42]

European public opinion doubted the Italians were fit for the task. When western journalists derided Italian imperial adventurism in Libya and Ethiopia, they were not really railing against colonialism itself, but questioning Italy's suitability for the heady responsibilities of colonial rule.[43] After touring the Dodecanese in the mid-1920s, Isabelle and C.D. Booth concluded that the Italians did many good things, having built roads and taken excellent care of antiquities, but they complained the Italians were over-zealous in policing the local population. The Booths concluded that this was a reflection of Italian immaturity, and that much could be learned from the more judicious and tempered methods of the British on Cyprus.[44] Italian colonial enthusiasts, however, never doubted the capacity of their countrymen to rule over foreign lands and peoples. With their massive road-building programmes and feats of engineering in Africa, and in transforming the Libyan coast into Italy's 'Fourth Shore', the Italians believed they had proved their worth.[45] So confident were they of their imperial calling that, like the French, they too felt duty bound to spread their culture, and expected the natives to adopt it gratefully. Social engineering, which represented the highest point of European conceit, required governmental structures which were far more professional, comprehensive and interventionist than those of the Ottomans.

After the Treaty of Lausanne had been ratified in 1924, the Italians felt they no longer had to ascribe to Ameglio's initial promise to the islanders of 'massimo rispetto alla vostra religione, ai vostri usi, alle vostre tradizioni'. The governor who was to have an enormous impact on island life was Mario Lago (1924 to 1936), an aristocrat from Peveragno in the Piedmontese province of Cuneo.[46] Under his aegis, the new administrative structure was installed to transform Dodecanesian society. As in the French and Dutch empires, colonial governors in each of Italy's overseas territories were invested with plenary powers.[47] The governor (*governatore*) of Dodecanese had his own civil service and budget, and according to a contemporary legal expert, the governor was the 'unico depositario di quasi tutti i poteri dello Stato italiano nel Possedimento'.[48] He could issue decrees, gaol and expel civilians without trial, appoint magistrates and administrative personnel, dismiss local government appointees and close down *demarchies*. He also had the power to establish and issue monopolies. Furthermore, the governor had little interference from government officials and departments in Rome, or from metropolitan agencies in the Dodecanese. The investment of such enormous powers in one individual was meant to enhance the effective operation of administration.

The governor's offices and residence were in Rhodes Town, and the islands of Rhodes and Halki came under his direct responsibility.[49] The rest of the archipelago was divided into administrative units based on older Ottoman divisions (*mudirs*), with the governor's representatives or *delegati* stationed in Kalymnos, Leros, Karpathos, Simi and Kastellorizo. Kos, the second most important island in political and economic terms, was initially appointed a *podestà*, and later a *reggente* (regent).[50] Assisting the governor in general administrative affairs was a *segretario generale*, whose responsibilities were quite comprehensive. They included education policy, official archives, budget accounting, registration of land, security and passport control, taxation, public health and hygiene, and port and customs services. The *segretario* was responsible for checking administrative abuse and corruption, he presided over contractual disputes, and was the official censor of local and imported literature.[51] Four major government departments or *direzione* attended to the more mundane operations of administration. The *Direzione degli Affari Commerciali* monitored commercial life among the islands, as well as external trade, particularly with Italy. The *Direzione dei Servizi Amministrativi* was principally responsible for the treasury, taxation, mortgages, land registration, and the government tobacco monopoly. The *Direzione dei Lavori Pubblici* took care of developmental projects, including ports, public buildings, architecture, roads and urban planning. The *Direzione dell'Agricoltura e del Lavoro* concerned itself mainly with agriculture, zoology and forestry. Another department, the *Sovrintendenza ai monumenti e scavi*, dealt specifically with scholarly research, archaeological excavations and the conservation of antiquities.[52]

As for the indigenous population, they were gradually removed from any meaningful political role in Dodecanesian life. Under Mario Lago, traditional local government continued to operate in most village communities and in some of the main towns, though these institutions suffered extensive interference. Government nominees were increasingly found in control of local government, but once Lago was replaced as governor by the *Quadrumviro* De Vecchi, local government was abolished altogether. The colonial government also paid considerable attention to policing the local population. As was common in conquered territories, the occupiers relied heavily on collaborators to inform on community members and report any seditious activities. More important were the *Carabinieri* and the *Guardia di Finanza*.[53] A detachment of the Royal Carabinieri (*Carabinieri Reali*) dealt specifically with the maintenance of civil order, while the *Guardia di Finanza* were meant to enforce the myriad of commercial and farming regulations, and were especially concerned with hunting down contraband goods. According to Dodecanesian oral tradition, both the *carabinieri* and the '*finanza*' were a pervasive, almost suffocating, presence.[54] In the event of serious public disturbances, the governor could always call upon troops stationed in Rhodes, Kos and Leros. In April 1935, for example, troops stationed in Kos were summoned to Kalymnos, where the *carabinieri* had lost control of a series of popular protests.[55]

Compared to what they had been accustomed to under the Ottomans, however, Dodecanesians felt the Italian colonial system, though highly regulated and restrictive, was much more progressive. Italian rule, as will be discussed in greater detail in Chapter 5, appealed to local conceptions on how society should operate, and hence in some ways the period witnessed a convergence of interests between the occupiers and occupied. The islanders came to believe that strong government was necessary for the maintenance of law and order, and that Italian administration provided a suitable model from which much could be learned. The occupation gave many of the islanders, especially on Rhodes and Kos, their first taste of civic government, as public issues like sanitation and sewerage were attended to swiftly and effectively. Dodecanesians were impressed by a bureaucratic system which extolled an ethos of professionalism and public responsibility. Memories of such impressive achievements prevented the islanders from being co-opted fully into Greek nationalist discourses on the Italian Occupation.

MILITARY AND ECONOMIC FUNCTIONS

When considering the *funzione* of their colonies, Italian commentators agreed that the prime function of the Dodecanese was military.[56] They often discussed Italy's strategic interests in the eastern Mediterranean, including how, for example, Greek, Turkish and British naval bases were within bombing range of the Dodecanese.[57] Mussolini's Fascists kept alive the dreams of their Liberal predecessors for an empire in the Levant, and the islands were still considered a good vantage point for further expansion in the area. The Dodecanese were therefore afforded a special status. Unlike the African colonies, which were the responsibility of a separate ministry, the islands came under *Ministero degli Affari Esteri* (Ministry of Foreign Affairs). The island group was classified as a 'Possedimento' (estate) rather than as a 'Colonia', and the indigenous were categorised as citizens of the Kingdom of Italy (*Cittadini del Regno*), though they did not enjoy all the rights of full citizenship, and males were not liable for military service. As one Italian commentator had put it, the Dodecanese Islands formed neither a province nor colony; their status was below that of a province and above that of a colony.[58] Local Greek historians have found the distinction congenial, largely because it seemed to accord the islanders a higher status than the 'races' inhabiting Libya and East Africa.[59]

For most of the interwar period, the Italians kept one infantry regiment in the Dodecanese, with one battalion stationed on Rhodes and another on Kos. Each of these islands also had an air base. There were small naval bases at Karpathos and Astypalea, but Italy's most important and heavily fortified naval base was Leros, which was blessed with a series of sheltered harbours, including one long, deep-water harbour re-named Portolago, which had destroyers, gunboats and submarines. The island could also boast 3 018 pieces of artillery, including 49 howitzers and 515 tonnes of ammunition. Over seven thousand troops were based on Leros, as were several hundred naval personnel, all of whom resided in a newly built, modern town (Lakki) on Portolago's shores.[60]

The Booths described Leros as another Gibraltar,[61] while locals were fond of calling their island 'the Malta of the Aegean' (i Málta tou Egéou). In a sense, the apparent international importance which the island had acquired did become a source of pride for Lerians. They were also over-awed by the heavy military presence; a popular local myth has it that the Italians brought so many armaments that they were forced to burrow deep into her hills to store them, leaving the mountains of Leros 'hollow' (ta vouná tis Lérou íne koúfia).[62] In the end, the Italians never made much use of their military bases in the Dodecanese, especially as British naval mastery in the Mediterranean was never seriously challenged. De Vecchi used submarines to attack neutral shipping in the Aegean in August 1940, and sank the Greek destroyer 'Elli' without permission from Rome.[63] Otherwise the Dodecanese did not further Italy's dreams of an empire in the eastern Mediterranean, nor did they give much assistance to the Axis during the war.

Nor did the islands offer Italy any substantive economic benefits. Economic arguments for empire in Italy were discussed after the fact, when the initial excitement of conquest had passed, and when the politicians in Rome were forced to face the true costs of empire. The government in Rhodes Town tried to use its comprehensive administrative apparatus to extract as much economic value out of the islands as possible. A whole series of taxes and charges were instituted, which included a land tax, poll tax, charges on local manufactured goods, customs and port dues, and stamp duties.[64] The occupiers also instituted monopolies and took over those established by the Ottomans. The most important was TEMI (*Tabacchi egei: Manifattura italiana*), which controlled the production and processing of tobacco, and became a major employer. The quality of TEMI tobacco and cigarette paper, however, was quite poor, and locals preferred to buy cheaper and better quality contraband tobacco from Anatolia and mainland Greece.[65] Other monopolies were farmed out to Italian companies. The *Compagnia Commerciale Italiana*, for instance, a Triestine establishment, gained the exclusive right to exploit a salt lake on Kos. The marketing and export of fruit and vegetable produce from Rhodes and Kos was leased to companies such as the *Compagnia Agricola Industriale di Rodi* (CAIR), which purchased currants at set prices and exported to Italy, Libya and Egypt. The olive crop, second in rank to currants in terms of export value, was also exclusively marketed and exported by Italian firms, which also controlled all the olive presses.[66]

With the colonial government targeting the more profitable sectors of the Dodecanesian economy, which were seized and squeezed by Italian interests, there was little room for established local interests to operate. Greek merchants were victimised by ruinous regulations and licensing which favoured Italian companies.[67] Such was the case with inter-island freight transport, where local operators could not continue their trade because they could not obtain government licences. Much of the heavy freight transportation was leased to the Italian firm *Compagnia Commerciale Italiana per L'Egeo*.[68]

Another policy which damaged some local interests was land expropriation, which particularly affected Greek and Turkish elites, and wealthier peasant families, who together owned most of the arable land.[69] The Italians introduced a colonisation programme primarily to create a modern, profitable agricultural sector. Six settlements were established in the Dodecanese under Mario Lago, four on Rhodes, two on Kos. Each settlement was founded in a fertile region with good access to water. The Rhodian colony of 'Peveragno' was publicised by the occupiers as their model settlement. Reports focused on its modern town plan, its functional homes, its paved streets, and more importantly, its agricultural specialities. From Salerno came pastoralists, from Romagna came fruit producers, and settlers from Padua brought with them their skills in cereal production.[70]

Balancing the budget, however, remained a persistent problem for the colonial government. The *Rassegna Economica Delle Colonie*, a contemporary Italian journal with up-to-date economic statistics, showed consistent negative trade balance figures.[71] Between 1928 and 1932, tonnage of imports outweighed exports ten-fold. Budget imbalances, though on a far grander scale, had also plagued Italy's African colonies, where difficulties were compounded by expensive military operations.[72] The empire was clearly a massive waste of Italy's limited resources, a huge burden on Italy's fragile economy, but reports in periodicals such as *Azione Coloniale*, *Gerarchia* and the *Rivista Coloniale* persisted in elaborating platitudes on the economic and strategic potential of the colonies. Italy's claims to being a major power were at stake, and her 'politically minded gentlemen' continued to believe that empire was crucial in maintaining their country's honour. Locals were also conscious that their occupiers had gone to great expense to develop the Dodecanese, which to some extent confirmed their image of Italians as benevolent and humanitarian, and yet raised questions in their own minds about the logic of the coloniser's programme. Many interviewees were of the opinion that the government in Rome paid great attention to the Dodecanese 'while their own people went hungry' (I dikí tous pinoúsan), that the Italians were giving privileged treatment to strangers such as themselves. If anything, or at least as far as Dodecanesians were concerned, it was the colonised who were profiting from Italy's expensive colonial ventures.

SHOWPIECES OF PROGRESS AND MODERNITY

In 1932, after visiting many ports in the Levant, Alfredo Lenzi felt that he was well placed to appreciate the difference that Italian rule had made on Rhodes. The island was like a modern oasis surrounded by Levantine backwardness, which was proof of the 'capacità organizzative della nuova Italia'. Fascist Italy believed it inherited the mantle of Imperial Rome, western culture's paradigm of order and civilisation. Like their Roman forebears, the men of the *nuova Italia* believed it was their duty to disseminate the civilisation of the metropolis, to build new cities, to erect monuments and construct roads, and to establish a new *Pax Romana*. As with many other Italian commentators who marvelled at what was being done in the Dodecanese, Lenzi used the record of the Ottomans as his frame of reference. Under the Turks, he claimed, agriculture was in 'desolante abbandono', and the forests had been half destroyed. In Italian hands, however, the islands had become part of the modern world within a handful of years, revitalising 'agriculture, building construction, roadworks, industry, trade, tourism, public education, archaeological research, sanitation, the judicial system and maritime trade'.[73]

The Dodecanese had indeed experienced a metamorphosis. As Denis Mack Smith points out, Fascist Italy expended more than any other imperial power on her colonial territories, which he claims would have been better invested in some of the depressed regions of Italy.[74] One of the major achievements of the regime in the Dodecanese, as in the African colonies, was to create a modern economic infrastructure. Road construction went on almost unabated through the interwar period, as Rhodes Town was finally connected with the island's forty-seven villages. Mechanised transport was introduced, port facilities were improved to cater for modern shipping, and airports large enough to manage major aircraft were opened on Rhodes and Kos. The Italians also excelled in town planning. The medieval section of Rhodes Town, built during the reign of the Hospitallers, was extensively renovated and restored, but outside its walls the occupiers built a modern town with wide thoroughfares and piazzas lined with neo-classical and modern architecture. Italian town planners also set to work in a number of rural centres (e.g. Peveragno, Linopoti), in Leros and Kos Town.

Thus while Italo Balbo was transforming the Libyan 'sandbox' into the 'Fourth Shore', Mario Lago was turning the Dodecanese Islands into showpieces of Italian civilisation.[75] In concentrating on the development and modernisation of her colonies, Italy was following an international trend in colonial governance, for as Raymond Betts points out, all the imperial powers by the interwar period had come to believe that the 'serious business of empire was order and development'.[76] Natives were expected to reap the benefits of British justice and administration, or the fruits of French civilisation. European ingenuity in engineering and science was to help raise the 'natives' out of their backward state. The Italians also believed their 'natives' stood to benefit enormously, but as elsewhere, the new paternalistic spirit of international colonialism also served to reify existing inequalities between rulers and the ruled.[77] Much like the other imperial powers, Italy was less concerned with how development would help colonial subjects than with how Balbo's and Lago's achievements would promote her reputation. In the following appraisal from the *Rassegna Italiana*, which is not untypical in its nationalistic and romantic tone, the basic purpose of Italian colonialism is made quite clear:

> This is the setting of beauty and poetry which Italy has created in the Aegean possessions, as Italy is visible in every manifestation of life in this corner of our country....[78]

The colonisers were keen to prove Italy's fitness as a ruling culture, and agricultural reform was one method of demonstrating this eligibility. Important groups like the *Società Agricoltura Industriale*, the *Società dei Tabacchi Egei Manufattura Italiana*, and the *Società Frutticoltura di Rodi*, experimented and demonstrated new farming methods to achieve qualitative and quantitative improvements. They also showed locals the benefits of using fertilisers and pesticides.[79] The Italians also experimented with new products, which included an attempt to make *spumante* out of local currants.[80] Modern farming methods and experimentation were conducted on expropriated land, with the assistance of Italian colonists, but local peasants were not slow to acknowledge these modern innovations. In Dodecanesian oral tradition, the Italians were remembered as having produced 'beautiful things' (oréa prámata), whose scientists or 'scholars' (epistímones) from Italy grew vegetables and fruit larger than had ever been seen before. The islanders also responded to, and drew their own meanings from, Italian public works and development policy, and these will be considered at length in Chapter 5. The rest of this section will discuss two particular fields which made a lesser impression on locals, but which were nevertheless construed by Dodecanesians as symbols of Italian civilisation and modernity. These were the tourist industry and the official promotion of high culture.

The colonial government likened high culture to Italian civilisation, and therefore the islands were adorned with monumental edifices, elegant neo-classical structures and the latest trends in Italian architecture. For the first time, opera, ballet and classical music were performed publicly in the Dodecanese, and artists and Italian theatrical companies gave regular performances at the Puccini Theatre in Rhodes Town, as well as at similar venues in Kos and Leros. The agenda for high culture events was set by the *Reale Instituto di Perfezionamento <<Dante Alighieri>>*, and all coming attractions were advertised in the official newspaper, *Il Messaggero di Rodi*. Regular features in the social calendar included lectures by visiting dignitaries on various subjects, including classical literature, law and Fascism.[81]

The regime paid great attention to the excavation, restoration and preservation of heritage items. As early as 1912, members of the Italian Archaeological School at Athens were invited to inspect the neglected antiquities of the Dodecanese. Two years later, a scholarly archaeological journal, *Clara Rhodos*, had begun publication, and a classical museum was set up in an old Hospitaller infirmary.[82] Much painstaking work went into the restoration of the medieval section of Rhodes Town and its fortifications. Its castle, the 'Palazzo del Gran Maestro', was the most pronounced landmark of Italian restoration work. It was virtually destroyed by a massive gunpowder explosion in 1856, after which the Ottomans used what was left as a gaolhouse. Restoration work commenced in 1933, which involved rebuilding two entire levels of 75 80 metres, which according to one estimate cost some 40 million lire.[83] Another major feat undertaken by the colonisers was the excavation of the Hellenistic and Roman levels of Kos Town, which took place after the town was devastated by an earthquake in 1933.[84]

A great deal of archaeological work was carried out in the Dodecanese, with considerable official encouragement. Archaeology was associated with bourgeois Europe's desire to explore and define its links with the Classical World, and official Italian promotion of excavations was meant to reflect Italy's standing as a progressive, European culture.[85] Archaeology was also employed to support official platitudes on Italy's legitimate place in the Aegean, as scholars developed a discourse which underlined the continuity of Italian influence in the Dodecanese since Roman times. As for the Classical and Hellenistic periods, these were presented by one Fascist writer as 'natural' antecedents of the Roman period, much as

Paganism was the 'natural' forerunner of Christianity.[86] The Middle Ages were also accounted for. The Hospitallers, or the Knights of St John, who were an international force, were claimed by the colonial regime to be as much a part of Italy's heritage in the Aegean as were the Genoese and the Venetians.[87] The regime also exploited historical monuments in other ways. More than any other structure, the imposing 'Palazzo del Gran Maestro', which dominated the whole of Rhodes Town, was meant to exude a sense of grandeur about the regime. On its completion in 1939, it became De Vecchi's residence, with its huge towers, canons, and turrets and crenellations. But the castle was too perfectly reconstructed, and like De Vecchi the man, the Palazzo was ostentatious and lacked subtlety. The hallways were adorned with large vases from the Far East, Hellenistic mosaics were transported from Kos to cover the floors, and ancient statues, fixed with heads from Renaissance period, lined the grand courtyard.

So proud were the Italians of their achievements in the Dodecanese that they hoped as many travellers as possible would visit. The colonial regime, mindful of its financial difficulties, also recognised the economic potential of tourism, and therefore sought to turn Rhodes into the *'centro turistico del Mediterraneo Orientale'*.[88] Italian writers extolled the archipelago's many attractions; its archaeological riches, the quaint customs and costumes of the indigenous, the panoramic scenery, and, of course, the regime's great achievements in public works.[89] Other features made the islands conducive to regular tourism. Long dry summers, coupled with the cooling effect of northerly winds, produced conditions ideal for holiday-makers in search of sun and sand. The Dodecanese were well placed on a busy tourist route between Venice and Egypt, and the colonial government made concerted efforts to entice travel companies like Thomas Cook to make Rhodes an established tour juncture.[90] Major European airlines *en route* to the Near East and Asia began to use Rhodes as a regular stop-over, including Germany's Lufthansa, Dutch KLM, and the Polish airline LOT.[91]

Much of the colonial government's investment in public works was directed towards transforming Rhodes into a first class tourist venue for wealthy holiday-makers. Visitors were not merely expected to enjoy their holidays but to marvel at the tourist industry itself, which was also set up as an advertisement for Italian civilisation. Several large hotels appeared during Lago's governorship, and among these was the *Grande Albergo delle Rose*, which had 160 rooms, 80 bathrooms, and first-class restaurants, and the *L'Albergo delle Terme*, which boasted 170 bedrooms.[92] Hotels were concentrated along beach-fronts to capitalise on the growing popularity of water sports and sun-bathing. The colonial government also created parks like *Rodini* on the outskirts of Rhodes Town, with its streams, ponds and lush vegetation, and what is now called the 'Valley of the Butterflies', so named because of the plethora of multicoloured butterflies which fill the park during the summer months. Other popular attractions included Mount Ilias and its forests, a popular venue for hunting sports, and the hot springs of Kalithea, with its futuristic-styled bathing complex. Italian Rhodes also catered for modern sportsmen, including golfers, cyclists and motor-car racers.[93] Initially, most tourists came from Italy, Greece, Egypt and the Levant, but by the late thirties, more were arriving from northern Europe, as estimates of tourist intake in the late 1930s began to reach up to 50 000 people per annum.[94] One of the government's lasting achievements was to prepare Rhodes for the advent of mass tourism in the postwar period. Rhodes became a major centre of the Mediterranean tourist trade, and the industry became the island's chief source of income and employment.[95]

RELIGION, LANGUAGE AND CULTURAL POLICY

Locals welcomed those Italian programmes and practices which improved material conditions among the Dodecanese Islands, and interviewees conveyed their appreciation by according the occupiers full credit for their efforts. At the same time, interviewees were ready to criticise and denounce unpopular Italian measures, particularly those which had posed a threat to their identity. The colonial regime pursued two policies which many Dodecanesians felt would destroy their culture: a religious policy, which some believed cloaked a secret scheme to convert the islanders to Roman Catholicism, and a policy of cultural assimilation, which involved making Italians out of Dodecanesians. The islanders were keen to accept the material benefits of foreign rule, but stood defiant against Italian social engineering schemes.

Not long after the Treaty of Lausanne had been ratified, Mario Lago set in train a religious policy which sought to sever the bishoprics of the Dodecanese from the Patriarchate of

Constantinople. He envisaged an autonomous ecclesiastical system headed by an independent bishop or 'Autokephalos' based in Rhodes Town, and he sought to secure this with the assent of the Patriarchate. Many precedents had already been set in Orthodox ecclesiastical history; the Church of Cyprus had been an independent see since the Council of Ephesus in AD 431, and once the Greeks had gained their independence in 1832, they created an autonomous national Church headed by the Archbishop of Athens.[96] One Italian commentator who took a special interest in the issue, Arnaldo Bertola, argued that it was conventional for Orthodox ecclesiastical boundaries to alter and align with changing political boundaries.[97] Political motives behind the ecclesiastical policy were not difficult to surmise, however. The local clergy proved themselves to be quite a nuisance during the first decade of Italian rule. Of Bishop Germanos of Karpathos and Kasos, one Italian general allegedly said, 'Your grace, you should have been an army officer, not a bishop.'[98] Bishop Apostolos of Rhodes was widely acknowledged as the leader of national protest movement in 1919, and his residence was the movement's *de facto* headquarters. In his memoirs, the bishop boasted that the Italians watched his every move, and that 'friends and enemies of the diocese admitted candidly that such energy and resourcefulness had never been displayed by the Bishopric of Rhodes'.[99] Lago hoped his policy would isolate the local clergy from the pro-Greek Patriarchate of Constantinople, and stop any more nationalist priests from being appointed to the Dodecanese. Moreover, Lago felt he would be better placed to exert his influence over the personnel and extensive structure of the Church, to keep troublesome priests in check and to control appointments and promotions.

Apostolos claimed he was aware that Lago's motives were political, but he went along with the scheme regardless.[100] Apostolos was personally attracted by the prospect of heading his own autonomous see, but he had also resigned himself to the fact that Italian rule was permanent, and that an independent ecclesiastical structure made good administrative sense. The other bishops, including Germanos, concurred.[101] This was a boon for Lago, who was aware that attaining the approval of the Patriarchate was a delicate matter, and he needed respected authorities like Apostolos to secure it for him. Lago also hoped that, with the support of the bishops, and with properly conducted negotiations with the Patriarchate, the lower clergy and the lay community would accept the new system.[102] This was not to be. Local elites and Dodecanesian organisations abroad denounced Lago's religious policy as an attempt to nullify the political power of the Church, and the bishops were condemned as collaborators.[103] 'The Autokephalo', as the controversy became known, drew passionate responses from among the lower clergy and the general population. Village priests questioned why their Catholic rulers should seek to meddle in their religious affairs, and why these 'Franks' were violating the sacrosanctity of Orthodoxy. The issue stirred a latent 'anti-papism' which was quite common among the lower clergy and some sections of the laity.[104]

The Patriarchate was quite conscious of the unpopularity of 'the Autokephalo', and after losing most of its ecclesiastical territories in Asia Minor after the Greek population had been expelled in 1923, it was not keen to lose any more. Official talks started in late 1924. Despite the Patriarchate's weak position, it managed to obstruct the negotiations by setting numerous conditions and by insisting on cumbersome procedures, all of which proved extremely time-consuming. In 1929 Patriarch Photius II set the most difficult of conditions; he demanded that 'the Autokephalo' must have a popular mandate, which Lago rejected.[105] By January 1934, the bishops lost patience and decided to act without the Patriarchate's approval. They met at the Monastery of Panormitis on Simi to proceed with 'the Autokephalo', effecting what was essentially an ecclesiastical schism. Schisms were not uncommon in the Orthodox world, but they were always treated seriously, particularly among the lower clergy who often conflated schism with heresy. To many Dodecanesian priests, the decision taken on Simi confirmed in their minds that the bishops had betrayed Orthodoxy. On Leros, for instance, a young priest named 'Papanastasis' tried to incite a protest, calling the faithful to the centre of the main town, Agia Marina, by ringing the church bells and then unfurling the Greek flag from the bell tower. He was duly arrested and deported.[106] In Kalymnos, locals were so alarmed by the actions of the bishops that they decided to keep their churches closed indefinitely. The Bishop of Kalymnos, Apostolos Kavakopoulos, who required heavy Italian protection after his return from Simi, was denounced by his lower clergy as an apostate and a traitor. When Kavakopoulos's supporters attempted to conduct a religious service in one of the main churches in April 1935, they provoked the most violent series of protests in the history of the occupation. Some Kalymnians used the occasion to agitate against Italian rule itself, but the chief driving force behind their protests was an ardent belief that 'the Autokephalo' was part of a Papal conspiracy. The Italians, they feared, sought to turn the islanders into 'Franks' (tha mas Frangépsoun).[107]

The belief that Lago planned to convert the islanders to Catholicism has since been widely accepted as a fact by Dodecanesian writers. They insist that Lago planned long-term conversion, though, and that the most likely outcome was that the Dodecanese Church would become a 'Uniate' Church, that is, one which would recognise the supremacy of the Papacy but continue to observe Orthodox or 'Byzantine' rites.[108] These assumptions lack supporting evidence, though the rumour of Catholic conversion stirred more passion in the Dodecanese than any political or economic issue. As De Vecchi himself noted when he assumed the governorship in late 1936, the popular rumour that the religious policy was connected with Catholic conversion was very difficult to dispel, and that the religious policy was not worth the trouble. During his tenure 'the Autokephalo' was given low priority.[109]

Dodecanesian nationalists in the diaspora hailed Mario Lago's recall to Rome in December 1936 as the end of a 'tyrant', but Lago was not remembered as such by most of the islanders.[110] Despite the unpopularity of his religious policy, the reputation of Lago in popular memory rested with the more progressive aspects of his governorship, especially public order and development. Lago had successfully promoted a popular self-image among the general population. He presented himself as a warm-natured and good-humoured man, and along with his equally popular wife, Octavia, he frequently toured the islands and mingled with the crowds. Lago believed quite firmly in the importance of cultivating popular consent, especially with such sensitive issues as religion, but as far as his successor was concerned, the islanders did not deserve to be cultivated. Like a true Fascist, De Vecchi believed that Dodecanesians had no choice but to obey the dictates of the ruling regime.[111] He cared little for their sensibilities, and his style augured a very different kind of governance, one based on bludgeon. For the islanders, De Vecchi's period would be regretfully remembered as the time 'when the Fascists came'.

His approach to cultural policy exemplified his Fascist-styled rule. A long term task of the colonial government had been to assimilate the islanders and make the Dodecanese a true extension of the metropolis. Lago believed the islanders could only be 'Italianised' over a long period of socialisation. In January 1926, he introduced one compulsory hour of Italian language for all school children, and this hour was gradually increased in later years.[112] Greek, Turkish and Jewish teachers were all required to attend Italian language and education courses at the 'Istituto Magistrale' at Rhodes Town, while all who wished to become teachers could only attain their degrees and training from Italian universities and institutions.[113] De Vecchi, a former Fascist minister for education, who believed education was not merely an instrument for moulding the hearts and minds of populace, but was 'the flesh and blood of the state', took a far more aggressive approach.[114] He expected that language attrition could be secured through force, and in his first year as governor, De Vecchi had all Greek secondary schools closed down, and made speaking Greek in public an offence. All children were forced to attend Italian schools and join the Fascist Youth or *Balilla*, and teachers who could not, or would not, teach in Italian were sacked.[115]

The effect of these measures was to galvanise local resistance against Italian assimilation policy. For the first time since 1919, the Italians were faced by widespread dissent, as community leaders successfully established secret language classes in nearly every Dodecanesian town and village. Children of all classes met in the evenings in secret locations, and as will be discussed in greater length in the next chapter, most participants felt they were taking part in a patriotic struggle.[116] Greek nationalist consciousness had hitherto been limited to local elites and the educated petite bourgeoisie, but De Vecchi's measures helped to make nationalism a popular anti-Italian ideology.

In general, De Vecchi's radical departure from Lago's benevolent style made many Dodecanesians decidedly anti-Italian, and they would remember the De Vecchi, or 'Fascist', period with a sense of bitterness. They felt that Italian rule no longer had much to commend itself, for not only did political conditions become far more oppressive, but by now the islands were also feeling the effects of Fascist Italy's worsening economic problems. Public and private investment in the Dodecanese gradually dried up, leading to rising unemployment. Conditions worsened further once Italy joined her Axis partner in war in 1940. Mussolini's invasion of Greece caused ethnic friction between colonial personnel and the occupied, while locals particularly resented the introduction of strict food rationing – interviewees expressed this feeling by complaining that they were not even allowed to pick fruit from their own trees.[117] For Dodecanesians, De Vecchi and Fascism represented repression and economic malaise. The next two governors of the Italian Dodecanese, General Ettore Bastico (Dec. 1940–July 1941), and Admiral Inigo Campioni (July

1941–April 1943) tried to tone down the excesses of De Vecchi's style, but by that time Mussolini's regime was nearing collapse.

NOMINAL ITALIAN RULE, 1943–45

On 8 September 1943, Pietro Badoglio called upon all Italian troops to cease fighting the Allies. Two days later, the British made contact with the Italian military in the Dodecanese to gauge whether they would support an Allied landing. The Italians appeared to hesitate over the matter, leaving enough time for a German garrison on Rhodes to read the danger signs and take control of the island.[118] The British had meanwhile sent troops to occupy Kos and Leros. Churchill believed quite strongly that Rhodes and her airfields would give the Allies total control of the Aegean and thus protect Egypt from possible air attack. He therefore argued strongly for the seizure of Rhodes, but Eisenhower insisted that Allied forces be concentrated on the invasion of Italy, and Churchill claimed the rebuff gave him the 'sharpest pangs'.[119] Kos was later seized by the Wehrmacht without much opposition, while on Leros, Italian and British forces put up dogged resistance in a desperate air and artillery battle which lasted four days.[120] With the fall of Leros, the Dodecanese came under German occupation.

The Germans were primarily interested in securing their military interests in the region, and, to a considerable degree, were content to allow their Fascist allies to continue to run the civil administration. Italian administration was thus maintained, but the reality was similar to that which would soon prevail in the Republic of Salò, where Mussolini was to rule without power. Italians continued to fill administrative positions in the Dodecanese, from governor to desk clerk, and the streets were still policed by *carabinieri*. On many occasions, however, the Germans did make it clear to the islanders who was really in charge, and they did not hesitate to humiliate their Axis allies when necessary. In November 1944, in what constituted a clear challenge to Italian authority, the Germans introduced popular councils or 'Volksbeirat' in which the *millets* (except the Jews) would meet and discuss important economic and social issues, thus encouraging the islanders to air their grievances against the Italian colonial government. The new occupiers also ignored Italian assimilation policy. The German military governor of the eastern Aegean introduced a weekly newspaper in Greek, though as one

Rhodian source complained, the so-called 'Greek News' only contained translated news from Nazi Germany.[121] The clearest challenge to Italian authority came in October 1944, when in response to local requests, the German military approved the re-opening of Greek schools. It had been six years since Greek language was taught in schools, and every town and village community eagerly set about restoring their education programmes. Such measures had convinced the local population that the Germans did not constitute an 'anti-Hellenic' threat, and on a social level, interviewees remembered the new occupiers as stern but civil. Yet, as on the Greek mainland, German reprisals against seditious activities were excessively harsh, and for the first time, Dodecanesians were to witness the horror of public execution. Despite the dangers, more Dodecanesians than ever believed it was their patriotic duty to resist. There was no guerrilla movement as such, but many of the islanders risked their lives to shelter Allied soldiers and send information on German activity to Allied headquarters in Egypt.[122]

While social relations between occupiers and occupied might have been civil, material conditions were desperate. German soldiers plundered the Dodecanese with as much rapacity as they did the mainland, taking as much food as they could find and making very little provisions for the welfare of the local population. Trade collapsed, a black market took its place, and production levels of all basic commodities plummeted. Between 1939 and 1945, oil production had halved, and wheat and tobacco yields had fallen to less than one quarter of pre-war levels.[123] Townspeople ventured into the countryside to scavenge for food, and hundreds of families escaped to Anatolia, from where they were transported to refugee camps in British Palestine. The former 'Privileged Islands' had been greatly reliant on food imports, and many of their inhabitants died of starvation.[124]

A more tragic fate fell upon the Dodecanesian Jewry. In July 1944, the Jews of Rhodes and Kos were ordered to assemble and prepare for deportation. A few Turkish passport holders were exempted, but the vast majority were shipped off to the Greek mainland and then to Auschwitz. Of the five hundred families which once lived in Rhodes Town, only three were spared.[125] Earlier, Italian troops who refused to continue fighting alongside the Germans were also annihilated, as happened after the failed Allied defence of Kos, when just under one hundred Italian officers were captured and forced to dig their own graves.[126] Though short in its duration, the German occupation was a harrowing experience, characterised by deprivation, death and famine. As the oral testimonies show, this period left a far deeper imprint in popular memory than did any other period, including the Italian occupation.

The Germans withdrew from the Dodecanese in March 1945, even though they had abandoned the mainland the previous October. Refugees slowly returned from the Middle East, and the Allies brought much needed food relief. For the next two years, the islands were placed under provisional British administration until the newly formed United Nations decided their fate. To much local consternation, Italians were maintained in key administrative positions, and Dodecanesian oral sources record much displeasure at the cold treatment they recieved from British officials, and Cypriot and Indian troops. On occasion, the British had to contain attempts by local elites to assert their own authority, as happened when British troops stopped Rhodian leaders from replacing Italian street names with Greek ones.[127] Most Dodecanesians expected the islands would be unified with Greece, but many local nationalists began to fear that the British were planning to keep the islands for themselves.[128]

Such fears proved groundless. As expected, unification with Greece was approved on 31 March 1947, and amid much fanfare, the Greek flag was officially raised in Rhodes Town on 16 July. To be sure, some Italian leaders did seek to retain some of their colonial possessions, and felt their nation's good record supported such claims. As one propaganda tract asserted, 'the Dodecanese had enjoyed a period of prosperity and progress as they had not seen since 1522 when the Knights of Jeruslaem (*sic*) were forced to abandon them...'.[129] Certainly, such positive views about Italy's colonial record would persist in Italian society despite the protestations of serious scholars, and Dodecanesian nostalgia would seem to suggest consensus between the former colonisers and the former colonised. The rest of this study seeks to avoid such simplistic conclusions by investigating the Italian occupation from an unusual angle, that is, to understand how the *indigenous* felt about it. It seeks to convey how the islanders understood the occupation, what meanings they invested in it, and the way this experience was incorporated into oral tradition. The historical overview presented in this chapter, being a more conventional coverage of colonialism, serves to provide the setting in which local thoughts and images were constructed. The following chapters will show how oral sources, properly used, provide a window into the mental world of Dodecanesians and what they made of the many changes which took place between 1912 and 1943.

3 Protest and Proto-Nationalism: Explaining Popular Dissent

The Greeks of the Dodecanese found many aspects of Italian rule impressive, even seductive, but they never accepted the legitimacy of the foreigner's presence. Their opposition was made quite clear in a series of plebiscites between 1912 and 1923, while anti-Italian sentiments were sometimes voiced during social protests which erupted intermittently during the following period. These social protests merit close study because they bring many of the social and cultural features of the relationship between dominators and dominated into stark relief. They are particularly helpful in understanding the latter, who were mobilised into action by threats to their welfare and values, and who expressed their concerns openly during the heat of protest. Social protests therefore reflect the mental universe of ordinary people in the past, and oral history is particularly useful here because the resulting source material is often nuanced and evocative.

Studying the behaviour of communities under foreign rule, however, is fraught with difficulties which are not necessarily related to historical methodology. Recent historiography has emphasised the extent to which a nation's image can be sustained or threatened by memories of wartime and foreign rule, how such public memories have been vigorously contested by competing interest groups, and the extent to which official readings of the past have dominated public memory.[1] As John Bodnar has pointed out, public memory is a serious matter which relates to 'rather fundamental issues about the entire existence of a society; its organization, structure of power, and the very meaning of its past and present'.[2] Smaller social units and individuals must therefore contend with the official line on the past, and must either adopt it, or must re-invent, conceal or defend their own. In Greece, where most of the population accept the official line on the nation's history, negotiating social and private memories has always been a vexed matter. Official history in Greece has held that Greeks living under foreign rule have always acted as heroes, that the

60

average Greek has been as brave as the warrior bandits of 1821, ever willing to risk life and limb for the nation. Anything less was deemed shameful.

The official line that ordinary people should be extraordinary was a romantic notion concieved without any reference to the real conditions and choices faced by ordinary folk under foreign domination. Most of the islanders were aware that heroics and foolhardy antics could very easily lead to personal ruin. Italian retribution could come in the form of incarceration, forced exile and even death, and as a consequence, the history of the Italian Occupation is not a chronicle of armed struggle, untold suffering and patriotic achievement. Interviewees felt obliged to defend their 'unheroic' record as they were ever mindful of the kinds of criticisms which non-Dodecanesians might level against them. Philipos Sofos of Asklepion, Rhodes, explained why locals did not fight as the warrior bandits of 1821; 'We couldn't fight them because Rhodes is not very big. If you resisted they could find you anywhere within days.'[3] Similarly, Mikhail Hatsinikolaou of Asfendiou, Kos, defended local *attendismo* by complaining, 'We were all alone! We had no help! Who was going to help us? The Greeks? We were left to fend for ourselves against a modern army.'[4] Their *attendismo* was an understandable response to a situation they were almost powerless to challenge, but with the retrospective imposition of a national moral code, what was once regarded as sensible behaviour was now potentially shameful.

The interviewees often indicated that patriotic expectations were unrealistic, for they sometimes acknowledged the foolishness of heroics, the stupidity of open dissent, especially when these actions put families at risk. Yet at the same time, they would maintain romantic notions of the innate heroism of the 'Hellenic race' and uphold other platitudes of nationalist ideology. As with other Greeks, Dodecanesians of all classes cherish their national culture, its myths and symbols, and accept the view that the Hellenes are an extraordinary 'race'.[5] The official line that Classical Greece created Western Civilisation has long enjoyed a general consensus, and it is a line which most social groups would vigorously defend. This claim has held particular attractions for a society which has identified with progressive 'Europe', but which introspectively admits to living physically and culturally on Europe's margins. This parleying of contrasting visions of self was reflected in Dodecanesian representations of the Italian period, for individual interviewees provided contradictory memories, that is, a characterisation which appealed to nationalistic expectations, and another which did not, yet which accorded more closely with lived experience.

The apparent confusion is evidence of the hegemony achieved by Greek nationalist culture, whose many contradictions have led to the widespread adoption of contrasting identities. Thus Greek society presents itself as 'European', 'western', 'progressive', while at the same time holding self-images as 'oriental', 'rustic' and 'backward'. Michael Herzfeld has shown how these conflicting self-representations have had a functional use in contemporary Greek life, as they can be deployed in a whole range of social contexts to convey meanings and project self-images. Herzfeld has dubbed this dialectical parleying as 'disemia', which describes 'flexible representations common to all societies, a balance of self-knowledge against the exigencies of collective representation to more powerful outsiders'.[6] Thus Dodecanesian interviewees would sometimes adopt a 'common sense' pose when justifying the practice of *attendismo*, and at other times would claim the image of a foolhardy patriot. At each turn Greeks are forced to contend with the expectations of their official culture, while never allowing themselves to be completely consumed by it.

Disemia helps explain why the oral historian is confronted by a plethora of contrasting images and contradictory subjective viewpoints. The overall confusion is most apparent in the oral testimonies of those who, because of their extensive schooling, were sufficiently socialised in the national culture. Illiterate and semi-literate interviewees, on the other hand, showed fewer traces of such official influence, and their testimonies showed there were many local ideas regarding protest and 'resistance' which pre-dated Greek nationalism.

The following microhistories will consider traditions of dissent which cannot be explained by any nationalist heuristic, and which tell us far more about perceptions of Italian rule than have officially acceptable interpretations of the past. Ironically, nationalist versions of the occupation have obscured the historical development of national consciousness among ordinary Dodecanesians, that is, when nationalism begins to have some resonance at a popular level. The last section of this chapter will explore the conditions which made the 'nationalisation of the masses' possible. This development is largely attributed to De Vecchi's attempt to 'fascistise' the islands, his tyrannical style, and particularly his policy of forced assimilation.

POPULAR PROTESTS IN THE 1930s

The protest movements which took place prior to the Treaty of Lausanne (1923) were overtly political in character. Methods were peaceful and orderly, consisting of marches and plebiscites, and aims were clearly defined, with unification with Mother Hellas the singular objective. Dodecanesian historians have also insisted that the small number of protests which erupted after 1923 must be seen as part of the struggle for liberation, but a closer investigation of extant sources suggests otherwise. These disturbances took place among the former 'Privileged Islands', where Italian investment was minimal, and where crises were fermented by a matrix of economic, social and cultural problems. Nationalism played a very marginal role at best.

On Kastellorizo, for instance, protests were reported in early 1934. Long accustomed to exemptions from taxes and duties under the Ottomans, the people of Kastellorizo found it difficult to cope with the removal of these privileges, particularly when the island's economic fortunes were in evident decline. In November 1933 duties were doubled on a range of items including petrol and flour, followed by another increase on 12 January. Local anger was partly focused on the colonial regime, but more was directed toward the *démarchos*, Ioannis Lakerdis, who was accused of failing to protect the interests of his community. As Evdokia Jackomas recalls, crowds sought to punish Lakerdis:

> I remember Tringali [Italian delegato]...with all the women in front of him and he was pleading. And they said to him: 'We don't want Italy to go. We want the keys to the *demarchia*.' They also said, 'Get rid of the thieves', by which they meant Lakerdis and Paltoglou and the rest of his committee. If you'd seen it you would not have believed it. To see Kastellorizian women marching in the streets.[7]

Though popularly elected in 1928 and in 1932, Lakerdis had spent much of his time of late on Rhodes attending to business interests, and many Kastellorizians felt he was conniving with the Italians to line his own pockets with some of the newly raised revenue. Kastellorizian women conducted a series of protests from January through to March 1934, during which reinforcements from Rhodes were required to restore order. There were several reports of clashes between the women protestors and Italian authorities, and in the meantime, Lakerdis required constant police protection. The movement climaxed on 25 March, an important date on the liturgical and national calendar, when Greeks commemorate the Holy Annunciation and the Greek War of Independence. After the morning church service, an inspired crowd attacked the *démarchos's* office and clashed violently with Italian soldiery. The Italians defused the crisis by announcing the removal of the unpopular Lakerdis.[8]

Much like the Kastellorizians, the people of Simi responded indignantly to the loss of cherished privileges, denounced their own leaders, and took matters into their own hands. The Simian *demarchia* had a reputation for enterprise which transcended the Dodecanese, and its many works are often recited in oral tradition. In September 1930, the women of Simi led a procession into the main square in response to the abolition of free elections for local government, and most were armed with rocks and wooden implements. According to one participant, Mikhail Mihalandos, the protesters set up a temporary 'womens' regime' (gynekokratía):

> They wanted to appoint a *démarchos*. But at the time, a 'womens' regime', as we then called it, came into being. The women...the women, they rose up and went against the Fascist government. Women were in front, and they were followed by teachers, priests, [giggles]...and my mother. They [the Italians] asked who put them up to it. They were released later of course....[9]

More protests were to follow. In early 1934, the *demarchía* had decided that free public health and pharmaceuticals could no longer be justified because of the island's diminishing revenue base. The continued decline of the sponge trade and mass emigration meant that Simi could no longer support its welfare schemes,[10] but whatever the economic justifications for the cuts, the community was in no mood for discussing the island's finances. Church bells were sounded, calling the women of Simi into the main square to protest. Violent clashes took place when they marched on the *demarchía*, but the *carabinieri* succeeded in warding off the protesters, who then marched to the residence of the Italian *delegato*. Here the women voiced their grievances, and, according to one Greek source, the *delegato* promised to refer their problems to higher authorities in Rhodes Town.[11]

Violations of traditional rights also prompted a violent reaction at Olymbos, the largest village on the island of Karpathos. Inaccessible by road and perched among the steep hills of the island's northern peninsula, Olymbos took great pride in its distinct customs, archaic dialect and autonomy. Their autonomy was guarded with a fierce passion, and was symbolised in its 'agrafo' status, which literally meant that local names were not recorded on any bureaucratic census. By May 1936, however, the Italians believed it was time the Olymbites were fully incorporated into the *Possedimento*.[12] Despite ominous threats, the villagers stoutly refused to submit their names to a census, fearing that taxation and the conscription of young males might follow.[13] A few days later, Italian troops were sent from southern Karpathos to force the Olymbites to comply, but the villagers were rallied into action. They abandoned their homes and set up an ambush for the oncoming Italians, who were greeted with a shower of rocks. Despite warning shots, the undaunted villagers, including women and children, continued to pelt their enemy. The *maresciallo* was so impressed by Olymbitan bravado that he promised the matter would be reconsidered. There were no reported arrests or serious casualties.[14]

The fragmentary evidence offers some clues about the nature of popular protest in the 1930s. Firstly, social protests were initiated and carried out by common folk, with little, if any, prior organisation. Each protest had a specific purpose and ended with few casualties. Secondly, women predominated. It was Dodecanesian women who took up the responsibility of defending moral community norms, and who committed themselves to violent clashes with armed police and soldiery. This phenomenon was not peculiar to the Dodecanese, nor can we assume that women had always led Dodecanesian social protests.[15] What we can safely conclude is that women felt confident enough to attack Italian soldiery without fear of bloody reprisal. Theirs was a calculated assessment of the enemy; they expected the Italians to recoil under concerted pressure, and they were confident that Italians would not shoot at women. As will be shown in Chapter 6, women interviewees consistently stereotyped the Italians as 'humane' and 'gentlemen', as well as 'soft' (malakí) and sometimes 'cowardly' (fovitsiárides).

Another general point can be made. Despite the air of desperation in these Dodecanesian protests – the Olymbites boasted that they were prepared to die for their rights – these were not rebellions. None sought to challenge Italian rule, nor did the protesters truly believe Italian intervention in their affairs could be stopped. For each of these communities, what was more important than keeping their privileges was not accepting intervention in a passive way. 'To show' (na díxis) defiance was a cherished value common to all Dodecanese island communities. Passivity was a source of shame. In the face of overwhelming odds, it was important to at least make an appearance of struggle and defiance. The importance of 'showing' defiance will be illustrated frequently in this study, suffice to say here that 'fatalism', a characteristic of 'Mediterranean' culture invented by western scholarship, was not a 'natural' feature of Greek peasant culture.[16]

Clearly, nationalism was not a motivating factor of these protests. Traditional rights rather than 'Mother Hellas' were uppermost in the minds of the dissidents. Nevertheless, our main source for these case studies, 'I Dodekanisiaki', a bi-monthly periodical of the 1930s, and published by the Athens based *Dodecanesian Youth League*, reported these protests as evidence of the undying spirit of Greek nationalism. Of the protest in Simi, the newsletter reported, 'The women of Simi have shown themselves as outstanding patriots', and in Kastellorizo, the islanders had 'given notice of revolution against the Tyrant'.[17] These reports worked on the unquestioned assumption that the islanders were continuing a tradition of patriotic resistance, and *I Dodekanisiaki* employed conventional nationalist imagery to convey the protesters' actions. These included phrases like 'they seized them' (tous ormísan) and the 'revolutionary ones' (epanastatiméni), phrases conventionally used for the warrior bandits of 1821. What is particularly noticeable about these reports is the ease with which traditional protests were re-interpreted as nationalist uprisings. The 'revolutionary' women of Kastellorizo and Simi probably knew little about national issues and values, yet nationalist meanings were effortlessly worked into their actions. The information used and presented by the periodical did not sustain its patriotic assertions, yet this did not seem a hindrance. Such has been the hegemony of Greek nationalism that details which contradict its interpretations do not always need to be omitted.

Much the same can be said for the extensive literature on the Kalymnian protests of 1935, which local historians have interpreted as a nationalist rebellion. A redeeming feature of this historiographical tradition is that some of it is based on original research, and much useful information is provided. The following case study of Kalymnos, for which we are comparatively well informed, provides greater scope for the study of traditional protest in the Italian Dodecanese, and allows us to elaborate on themes which have been outlined above.

THE 'ROCK WAR': KALYMNOS

Of the former 'Privileged Islands', Kalymnos was the largest in population and most vociferous in defending its autonomy. When the colonial government decided in January 1926 to control the curriculum in Greek schools, no island was more obstructive than Kalymnos, so much so that by October the Italians had dismissed the island's *demarchía*.[18] Free elections for local government were restored in early 1929, but the *demarchía* continued to be unco-operative with the colonial government, failing, for example, to comply with the introduction of duties on wine imports, and refusing to grant the Italians a centrally-located site for a new administrative building.[19] Continuing friction between the colonial government and the *demarchía* led to the latter's permanent dismissal in March 1933, and the appointment of a *podestà*, though not without loud public protest.[20] Kalymnian leaders had exemplified the notion of 'showing' the enemy, of not accepting any intervention in local affairs without a fight. Their dismissal, however, left a leadership vacuum, and as often happened in Greek tradition, the vacuum was filled by the clergy.[21]

One contentious issue which had long been fermenting was the so-called 'Autokephalo', where the bishops of the Dodecanese sought to establish an autonomous Church. Among these bishops was Apostolos Kavakopoulos, Bishop of Kalymnos, Leros and Astypalea, who, because of his association with the 'Autokephalo', did not enjoy the support of his lower clergy. In January 1934, the bishops, frustrated by their failure to gain permission for their new Church from the Patriarch of Constantinople, decided to proceed with their project without his permission, thus precipitating a schism. The Kalymnian lower clergy immediately denounced their bishop on religious grounds. Given that the bishops were in league with the colonial government, the lower clergy became convinced that the 'Autokephalo' had the Catholic Church behind it. The schism was regarded as part of a papal conspiracy, the first stage in an attempt to convert the islanders to Catholicism. The priests of Kalymnos gathered in the Church of Ippapantis on 19 October, placed their hands on the Bible, and swore undying opposition to the papal threat. The occasion heralded the formation of the 'Kalymnian National Union', led by Mikhail Tsougranis, a highly respected priest with a fiery temperament.[22] The 'Union' formally denounced Bishop Apostolos Kavakopoulos as a papal stooge, and on 19 January

1935, the clergy took the unprecedented step of having every parish church closed indefinitely.[23] All major events on the liturgical calendar, including Easter and Christmas, would not be celebrated, and important rites such as baptism and marriage had to be performed in secret locations.[24] Though the clergy had dubbed themselves a 'national' organisation, their sole task was to defend Orthodoxy, to vouchsafe its spiritual legitimacy and purity for future generations. The closure of the churches was a gesture meant to highlight the gravity of the situation and to symbolise their defiance against the papal threat.

Significantly the lower clergy had the support of the wider lay community. When the Italians tried to have Tsougranis arrested, the women of his parish rallied to his aid, mobbing the *carabinieri* as the old priest was swiftly shuffled through the narrow back streets to safety. He was later smuggled across to Turkey, from where he made his way to mainland Greece. Tsougranis is remembered as the man who started the Kalymnian 'resistance', and his role has since been commemorated with a statue in the main square, and by one patriotic play.[25]

Meanwhile, Kavakopoulos had become a public enemy. The bishop required constant police protection and was terrorised with death threats. He was eventually forced to transfer his seat of residence to the relative safety of Leros.[26] Another hated 'collaborator' was Themelis Tsangaris, or 'Papa Yanaros' as he was popularly known, an elderly priest and an original member of the National Union. He had been arrested and sent to Rhodes, where during his incarceration he converted to the pro-Autokephalo camp.[27] On his return to Kalymnos, rumour spread quickly that Yanaros had joined the collaborators, and now he too required police protection. In 'Horio', the adjoining village to the main town, where Yanaros was a parish priest, villagers staged a mock carnival during the fifth week of Lent in 1935. In what seemed to be a Greek form of *charivari*, an effigy of Yanaros was carried through the streets of Horio. According to Mikhail Hatsithemelis, he was dubbed the 'pseudo-Judas' (o pséftikos Ioúdas):

> We then made a effigy made of cloth, and we named it the 'pseudo-Judas'. It was just before Easter, and the people of the village paraded him through the streets. Of course it was meant to be old Papa Yanaros. That is why the Italians tried to arrest us.... They chased us....[28]

The *carabinieri* tried to break up the procession and arrest the culprits, but then a riot ensued, as the *carabinieri* were attacked by a large group of women. Hatsithemelis, a tailor by trade and the suspected maker of the effigy, remembered a mob of women coming to his aid as the *carabinieri* tried to arrest him. Among them was his mother:

> they [the *carabinieri*] grabbed me, and tried to drag me away. But then my mother got in the way. 'You're not taking him', she said. Other women started to push them off. Yes.... Then my mother took me home.[29]

He was arrested sometime later and, as was common for political prisoners, was tortured. Hatsithemelis was exiled to Kos along with his brother, who was also regarded as a troublemaker.[30]

The so-called 'Rock War' (Petropólemos) began a few days later on 5 April, when people heard that Yanaros, along with a group of lay 'collaborators', was about to open one of the main churches to celebrate the Akathist Hymn, the last in a series of Lenten services in honour of the Virgin Mary, for which he had the blessing of Kavakopoulos in Leros and the Italian authorities. The church in question, 'Christ's Church' (O Hristós), is situated on the eastern side of the town's main square, and adjacent to the main harbour. Early that evening, Yanaros and his followers opened the church and held a religious service as *carabinieri* stood guard outside. According to the historian of Kalymnos, Ippokratis Frangopoulos, the mere fact that these men had opened the church 'was regarded by the people as an act of aggression'.[31] Given that the church closures symbolised the community's stand in defense of Orthodoxy, the re-opening of 'Christ's Church' was interpreted as a challenge to community resolve. Word spread quickly through the neighbourhoods of Kalymnos that Orthodoxy was under threat. Nuns from the Monastery of St Katerina marched to the centre of Kalymnos to protest, and as their procession descended into the main square that afternoon, large numbers of women joined them. According to one participant:

> from all over...they came down...women, old ladies, young girls, young boys of fourteen and fifteen....We placed one of the nuns from St Katerina in front of us....Then we advanced. This was happening in all neighbourhoods.[32]

Hundreds of women gathered near the church, from where they railed and taunted Yanaros and his followers. The protest seemed peaceful enough at first, but when Yanaros's followers rang the church bells, a riot ensued. Sounding the church bells was accepted practice on important religious occasions, but the women protesters believed the collaborators inside were making a mockery of Orthodoxy. In this emotionally charged atmosphere, violent scuffles broke out with the *carabinieri*. As one participant recalls:

> Then came the crucial moment, when we heard the church bells of Christ's Church ringing. We all became enraged, and suddenly we felt a new sense of urgency and power.... One [woman] was hit in the back, another was hit on the head,... all of us around me were screaming, shouting, punching, slapping....[33]

The *carabinieri* managed to contain the riot, but Yanaros and company had to be escorted to the safety of their homes. Thereafter, these 'collaborators' were labelled 'cabanelli', a mock Italianisation of the Greek word for 'bell ringers'.

Unperturbed by Friday's events, Yanaros and the 'cabanelli' were determined to press on and conduct church services the following day. That Friday evening, community anxieties were exacerbated by the news that, by order of the *podestà*, children were to be taken from school to attend church on Saturday morning.[34] Targeting the children was seen as underhanded and immoral, and Kalymnian leaders quickly distributed an encyclical, warning parents to keep their children at home:

> Greek people of Kalymnos, our Religion is again in danger. Again our religion is threatened with extinction, because the hands of certain dark officials are trying to manipulate our religion and deliver it into Italian hands. We true Kalymnians, true children of Diakos, Kolokotronis, Miaoulis, and Kanaris,[35] need to seize and bury these outrageous plans and the collaborators. Long Live Orthodoxy. Long Live Kalymnos.[36]

School children stayed home the following day, and the authorities retaliated by arresting teachers and other alleged conspirators. Once again, Kalymnian women marched into the main square, this time led by an octogenarian mother superior called 'Magdalini', who carried a large wooden cross. More violent clashes between the women and *carabinieri* followed, and at one stage during the riot, 'Magdalini' was struck on the head. She dropped the cross and fell to the ground, but a young girl ran up to raise the cross again, as if it were a battle standard.[37] The women tried to enter the church from a number of angles and failed, but they proceeded to humiliate the *carabinieri* by punching and scratching them, and tearing their uniforms. The protesters were emboldened by the belief that they were guardians of Orthodoxy, and encouraged by the lack of ruthlessness in the Italian response. While the Italians did manage to keep the women at bay, they felt there would be more protests to come, and troop reinforcements were called in from Kos.

When Italian reinforcements disembarked the following morning, they were greeted by a shower of rocks. Troop access from the wharf to the main promenade was hindered by a host of stone-throwers who had secured a position behind a ridge directly above. The Kalymnians had organised themselves into three groups; one group gathered rocks from hill sides, another carried these rocks to the throwers, and then there were the rock throwers themselves. All the throwers were women. Whilst males were allowed to participate in the first two groups, only women were allowed into the front-line of rock throwers. Most believed that the Italians would not shoot at women, and according to participant Maria Pizania, males who tried to join the throwers were pushed to the back:

When the men came near, so they could also throw rocks, the women would shout, with one voice, 'Men get back', so they would not get killed, so we stayed in front....

The sky was darkened because of the shower of rocks. And don't assume that the rocks we threw were small; they were 'boulders' (kotrónes). Where did we get so much energy? I think back and wonder....[38]

Eventually a male forced himself into the fray, a young shepherd named Manolis Kazonis, who happened to be in the neighbourhood selling milk. He dropped his milk cans, left his donkey behind and ran off to join the fighting. Kazonis was a tall man and an easy target for the troops positioned below. He was shot in the head and died immediately. The rock throwing ceased and the women returned to their homes.

The people of Kalymnos had 'showed' their enemy (tous díxan); they had made their gesture of defiance and retained their honour, but the young man's death took the issue beyond acceptable limits. The Italians had quickly regained control of the town. The official Italian explanation for the riots was that they were provoked by religious fanatics who took advantage of the heightened religious feelings of the Lent period. The suppression of the Rock War was explained as a victory over religious intolerance.[39] That Sunday evening, the *carabinieri* made a large number of arrests, though few of those arrested were women. Priests, doctors, teachers and other community leaders, men whom the Italians had assumed had instigated the protests, were sent to the old Hospitaller dungeons in Kos and Rhodes where they awaited trial.[40] Prison sentences were handed down ranging from two to six years, but later that year all were granted an amnesty.[41] Church doors remained closed until February 1937, when, with the blessing of the Patriarchate of Constantinople, Kalymnos was withdrawn from the territorial jurisdiction of Bishop Apostolos Kouboukalas, and was placed in the diocese of Kos and Nisyros. As this particular diocese was not associated with the 'Autokephalo', the Kalymnians found the change acceptable.[42]

THE MEANING OF THE 'ROCK WAR'

In the encyclical sent to parents during the evening of 5 April 1935, Kalymnian leaders told their community to take inspiration from patriotic heroes of the past: 'We true Kalymnians, true children of Diakos, Kolokotrones, Miaoulis, and Kanaris...'.[43] From the outset, Kalymnians had been encouraged to view the Rock War as a nationalist rebellion. Contemporary expatriate reports in Athens claimed a golden page of Greek history had been written, and that the Rock War augured a general Dodecanesian uprising.[44] Kalymnian writers have since continued to develop the 'war's' alleged patriotic significance. The women protesters, for instance, have been compared to the 'Souliótises', the legendary women of an Epirot community who, during the War of Independence, on seeing the approach of the marauding Turks, performed a ceremonial dance near a cliff face and, one by one, leapt to their deaths. Like the Souliótises, the women of Kalymnos have been described as patriotic heroines and soldiers of 'Mother Hellas'.[45] Numerous publications have interpreted the Rock War as a revolt against Italian rule, and Kalymnians as 'revolutionaries' (epanastátes).[46] Official appropriation of the 'war' has, among other things, involved the demotion of its folksy name and its replacement with the more 'serious' title, 'The Nationalist-Religious Resistance' (H Ethniko-Thriskeftikí Antístatsi). As the extract below demonstrates, rhetorical excess is a typical feature of this patriotic literature:

> The Fascist tyrants poisoned the Greek heart of all the Dodecanesians, and thus there developed a mighty anti-fascism, which resulted in the outbreak of the Kalymnian Resistance of 1935!
>
> The Resistance of the Kalymnians showed their virtues, their big-heartedness, their struggle-natured soul, their fantastic religiosity and their yearning for Freedom![47]

The official view of the Rock War as a 'nationalist' revolt, which all educated Kalymnians would subscribe to, is the only view found in print. Yet balanced against this dominant patriotic version is an enduring repository of counter-memories. The elderly and illiterate in particular, who have not been socialised in national ideology, have retained a radically different understanding of the 'war'. Their testimonies confirm that it was not a nationalist rebellion but a womens' protest in defence of Orthodoxy. The fear of a Catholic conspiracy saw the womenfolk take to the streets in protest. At best, nationalism was a marginal influence.

The sheer scale of the Rock War, and the daring shown by the protesters has served as an inspiration for many generations of Kalymnians. Such has been its importance in popular memory that its meaning has been contested, though by 'contest' I do not necessarily mean public debate. The nationalist interpretation has never been a subject of public disputation, and interviewees never consciously criticised the official line. Popular discourse has produced a variety of interpretations which remain in oral form, and which co-exist quite comfortably with the written version, even though they often contradict each other. Contested meanings only become manifest in subtle ways, and the 'contested-ness' of these meanings is never addressed directly. This became apparent when interviewees seemed untroubled when they offered contradictory meanings of the Rock War in the course of their oral testimonies. As critical debate has never been a customary feature of Dodecanesian scholarly life, and as the nationalist interpretation is quite secure as the official line, the 'contested-ness' of the Rock War has never been addressed. This has allowed the significance of women to be considerably compromised.

Kalymnian male writers, for instance, have essentially ignored the women protesters. As historical evidence for Kalymnian social protest before 1935 is scarce, we do not know if women's protests represented an age-old local tradition, though quite similar and near synchronous protests in Simi and Kastellorizo might suggest a 'Dodecanesian' tradition. We are on safe ground in claiming that womens' protests constituted a shrewd and calculated response for dealing with the Italians. As mentioned previously, locals had long realised that the Italians were unlikely to shoot at women, for they were not thought to be 'barbaric' or ruthless enough. Italian reports also confirm that the protesters were of a varying age and represented all social classes, including, as the *podestà's* official report notes, 'girls from the best families'.[48] Their social make-up, and the fact that the women came from every neighbourhood, suggests the Rock War reflected anxieties which were being felt throughout the island community. The extant evidence shows that the protests were initiated, orchestrated and carried out by women.

But for Kalymnian males, the Rock War is too important a myth to be conceded to their women folk. Its importance in the island's cultural life is exemplified by a strong written tradition which has included histories, poems, drama, short stories and biographical sketches. Most of these works mention the women protesters, but the full significance of their role has been diluted by undue focus on male heroes such as Tsougranis the priest and the martyr Kazonis. Moreover, local writters have worked on the premise that the protests were planned by male elites, who sat 'behind the scenes' and directed the course of events. Giorgios Sakellaridis, a prominent local writer, confirmed in his oral testimony that the 'resistance' was masterminded by great Kalymnian patriots:

> The Italians faced a very effective campaign, and it was all a result of the subtle planning of Kalymnian leaders. They met in the *Anagnostirion* [cultural centre] and organised every move. The absence of men [in the protests] was a deliberate ploy. This was a good move. See what happened when Kazonis joined in. He was a man and he was shot....[49]

Male oral testimonies often reiterated the assumption that men *allowed* their women to take the centre stage. They suggest that husbands sent their wives and daughters into the streets, confident the Italians would not harm them. In his oral testimony, Loizos Loizou, who carried rocks to the throwers in the last phase of the 'war', made sense of the event with following male perspective:

I was too young and short to throw rocks. Anyway, only women were supposed to throw rocks. The Italians didn't want to shoot the women, so we let the women do the fighting. They would have shot at us if they saw men.[50]

The official Italian view was quite similar. The *podestà* also believed the women were put up to mischief by their menfolk, for as he complained in his report, none of the men tried to control the female rioters.[51] Many Kalymnian males did encourage the women, but this does not necessarily mean that women simply followed orders.[52] The chief problem with male versions of the Rock War is that the oral testimonies of the protesters themselves have given no indication that women were following male directives. It is significant that by far the best, and most detailed, study of the Rock War has been written by a Kalymnian woman named Themelina Kapella, who, having interviewed many of the protesters, demonstrates how women took matters into their own hands. Her interviewees never mentioned any male involvement, save for the unfortunate Kazonis, and while Kapella never refers the male usurpation of the Rock War myth, her silence on the matter is loud.[53]

The attractions of the myth for Kalymnian males has a sociological explanation. This hardy, seafaring community has long prided itself as being a tougher breed than other islanders, and the 'war' has been remembered as an exemplification of this greater masculinity. The physical environment has been the enduring source of Kalymnian grievances and ideas of masculine identity. While most localities have taken pride in the distinctiveness of their natural environment – the fertility of Kos, for instance, is treasured by Koans and is used to assert their ascendancy over other islanders – the Kalymnians have been somewhat embarrassed by their own arid landscapes. Nevertheless, 'the rock', as locals jokingly call Kalymnos, compelled its inhabitants to be more resourceful and enterprising than others. They were forced to eke out an existence at sea, and with the success of the sponge trade, they triumphed. This triumph allowed them to build a flourishing community on their beloved 'rock', which they endowed with a wealth of neo-classical buildings and churches. Kalymnians have regarded this as an extraordinary achievement, and this has underpinned self-conceptions of Kalymnians as being more resourceful and having more spine than other Dodecanesians.[54] Locals have extrapolated from the Rock War myth that only the Kalymnians had enough strength of character to resist Italian rule. For Panormitis Menouhos, other Dodecanesians had effectively submitted: 'They bowed their heads (skípsan ta kefália tous). They gave in. They were fascists.'[55] As Loizos Loizou asserted in his testimony, only the Kalymnians had enough mettle to defend their convictions:

> We are not like the others [Dodecanesians]...they don't care. We cared....We [Kalymnians] were the only people with integrity and a sense of what is proper.[56]

It follows that local males could hardly sustain their masculine self-image if they also acknowledged the true significance of women in the Rock War. Male Kalymnians would be derided as cowardly and unmasculine by their inter-island counterparts.[57]

Another contested meaning of the Rock War, though a much more subtle one, is related to the importance of anti-Italian feeling. Kalymnian interviewees often characterised the relationship between locals and Italians in terms of 'hatred' or 'misos' (mísos), and local writers have also promoted this notion of rivalry in their patriotic representations. The mere fact that the Rock War was likened to a 'war' (pólemos) does not only reflect the monumental scale it has assumed in Kalymnian imagination, but also conveys how locals, driven by their *mísos*, had the audacity to challenge the might of Fascist Italy.[58] The historian Frangopoulos has claimed that locals were not over-awed by the might of the Italians, 'despite recent military successes in Abyssinia'.[59] In written tradition, the 'war' has been represented as a battle between Kalymnians and Italians, suggesting an equal contest.

In the inter-island context, this equal contest is meant to elevate the Kalymnians above other Dodecanesians. Thus while most elderly Dodecanesians hold fond memories of Italians and Italian rule, Kalymnian interviewees are keen to point out their experience was different, and that unlike other communities, they challenged the might of Mussolini. When questioned about the validity of the popular Dodecanesian saying, 'the Italians were good people' (i Italí ítan kalí), Mikhail Hatsithemelis snapped, 'No! Don't listen to them, don't listen to them. No, they were not good....' (Ohi. Min kous, min kous. Ohi, then ítan kalí...).[60] As a rule, Kalymnians insist that Italian rule had no redeeming features, but quite often during the course of an interview, even the most recalcitrant locals would inadvertently concede that the Italians had many positive attributes. Women interviewees would admit, 'off the record' of course, that Italian males were handsome and well-mannered. After giving the conventional negative picture of Italians, interviewees would later relax and consider themes and issues which would contradict their initial negative picture. Sevasti Kortesi, for instance, stereotyped Italian males as gentlemen, and claimed they were good marriage prospects.[61] When asked what conditions were like before the Rock War, Loizos Loizou and Mikhail Hatsithemelis instinctively responded in their interviews with an identical phrase: 'Before we lived well' (prin pernoúsame kalá).[62] The revealing phrase 'we lived well' is commonplace in Dodecanesian oral tradition, suggesting congenial relations between occupiers and occupied. In using this and other popular phrases, Loizou, Hatsithemelis and other interviewees showed how Kalymnos has also been linked with a general Dodecanesian tradition. The contradictions revealed within Kalymnian social discourses on the Italian period show the workings of disemia within a local, popular context.

The myth of the Rock War has also been important in symbolising local claims to exceptional religiosity. Kalymnians have long enjoyed a wide reputation for their religiosity, as made apparent by the island's extraordinary number of churches and monasteries. For Mikhail Hatsithemelis, religiosity was part of the Kalymnian character:

> They [the Italians] wanted to give us the 'Autokephalo'. All the other islands signed up. Kalymnos, however, never did, because we Kalymnians are very religious.... All islanders are good Christians, but as believers the Kalymnians have something extra.[63]

Anxieties about the future of Orthodoxy permeated Kalymnian thinking in 1934 and 1935. Clergy and parishioners alike were convinced of a papal conspiracy, as shown in the oral sources by recurring phrases like: 'they wanted to turn us into Franks' (thélan na mas fragképsoun), and, 'they wanted to change our religion' (thélan na láksousin tin písti mas).[64] Locals regarded the perceived attack on their religion as an unprecedented outrage, as some interviewees correctly noted, not even the 'barbaric' Turks had ever 'put their hand' (válasin héri) into local religious affairs. Mikhail Hatsithemelis's following reference to religious freedom under the Ottomans was echoed by other interviewees:

> They [the Italians] wanted to 'Francisize' us. Why did they try to do it? We had the Turks for four hundred years, but they never tried to make us worship Allah.... We didn't accept changes....[65]

Nevertheless, as a motivating factor for the Rock War, fear of conversion is not an explanation which should be taken at face value. There is a subtext to the religious interpretation, for the protesters never actually thought that they themselves would be converted to Catholicism. It was highly unlikely that the faithful, sufficiently guarded against the papal threat, would then be its victims. A better explanation is that Kalymnian anxieties were really focused on the distant future. If the papal threat was not countered from the outset, then unwary later generations might fall prey to the pressure and propaganda of their Italian rulers. This fear reflected traditional Kalymnian distrust of bureaucracy, and, in a sense, was a tacit acknowledgement of Italian power. More importantly, it also reflected upon local conceptions of time. The islanders understood their role as custodians of culture and values, which was a solemn responsibility carried out for the benefit of descendants. This sense of duty, and understanding of place in time, was conveyed in the testimony of Maria Economou Pizania, who was one of the protesters:

> It was shameful to stay at home during those days. If someone [a woman] stayed home to do housework, or if she was not feeling well, others would pass by and they'd say, 'What are you doing inside, shame on you! Come, let's go, leave your housework, you'll find it here when you come back. But if we lose our religion, we'll never find that again!' There was no need for more words, you just left everything and you went along with them.[66]

Another participant, teacher Sevasti Rigas, recalled being threatened by an Italian officer while on her way to the protests. The *maresciallo*, however, could not deter her from carrying out her obligations to posterity:

> From a balcony up high, *maresciallo* Nardone saw me, and he shouted, 'Teacher, tomorrow we will settle accounts.' But he did not scare me. I felt like I had been doing my duty....[67]

Leaving a legacy of dissent was an important consideration. Failure to 'show' dissent would bring shame on the community and reflect badly in collective memory. These oral sources lend support to critics of 'fatalism', a concept popular among some anthropologists who have subscribed to the notions of Mediterranean cultural unity, and who use fatalism to explain the region's under-development. As

Michael Herzfeld has pointed out, 'fatalism' has enjoyed much currency in western scholarship, but it is not a concept which the Greeks would accept. Indeed, in Greek culture, fatality is considered a shameful characteristic which they have often applied to other 'lesser' peoples, especially the Turks.[68] In the Italian-occupied Dodecanese, 'showing' dissent was an honourable alternative to resignation to fate. For a proud society enduring the humiliation of foreign rule, 'showing' dissent served as moral consolation. As one writer explained in his dramatisation of a failed protest in the Rhodian village of Gennadi in 1913:

Is this not really a victory? A victory against fear, against mere silence? Victory is every protest (xesíkoma), despite the number of people involved and the result, because it sets an example to the young.[69]

Many Dodecanesians outside of Kalymnos shared similar forebodings about the 'Autokephalo', especially educated elites. The consensus among Dodecanesians living in Athens and Egypt was that the scheme was closely related to the regime's assimilation policy.[70] For most ordinary Dodecanesians, however, an impending papal threat was not really apparent, and many couldn't appreciate the anxieties felt in the Kalymnian community. Resentful of Kalymnian claims to greater patriotism and bravery, other islanders have often reacted by accusing them of 'hysteria' and 'self-delusion'.[71] As Ioannis Alahiotis of Kos sardonically argued:

They [the Kalymnians] say they [the Italians] wanted to make us Catholics. I ask you, did we become Catholics in the end? I'm still Orthodox. Everyone else is still Orthodox![72]

Of course, there are more objective explanations for why the Rock War took place in Kalymnos rather than any other island. A strong sense of autonomy and tradition of protest was quite important, as was the ability of the lower clergy to mobilise popular opinion. Of the former 'Privileged Islands', only Kalymnos was still a substantial centre, with 15 000 inhabitants recorded in 1936. The island was also the most densely populated in the Dodecanese.[73] The inhabitants were concentrated in tightly-knit neighbourhoods, living among a maze of narrow, winding streets which the *carabinieri* found very difficult to control. Yet locals have preferred to explain the Rock War in terms of Kalymnian character. The 'war' remains a myth from which many ideas about local identity are drawn, and until historical debate becomes accepted practice in public life, the Rock War will remain just a myth about Kalymnian patriotism and character.

THE ORIGINS OF POPULAR NATIONALISM

Overall, nationalism had very little to do with Dodecanesian popular protest, nor was there much sign of popular national consciousness, at least during Lago's period as governor. Under De Vecchi, however, a new era of popular dissent had begun, in which Greek nationalism had started to become influential. The following section will consider the forms and motivations which characterised this new phase of dissent, and how the highly repressive conditions of De Vecchi's governance fostered the emergence of a nascent popular nationalism.

The following story illustrates some of the ways in which common folk viewed their national culture before De Vecchi's arrival. This culture was, to varying degrees, familiar to most common folk, but it was still very much 'other'. The place of Eleftherios Venizelos in Dodecanesian life is a case in point. Venizelos was the dominant figure of Greek politics in the early twentieth century, and most Dodecanesian leaders regarded him a national hero. Sometime in the 1920s, a Lerian café owner called 'Toulantas' got himself into great trouble when he refused to remove a portrait of Venizelos from his café. This story was related to me by his granddaughter as a humorous anecdote:

> My grandfather, he had a picture of Venizelos and a Greek flag up on his [shop] wall. Back then, the *finanza* did inspections, like the police do now. They did inspections. So they said to him, 'Who is that up there?', pretending they didn't know.
>
> He proudly boasted, 'It's Venizelos!'
>
> They said, 'You must take it down!' ... they said to him, 'Take it down!', but he didn't.
>
> Anyhow the police left and the picture was still up there. They came back a few days later and they smashed it. They stepped on it. He [her grandfather] then said a few ugly things to them and they dragged him away. They took him to the police station. Then someone went and told my grandmother:
>
> 'Ephrosine, they've put your husband "inside" [gaol].'
>
> 'Oh Mother! (mána mou)', she said, 'Whatever for?'
>
> 'Because of Venizelos!'

'Because of Venizelos?'

The poor woman dropped what she was doing, took off her apron, and grabbed her little children. She took them with her to the police station so they'd feel sorry for her. So they would let him go. Because my grandfather had a café to run!

She asked: 'Why have you locked him up?' The Italian said he was staying and told her to go.

'I curse your Venizelos', she said to him [her husband]. 'Why don't you call Venizelos to come here and look after these [children]?'

She went back the next day but the Italians told her to go away again. Again she told her husband:

'Hey Venizelos! Mr Venizelos! Yes you! What are you doing in there! Who is going to feed these young children now?' [interviewee laughs]

'Shut up', he told her. 'Shut up and get out of here you "rag" (patsavoúra). When I get out of here I'll fix you up.' [more laughter]

This story was told to me by my grandmother.[74]

Much of the humour of this anecdote is lost in its written and translated form. Missing is the old Lerian accent mimicked by the story-teller, and colourful idioms she used in the dialogue between her grandparents. More importantly for our purpose was her play on familiar stereotypes. Her grandfather is the pretentious, well-to-do peasant, now café owner, who likes to think he knows something about high politics, and who tries to 'show' he is a patriot; and then there is his wife, the hard-headed peasant woman, who sees through his pretentiousness and reminds him of his familial priorities.

Most Dodecanesians were not patriotically-minded, but they did have what Eric Hobsbawm has called pre-existing 'variants of collective belonging', or 'proto-national' bonds.[75] The success of nationalism in replacing 'real' communities, explains Hobsbawm, must be partly attributed to its ability to turn these 'proto-national' bonds into national bonds. The Greeks of the Italian-occupied Dodecanese identified themselves as 'Greeks'; they displayed some degree of ethnic chauvinism based mainly on language and religion, and they identified to limited degree with the Greek state. But nationalism was not yet a fully internalised ideology, for as the above anecdote shows, sentimental attachments to Hellenism and its symbols were still weak. Yet the basis for developing these attachments was there. After all, the common folk had already supported their patriotic elites in pro-Hellenic protests and plebiscites during the first decade of the occupation. One of the more difficult questions in the study of nationalism is when nationalism becomes genuinely popular. When do the masses acquire an emotional attachment to nationhood?

According to Miroslav Hroch, an important precondition for the development of a popular national movement is a major conflict of interest between the occupied and occupier, when the occupied begin to interpret the conflict as 'nationally relevant'.[76] De Vecchi's assimilation policy fostered a crisis which an increasing number of locals regarded as a national, rather than a Dodecanesian, issue. De Vecchi wanted to 'Fascistise' the islands, and his methods bore many of Fascism's more negative hallmarks, for between 1937 and 1941, the islanders received a strong taste of the sort of cultural oppression experienced by ethnic minorities in Venezia Giulia.[77] Locals saw De Vecchi's 'Fascist' rule as excessively brutal, but what they were not prepared to tolerate was De Vecchi's openly avowed intention to destroy a basic tenet of their cultural identity. On 21 July 1937, De Vecchi abolished the teaching of the Greek language in all schools as the first step in an undisguised programme of Italianisation.[78] His preparedness to use violence, however, deterred the occupied from deploying traditional forms of protest. It was in these anxious times that nationalism became increasingly relevant to popular needs.

To be sure, Mario Lago also wanted to assimilate the islanders, though he recognised the need for subtlety in carrying out such an ambitious agenda. He believed that assimilation policy could only effect change over generations. The interviewees, perhaps only in hindsight, recognised the guile of Lago's approach by frequently asserting that Lago 'wanted to make us love them' (íthelan na tous agapísoume), and 'to make us Italians slowly, slowly' (íthelan na mas kánoun Italoús sigá, sigá).[79] The role played by education was important in his long term programme. There were three school systems in operation in the Dodecanese; Italian schools which used the Italian national curriculum, village schools which were subsidised by the colonial government and employed elements of the Italian curriculum, and the *demarchía* schools, which were supported by local communities and followed their own curriculum. The vast majority of Greek children attended *demarchía* primary and secondary schools, and lessons were taught in Greek. In January 1926, Lago introduced an number of measures which established

Italian authority in all school curricula, which included the appointment of school inspectors, and most importantly, the introduction of one compulsory hour of Italian language per week.[80] *Demarchía* leaders protested immediately against this violation of traditional rights, especially in Kalymnos, where the implementation of this policy was actively obstructed.[81] But the failure of Dodecanesian common folk to support their elites revealed the cultural divide which existed between them, for at a popular level, Lago's reforms received a much more positive reception.[82] Indeed, common folk believed that their social betters had over-reacted, for as their oral sources suggest, learning Italian was not thought to be a threat to Greek culture, and in any case, learning a European language was seen as socially progressive. In explaining the beneficial aspects of Lago's education reforms, Gabriel Kosaris's apologetic tone showed he was mindful of an old dispute with more zealous patriots. His insistence that 'learning another language is a good thing' (na máthi kanís mia glóssa íne kaló práma) was repeated by many other interviewees:

> I learned the language for good reasons. I did not think of patriotism. I believe learning another language is a good thing. I loved languages. Others didn't because of [patriotic] fanaticism. This is bad. Why blame the language? Italian is a beautiful language. That writer, what is his name?...eh, Dante, who wrote <<L' Antico Amore (*sic*)>>...this is a beautiful thing.[83]

Most people felt comfortable with Lago's reforms. There seemed to be little official pressure to learn Italian, as reflected by the fact that adults often volunteered to take up evening classes, while students boasted of regular truancy from compulsory classes.[84] For Christoforos Fournaris, a young student in the late 1920s, escaping from these classes had become a proud ritual, though he later admitted in his testimony that learning Italian was not a bad thing:

> They started to put their hands into the schools. They wanted to put Italian teachers into our schools. They wanted to have us learn two half-hour classes in Italian. We had [been taught by] a Constantinopolitan who was a policeman, another teacher was an officer in the *finanza*, and another was a secretary from Rhodes. But we showed as students, to the three of these teachers...we didn't like this. Every now and then, we'd say to the teacher, eh << Signore, permette...>>, 'Can I go outside to the toilet?' 'Yes',

he'd say, 'You may.' I went out. Our toilet had a very small
window which we could squeeze through and we'd fall out head
first. And then we'd run off. Then next morning we'd start our
Greek lessons again. But it was the complaint of every Italian
language teacher that they were never able to finish a lesson with
at least ten students. Our class had at least twenty-seven students,
but only ten would be left.... [85]

In retrospect, many interviewees realised that Lago had an
assimilation programme in train. In order to defend their apparent
failure to combat this plan, interviewees were keen to note the
shrewdness and cunning of Lago's 'slow, slow' approach. Some
admitted that the increase in compulsory Italian classes to four
hours per week in 1932 made them suspicious, but overall, Lago
was regarded as too canny an operator.[86] He was clever enough to
make assimilation policy seem unthreatening, unlike the blustering De
Vecchi, who had none of Lago's talents. The oral sources presented
De Vecchi as the one who exposed the Italian agenda and spoiled a
very clever strategy. As Mikhail Hatsinikolaou pointed out:

In 1932 I went to school for the first time.... I started doing one
hour of Italian every week. Until 193...4, we had one hour. Then
they increased Italian to two hours. By the school year of
1936,...no after this, 1937,...they stopped Greek and they made
Italian compulsory. This was proof to us that they wanted to
make us into little Italians.... Even during breaks in the school
playground, we were supposed to speak Italian. Outside the
school, we could speak Greek, but inside it was all Italian.[87]

De Vecchi's 'reforms' were applauded by commentators in Italy for
raising the standard of Dodecanesian education to the same level as
the 'rest' of Italy.[88] De Vecchi's intention was to hasten the islands'
integration into the metropolis, but his 'Fascist' style was never going
to capture hearts and minds. He believed pure Fascist will, rather than
Lago's plodding strategy of cultivating popular consent, brought
quicker results. He thought the islanders would embrace Italy and
her culture more swiftly if they were forced to do so. Unsurprisingly,
his approach provoked widespread opposition. The islanders
immediately saw him as 'anti-Greek' and cast him as a hated enemy.
Interviewees often recited anecdotes which illustrated his belligerent,
'anti-Greek' nature, including the story of his first visit to Kos as
governor, when he publicly shunned Greek Church dignitaries

because they could not speak Italian.[89] In his memoirs, Apostolos Papaioannou, then vicar-general, noted that during a lecture by a visiting Italian archaeologist, De Vecchi interrupted proceedings when the speaker used the Greek word 'Leros'. He was sternly told to use the Italian '..."Lero", without the "s", professor, for that ["Leros"] is Greek'.[90]

Many parents began withdrawing their children from school, despite threats of retaliation from the authorities. This became a commonplace form of dissent. Given the importance ascribed to schools for social advancement, ending a child's education was a very difficult choice to make, but many parents feared that their children would become 'little Italians' (Italákia), and worse still, young Fascists. De Vecchi required that all children be enrolled in the 'Balilla', and to participate in parades and other Fascist celebrations. Some interviewees privately conceded that they found Fascist Youth uniforms quite attractive – they loved the boots and hats especially – though predictably, all vehemently denied being influenced by Fascist propaganda. Mikhail Hatsinikolaou remembered that the assimilation programme involved political indoctrination:

> They tried to make me go to their schools, but this meant 'politicising' me (na politograftó). I'd have to become a 'Balillas' (*sic*), a <<Giovane Fascista>>. I'd have to become...a young Fascist. Mussolini wanted to impose Fascism on us. So he started with youth, he started in schools, with children....So I did not continue on with normal schooling because I didn't wanted to be 'written' as an Italian....[91]

Kalliope Harapas claimed in her testimony that her father kept her at home in protest against Italian education policy:

> We did not want to go to school....Why? The reason was they wanted to make us Fascists. We had to dress in black, the *camicia nera* as they called it then, to be in their parades, this and that....We, the people of Kos, we did not like this. Our parents kept us at home. My father did this. I, of course, read and write Italian very well....[92]

The most inspired response to De Vecchi's assimilation programme was 'the secret school' movement (to krifó scholió). Many teachers were left unemployed in the wake of De Vecchi's education reforms, forcing some to leave for Greece and others to teach students in secret locations. Conducting illegal Greek language classes to large groups of children was fraught with danger, given the network of school inspectors, collaborators and *carabinieri*, and the possible indiscretion of the children themselves. Interviewees who were students at the time remembered their secret schooling as period of adventure. Many were keen to recall 'near thing' instances in order to convey the danger and excitement of the times. Mikhail Hatsinikoloau related the following typical experience:

> The teacher would write things up on the board, we'd try and remember it all, and then the teacher would have to rub it all off. The teacher, he is dead now, God bless his soul. He opened up a section of the school, where we went at nights, with a kerosene lamp, and we did language exercises on the black board – grammar, conjugations, – the rest we read about at home.... But one night we had bad luck after which the teacher was forced to flee, and I left too. We forgot to rub out our Greek writing on the blackboard. The next morning, the inspector came, <<*ispettore*>>, and he found the Greek writing on the board, and he asked for explanations. The teacher immediately denied doing it. He claimed outsiders did it, they forced their way in....
>
> I continued to work at nights.... With fear of course, there was danger. They [the Italians] did all this so we would become Italians.... It was a dangerous time....[93]

Such 'secret schools' were a regular feature of Dodecanesian life after 1937. The nature of the movement differed from island to island. On Rhodes, for example, the movement was quite efficiently organised by the Church, while ou Kos, 'secret schools' appeared and operated without any central organisation.[94] Gabriel Kosaris was a church chanter who could read and write, and for much of the De Vecchi period, he took up the responsibility of teaching children in his village. He regarded his work as part of a noble mission to preserve Hellenic culture:

> I for one would invite a number of children into the church, to give them lessons on our religion, on our Fatherland. Our teachers had been 'stopped' [dismissed], and I did it even though there was fear that, shall we say, I could go to gaol or be sent into exile. But many did as I did in the Dodecanese. And they did even more work than I did....[95]

Admittedly, Greek language was permitted within school hours for the purpose of teaching scripture, as priests and lay theologians were allowed to teach religion at least one hour per week.[96] This inconsistency in Italian education policy was exploited by the Church at Rhodes. A team of scripture teachers, headed by Apostolos Papaioannou, ensured that most of the island's forty-seven villages had regular 'scripture' lessons, during which children were really taught the basics of Greek language and history.[97] 'Zaharia' of Asklepion remembered an number of teachers coming to his village during the dark De Vecchi years:

They took our schools, under De Vecchi. 1937, I think, 1936? Before that they took the schools. We did four hours of Italian a week. They had closed the secondary schools.... We had 'the secret school' later. A priest would come from [the village of] Lardos and acted as if he was giving us scripture lessons. Another fellow, 'Hondros', he gave lessons here. We learned our 'alpha-beta'. We learned this stuff at night, because the children otherwise knew nothing. Papa Vangelis would come over too.[98]

For interviewees and local historians alike, the suppression of the Greek language was the most sinister feature of the Italian occupation, one which excited the most impassioned reaction and emotive language. One author from Karpathos, Mikhailidis-Nouarou, made parallels between De Vecchi and King Herod, for, 'Like a new Herod, De Vecchi tried to cut off the tongues of Dodecanesian youth, so they would no longer speak or read in Greek....'[99] The same author goes on to claim that the Italians sought to demote Dodecanesians to a level where they would be no different than 'Hottentots or Zulus'.[100] As Apostolos Papaioannou claimed in his memoirs, the issue was a rallying point for the Greeks of the Dodecanese, as 'parents, priests, theologians, teachers.... foiled the designs of the "European" and "Christian" assimilators'.[101] In a recent study of Kos, one Alekos Markoglou reiterated the impression given by most interviewees that De Vecchi's education reforms fostered a 'people's' resistance, but like other writers, Markoglou could not resist interpreting the movement as a patriotic 're-awakening'. He claimed, 'the People again resisted, because in their hearts was deeply embedded the feeling for resistance against the occupiers'.[102] Yet while assuming a 're-awakening' of nationalist consciousness, local historians inadvertently identified a rather new phenomenon in popular history.

Local historians have predictably drawn parallels with the legendary 'secret school' movement in Greece before the War of Independence.[103] Put simply, the myth held that during the 'four hundred years' of Turkish rule, the Ottomans tried to extinguish the flame of Hellenism by prohibiting education. Children were forced to go to 'the secret school' at night time, guided on their way by the moonlight.[104] Many romantic icons, which nowadays hang in every Greek school, show children sitting at the feet of their mentors, usually a priest, and in the dead of night the children were taught the alphabet, and about what it meant to be a Hellene.[105] The myth has had immense symbolic importance in modern Greece for a number of reasons. Firstly, it perpetuated the image of 'the Turk' as 'unlearned' and 'uncivilised', who has hence been blamed for having retarded the forward march of Greek civilisation. In everyday social discourse, 'the Turk' has been a convenient scapegoat for many contemporary social drawbacks, and stands as the symbolic contrast to the innately 'civilised' Greek. Secondly, the myth holds that the Greek language and spirit had only survived centuries of Turkish rule because of 'the secret school', as it was supposed to have kept the link between ancient and modern Greek civilisation intact. Thirdly, 'the secret school' was seen to exemplify the 'natural' resilience, or the characteristic 'resistance', of the Greek people.

All participants in the Dodecanesian movement drew patriotic lessons from their recollections, as interviewees consciously associated their secret tuition in the De Vecchi period to 'the secret school' of national mythology. As a village priest, Kosaris was keen to assert the role played by the Church in his memories of his 'secret school'. He tried to convey how the Orthodox Church played a crucial role in both 'secret school' movements:

> As in the Revolution of 1821, it started from them, the Church. The 'Palaion Patron Germanon' [cleric and war hero], raised the flag, 'Freedom or Death'. Meaning, we Greeks have this as our basis. The Ancients did the same... at the Oracle of Delphi....
> We Orthodox Christians have had the Church as our base.[106]

When organising their resistance to assimilation policy, the islanders looked increasingly to 'Mother Hellas' for inspiration. Nationalist ideology armed them to meet a very new kind of threat, against which traditional forms of protest were recognised as inappropriate. 'The secret school' movement was crucial in the development of nationalist consciousness at a popular level, for the islanders could directly relate their experiences to the 'enslaved' Greeks under the barbaric 'Turk', and hence place their experience within a national cultural context. If the children could not see the allusion themselves, their patriotic teachers would have surely drawn it for them. The next chapter will deal at length with those teachers and other patriots who developed this process of socialisation, suffice to say here that the De Vecchi period saw, at the very least, the initiation of this process. Popular use of the phrase 'the secret school' is in itself revealing, as the definite article 'the' and the singular 'school' is a clear allusion to the national myth.[107] Another function of the myth was that interviewees could use their involvement in the movement to highlight their own patriotism and show how they too were part of a patriotic struggle. In so far as the Dodecanesian 'secret school' operated through common effort to resist political oppression, parents, teachers and students were indeed involved in a form of 'peoples' resistance'.

CONCLUSION

This chapter has sought to dispel a number of myths created by Greek nationalist ideology and historiography in order to discern a more plausible picture of dissent during the Italian Occupation. The unspoken assumption which pervades nationalist discourse, that Greeks have been patriotic since antiquity, and that patriotic convictions have made them zealously hostile to foreign domination, has engendered an unsophisticated understanding of the experience of occupation. Oral sources do not merely serve to dispel the myths created of nationalism, they actually give us a more reliable insight into the development of nationalism itself. Lago's governorship witnessed the persistence of traditional forms of protest which were motivated by traditional moral concerns. In contrast, new forms of protests were devised to combat De Vecchi's assimilation policy. The *Quadrumviro*'s style effectively hastened the spread of patriotic values and morality, and during the German Occupation which followed, this process was hastened even further. In March 1945, when the Germans had withdrawn completely from the Aegean, common folk in the Dodecanese brought out their Greek flags and rejoiced in the prospect of unification with Greece. By then, most ordinary Dodecanesians no longer needed their educated elites to guide them in such matters.

4 The Poetics of Patriotism: Italian Rule and Greek Nationalist Consciousness

In the previous chapter, I argued that traditional views about the influence of nationalism on popular dissent needed radical qualification. Nationalism remains, however, an important theme for our understanding of Italian rule because it constituted the only articulated and sustained anti-foreign ideology. The basic features of Greek nationalist thought need to be defined in order to describe how patriots saw their Italian occupiers, and to assess the significance of their 'patriotic' actions. This chapter will continue to revise nationalism's historical role in the Italian Dodecanese by focusing on those islanders who happened to be 'patriotically-minded'. Nationalist values informed the outlook of a small but growing number of individuals whose movements were monitored closely by a wary colonial regime. This important minority of Dodecanesians, who hereafter shall be referred to simply as 'patriots', experienced a different kind of occupation to the common folk. This alternative patriotic experience was heavily influenced by their higher social status in community life, the special attention they attracted from the colonial regime, and their patriotic mentality.

Their outlook was informed by values acquired through educational socialisation, in which the Greek nation was attributed the highest moral significance. Patriots were distinguished by their deep emotional investment in the vicissitudes of the Greek nation, expressing genuine joy in its successes, and sorrow and outrage at its failures. Patriotism was thus firmly anchored in high politics, as national concerns rendered all other matters, especially parochial concerns, trivial in comparison. One of the utilities of national morality was that it allowed for quite definitive judgements of Italian rule. Simply put, patriots regarded the Italians as morally repugnant because they had acquired territories which were Greek. They denounced Italy not so much because she had occupied the Dodecanese Islands, but because she infringed upon Greek national interests. The common folk did not share this moral certitude. Their attitudes towards the occupiers were ambiguous, consisting of a mixture of positive and negative impressions. Patriots have explained this common folk 'confusion' as a reflection of their ignorance, but as later chapters will show, these 'confused' memories provided as much insight into life under Italian rule as did patriotic representations.

This 'failure' on the part of common folk to appreciate the significance of the Greek nation was indicative of the social cleavage which existed between them and the patriots. In social terms, patriots were upwardly mobile and educated. In his useful studies on the development of nationalist movements in nineteenth-century Europe, Miroslav Hroch has noted that minor nations usually experienced an early phase in which nationalism meant little to most people, and when the spread of patriotic ideas was undertaken by a small number of committed individuals. These patriots, who sought to 're-awaken' a dormant national consciousness among the masses, also happened to be socially mobile.[1] The study of Greek nationalism in the Dodecanese should be considered within its social context, as patriotic ideas were spread by the most dynamic and pivotal social class in that society. Patriots were not merely acknowledged by common folk as community leaders, but as harbingers of modernity, and nationalism was seen as an integral part of that modernity.

Did the patriots of the Italian-occupied Dodecanese behave as 'patriots'? What did patriotic behaviour involve? Faced by the realities of Italian power, the patriots found the substance of their convictions tested. Nationalism pressured its patriots to be active and heroic, and if possible, to fight like the warrior bandits of the Greek War of Independence. But Italian political repression after 1923 was such that many patriots proved unable to translate their ideology into a code of practice, particularly as the Italians had targeted educated locals as potential leaders and dissidents. Some patriots failed to live up to nationalism's exacting standards, forcing them to reassess their understanding of nationalism's demands, including conventional conceptions of 'collaboration' and 'resistance'. Yet while Greek nationalism may have failed to provide any practical prescriptions for combating Italian power, patriots performed rituals which advocated their anti-Italian feelings in less obtrusive ways. These rituals could take the form of writing propaganda tracts, relating one's patriotic feelings in private conversation, or by shedding tears after hearing a patriotic song. This chapter will consider the meaning of such performances and convey their function as a substitute for open dissent.

As Hroch has confirmed, class is an important factor in understanding the historical development of nationalist movements. In the Italian Dodecanese, two distinct phases in the development of nationalism can be identified. The first period extends from 1912 to 1923, when patriotic leadership came from the uppermost echelons of Dodecanesian society. These included the wealthiest landholders, the most successful merchants and distinguished professionals. Their patriotic struggle involved organising demonstrations and plebiscites, and lobbying Great Power leaders. From 1923 to 1943, after their efforts had completely failed, the nationalist struggle was carried on by *petit bourgeois* patriots, particularly primary school teachers. Their patriotic duty was to provide leadership and inculcate political awareness among the common folk. Patriots of both phases shared what was, by local standards, an extensive educational background, which gave them a high social status, and a patriotic morality which served to re-inforce that status.

EDUCATION AND 'THE LEARNED-ONES'

While trekking through the villages of the Peloponnese in the early 1930s, the classicist H.D.F. Kitto identified what seemed to be a new social class. He pointed out that villagers who had returned from the United States enjoyed high social standing in community life. Every village seemed to have at least one returned émigré who 'inevitably feels superior to the peasants who do not (speak English)... and (who) reduces them to awed silence while he tells the story... of his successful candy store in some small American town'.[2] Throughout the Greek-speaking world, peasants had long acquired a sense of their own parochialness. They had come to view themselves as 'backward', recognising that progress was taking place beyond the microcosm of the village. In the Dodecanese, this commonplace attitude was symptomatic of fundamental changes which had taken place in the last decades of Ottoman rule. The penetration of western capital, which had drawn the empire more fully into the capitalist world economy, as well as the protracted efforts to rationalise the Ottoman imperial administration, were the two main themes of Ottoman modernisation.[3] These trends opened new kinds of employment opportunities in commerce, the bureaucracy and the professions, all of which represented fresh avenues for upward social mobility. The expansion of education facilities also made social mobility attainable through merit. The Greeks of the Ottoman Empire profited greatly from modernisation, as suggested by the significant growth in the number of Greek primary and secondary schools, and of higher education and learned societies.[4]

In the Dodecanese, symptoms of change were especially felt towards the end of the nineteenth century, in the transition from subsistence polyculture to market agriculture, and in the rise of the sponge trade. Merchant numbers increased, as did accountants, bureaucrats, teachers, doctors and lawyers. By the end of the nineteenth century, Dodecanesians of all classes were according more and more importance to literacy and learning, as almost every Dodecanesian village had an established primary school, while most of the main towns would eventually have secondary schools (Kalymnos in 1905, Rhodes Town in 1910, Kos Town in 1918, and Simi in 1922).[5]

Dodecanesian patriots were a product of this great era of social, economic and political change. To those who could afford it, education offered a way out of the tedium and insecurity of peasant life, and from the dangers of life at sea. It also presented an alternative to that other escape route: emigration. Working 'with words' (me ta grámmata) meant a much brighter future, a more comfortable existence. Education was an essential pre-requisite for 'clean work' (katharés douliés) as teachers, clerks, inspectors, bank tellers and customs officials. Envious peasants worn-out by hard toil would disparagingly refer to members of this privileged professional class as 'unworked' (adoúleftos). Heracles Karanastasis of Kardamena, Kos, was the son of a major landholder and a self-confessed 'unworked'. During one of his school vacation breaks he worked as a labourer on a tobacco farm, but the experience had convinced him that being 'unworked' was a privilege:

> Unaccustomed since childhood to hard work, which required a strong back and powerful arms, I could not bear it. My family saw me returning home half dead from digging and planting, worried that I might get sick. They refused to allow me to work any longer.[6]

Not only did the 'unworked' have an easier life in dealing 'with words', they were accorded great respect and courtesy. After completing their secondary school studies in Kalymnos in June

1922, Heracles Karanastasis and Mikhail Diakomanolis returned to their native Kardamena, a small village on the south-western coast of Kos. As Karanastasis recalled in his memoirs, the whole community came out to welcome home the graduates:

> We two...graduates of...secondary school, were honoured for being the first members of our village to have attained a secondary school diploma. And naturally, now we were the most...learned.
>   ...Salutations, merriment, entertainment, and much pomp and ceremony followed.[7]

Karanastasis was eager to continue his studies immediately at the University of Athens, but village elders requested he postpone his departure so that he might share his acquired wisdom with the village children.[8]

The learned ones were given respect because they were the main link between the moral community and the modern world. They advised common folk on countless matters, from explaining legal documents to imparting their knowledge of international affairs. As ethnographic studies have shown, educated members of village communities were accorded high social status in much of the Greek-speaking world. In his study of a Cypriot mountain village in the early 1950s, John Peristiany noted the deference which the peasants gave to their resident teacher, partly because he had completed secondary school (which gave him higher standing than the priest, who had only completed primary school), and partly for his symbolic connection with the outside world. He represented 'progress' because he knew the mind of the townspeople.[9] In the late nineteenth and early twentieth centuries, educated Dodecanesians had acquired many of the cultural characteristics which symbolised modernity. The learned ones discarded their local accent and adopted the 'correct' or 'clean' (katharí) speech of the capital. They also wore western-styled clothing. Male peasants continued to wear baggy trousers (vrákes) and black boots, but the learned ones wore *pantalons*, laced shoes, shirts, jackets, and the *fedora* or a beret.[10]

The village teacher was the most pervasive representative of the learned class. He was usually referred to as 'master teacher' (kírie dáskale), and as a mark of respect, he received preferential treatment as a guest at weddings and at other communal celebrations.[11] As a symbol of social progress, the village teacher also had the effect of highlighting the 'backwardness' of those around him. Members of all social classes, to some degree, shared the feeling that the Greeks were indeed a 'backward' people, and the learned ones in particular felt modern Greek society was unworthy of its historical inheritance.[12] Through education, there was hope of making Greeks worthy of this inheritance by turning former Turkish subjects into modern 'Europeans'. Education was regarded as a means of self-realisation, a way of redeeming a suppressed inner spirit which had once made the Greeks great. The official line was that education did not merely socialise, it fostered a metamorphosis. The Greek term 'morphosis' (mórfosis) or 'learned-ness' conveys an air of sublimity, denoting spiritual elevation and enrichment. Karanastasis proudly referred to himself and his friend Diakomanolis as the most learned or 'morfoméni' (morfoméni) of their village. A Rhodian clergyman boasted of his local secondary school as, 'the primary weapon which existed for *spiritual* growth and enlightenment' (my italics).[13] According to Christoforos Fournaris of Kos Town, who attended secondary school in the mid-1920s, education was a cure for 'backwardness'. 'I wanted to be either a teacher or a doctor,' he claimed, 'for the doctor cures the body, while the teacher cures the soul.'[14] Education was thus seen to have a mystical quality which would awaken a dormant spirit in Greek consciousness. Its awakening would lead to national regeneration. 'Mórphosis' and nationalism thus worked in concert to make the Greeks great again. As Minos Venetoklis, who had endowed Rhodes Town with its first secondary school claimed, 'Education, education...only education shall securely steer us to the blissful thing we have longed and suffered for, our beautiful and sweet fatherland....'[15]

While education performed a crucial patriotic role, it also fostered class segmentation, for most Dodecanesian children could only afford one or two years of schooling. The first priority of each child was to acquire a functional education, but the 'clean jobs' were only open to students who could progress through the education system, at least to secondary school level. Throughout the Italian Occupation, only a minority of Greeks were wealthy enough to complete secondary school because tuition involved a considerable financial sacrifice. As mentioned earlier, Karanastasis's father was a major landholder in Kardamena, but even he found the ordinary school expenses exceptionally high. The cost of uniforms, stationery, food and lodgings was exorbitant, and Karanastasis remembers, perhaps with some exaggeration, his father's anxieties:

I will make possible what seems impossible and educate both of you; you and Tasos [his younger brother]. I will work hard and twice as long. I will sell my boat, I will bear much hardship, just so I could see you both one day as men of higher status and distinguishable from the rest.[16]

Graduates were rare and hence valued. This was shown throughout Kos where graduate numbers were a focus of inter-village rivalries. Kardamena was a relatively new village which was keen to establish its own landmarks and identity, and as Karanastasis and Diakomanolis were the first sons of Kardamena to complete secondary school, the whole community celebrated their graduation. Karanastasis boasted that Kardamena could now rival the neighbouring village Antimachia, which prided itself in the number of children it had in secondary schools. In Antimachia, he recalls, it had become accepted practice among wealthier peasants to sell land in order to finance their children's studies.[17]

If *mórphosis* and 'clean jobs' were restricted to a privileged minority, then so too was national consciousness. Only the *morfoméni* knew what it meant to be a 'patriot' (*patriótis*), and common folk expected they too would know what it meant once they had climbed the social ladder. Like western clothing and 'pure' accents, nationalism was a distinguishable mark of *mórphosis*.

THE PATRIOTIC MENTALITY: KEY FEATURES

Unlike the common folk, *morfoméni* claimed they understood the significance of the Greek nation because they claimed to understand History. Armed with this knowledge, they were able to make quite confident interpretations of past and present events. The official version of the Rock War, as discussed in Chapter 3, is a case in point. Kalymnian oral tradition remains ambivalent about its meaning, for while the Rock War celebrates positive aspects of Kalymnian character, the event also involved the death of a young man. Consequently, some interviewees remembered the Rock War as 'the big calamity' (to megálo kakó). When Nikolaos Poulas (born 1897?) told the story of the Rock War in his testimony, he delivered his presentation of Kazonis's slaying in a sad and muted tone:

Then happened the 'great bad'. The boy Kazonis was selling milk near St Nicholas's. He joined the others and started to throw stones at the Italians. But then one [bullet] caught him in the eye. He fell back and there he remained.[18]

Many of Poulas's generation saw it as a tragedy from which little joy could be taken. In contrast, *morfoméni* had given the event a positive symbolic meaning even while Kazonis's corpse was still warm. The same evening that Kazonis was buried, Ioannis Zervos, secondary school principal and highly respected local writer, composed an ode to the fallen shepherd. Zervos found solace, even reason to rejoice, in the patriotic significance of Kazonis's death:

> To Cry? Oh! To be filled with joy!
> And where is the blood of the first [patriot]?
> The soil where I may pay my respects to you?
> The pain. The Joy. The first blood,
> For Liberty such true blood spilt.[19]

Kazonis was an obvious choice for martyr and symbol of the Rock War; he was struck down in the heat of battle, in dramatic fashion, and for a noble cause. He came to symbolise the patriotism of the Kalymnian people. However, Kazonis probably knew very little of, and possibly cared little for, conceptions of 'Mother Hellas'. A poor shepherd was less likely than most to have had any formal schooling, and Kazonis probably spent most of his short life tending his herd and selling milk. Nevertheless, educated Kalymnians like Zervos saw much that was profound in his 'martyrdom'. There was no doubt in their minds that Kazonis – whose body, legend has it, was wrapped in a Greek flag before burial – had died for 'Mother Hellas'.[20] That Kazonis would not have understood the meaning of his martyrdom is immaterial. It was the role of *morfoméni*, as keepers of higher knowledge and national values, to know the significance of such things. They spoke on behalf of Kazonis and explained what his death really meant.

Written and oral traditions, which have provided alternative perspectives on such matters, have co-existed quite comfortably.[21] Each has played to different audiences, but the oral version of the Rock War has been restricted to local consumption, for it is too unsophisticated and fails to relate the patriotic significance of the 'war'. For *morfoméni*, History has always been about Hellas. Representations of the past have had to relate to the Hellenic nation or they are not 'serious' history. Unlike the common folk, local *morfoméni* have regarded themselves primarily as members of a national community. Consequently, historical representations of the Dodecanese, whether in oral or written form, must evoke a patriotic significance. The *morfoméni* of Kalymnos, who had re-named the Rock War 'the National-Religious Resistance', did their duty by giving the 'war' a significance within the context of nationalist discourse. They presented Kalymnos as a bastion of Hellenism, transforming the Rock War into a myth about Kalymnian patriotism, and thereby presenting the islanders as 'resisters'.[22]

As shown in the case of Kalymnos, local history is important because of its implications for community reputations. These reputations have been upheld by local amateur scholars whose traditional task has been to extol the patriotism of their island, and to show how Dodecanesian history is a worthy and integral part of Greek national history. Thus local historians have always made conscious comparisons between the Italian-occupied Dodecanese and the Greek mainland under Turkish rule. According to mainstream Greek historiography, the initial uprisings of 1821 ignited a national 're-awakening' which spread throughout the Greek-speaking world. The pre-independence period is significant in nationalist thought because the Greek people allegedly suffered untold cruelties at the hands of their oppressors, and yet, as shown in 1821, their national spirit re-emerged like a phoenix rising from the ashes. In their attempt to tie Dodecanesian history to that of the Greek nation, local scholars have sought to show how their region had endured an equally 'barbarous' regime, and that the islanders also had a national 're-awakening'. Hence their concentration on the themes of 'foreign oppression' and 'patriotic struggle'.

These priorities have ensured that patriotic representations of Italian rule have been resolutely hostile to it. The resulting historiographical tradition is therefore almost indistinguishable from anti-Italian propaganda of the occupation period. Local historians today would approve of the following characterisation of the Italian-occupied Dodecanese, written by an expatriate propagandist during the Second World War:

> The inhabitants were imprisoned, abused and humiliated for the merest trifle, their life made hard and impossible, forcing them to leave their country and seek shelter in free Greece. Those that in spite of all stayed on behind (*sic*) were under a cloud of terror.[23]

The patriotic credibility of this representation of Italian rule lies in its emphasis on 'oppression', and because it demonises Greece's national adversaries.

The oral testimonies of educated Dodecanesians show the same priorities. Among them was Giorgos Koulianos, a school teacher who taught for many years in Kos, Rhodes and Leros. He began his oral testimony by outlining the politics of Italian rule and its implications for Hellenism:

> The Italians wanted to destroy Hellenism and make this place [the Dodecanese] Italian. Their method was to attack the twin pillars of Hellenism: [holding up two fingers, vigorously grabbing each in succession] our religion, and our language. They therefore victimised the priests and the teachers.[24]

In beginning his testimony with a textbook history lesson, Koulianos revealed a habit followed by most of the educated interviewees. Ioannis Alahiotis, an autodidact peasant from Asfendiou, Kos, started his testimony with an overview of Italian expansion since the Risorgimento, with the intention of presenting the Dodecanese as a victim of imperialism.[25] Fellow-villager and school-master, Manolis Kiapokas, a young student at the time of De Vecchi's education reforms, opened his interview with an emphasis on 'oppression'. He contextualised his experiences in History:

> Having been born in 1930, I was of the generation which suffered most when it came to education.... We saw [experienced] the De Vecchi laws – certainly all the boys in my village did, and probably Dodecanesian youth in general – as something which was horrifying. For students, and of course their parents, it was a source of deep concern.... The Italians, of course, wanted to Catholicise us, to make us Catholics, and to Italianise us,... to make us into Italians.... These were, of course, hard times for Dodecanesians.[26]

These oral representations were intended to confirm the official view of history. *Morfoméni* believed that the function of history was to serve the state, to chart the forward progress of Hellenism, and to celebrate the exceptional qualities of the Greek people. Information volunteered in these testimonies was meant to uphold this patriotic purpose. Alternatively, presenting a more balanced view was thought to be unpatriotic, as unqualified hostility for Italian rule characterised the writings and oral testimonies of all *morfoméni*. Privately, many

morfoméni harboured more measured views of the experience of
occupation, and as will be shown in the last section of this chapter,
they occasionally revealed such views in their testimonies.
Nevertheless, most *morfoméni* sought to project a self-image of an
undying patriot.

Morfoméni claimed, often with some exaggeration, to have hated
their occupiers with a passion, and the manner in which they
expressed this passion revealed much about the culture of
patriotism. Since nationalism was one of the factors which
distinguished *morfoméni* from common folk, it was quite important
for *morfoméni* to flaunt their patriotic feelings. 'Showing' their feelings
in highly emotive ways was meant to reveal the depth of their
patriotism. The mere presence of the Italians was too irksome for
some. 'I could not bear it', cried the Kalymnian writer Ioannis
Zirounis. 'We did not lose a war... yet the islands were now LE
ISOLE ITALIANE DELL'EGEO, as the proud Italians called
them.'[27] For one Koan patriot, the occupation caused such
emotional stress that it proved fatal, or so we are told by the
historian of Kos, Vasilis Hatsivasiliou. The patriot in question was
Nikolaos Partheniadis, one time *démarchos* of Kos Town, who
died on 15 August 1912 because the occupiers were secretly planning
never to leave the islands. According to Hatsivasiliou, Partheniadis's
patriotic anguish was such that he could not bare the thought of
the Dodecanese staying under foreign rule. 'His irrepressible
enthusiasm', writes Hatsivasiliou, 'came to symbolise the feeling of
disillusionment and resignation with which the people held their
destiny.'[28] The fact that so careful an historian as Hatsivasiliou
could incorporate such an implausible anecdote in his 'serious'
historical work reflects the extent to which Italian rule has been
deemed a moral issue.

Displays of anguish and emotion were considered virtuous by
morfoméni because they conveyed the depth of one's commitment to
the nation. During the occupation, numerous Dodecanesian
morfoméni in the diaspora committed their anxious thoughts to
paper in order to share their pathos with other *morfoméni*. These
writings varied in terms of quality, but all evoked a passion for their
nation. Two examples will suffice. Gerasimos Drakidis's *Notes on the
Dodecanesians*,[29] one of the earliest anti-Italian tracts (1913), begins
with a long poem set against an elegant pictorial background of
Rhodes harbour. An allegory of 'Mother Hellas' sits on the horizon,
accompanied by a two-headed Byzantine Eagle and flanked by Greek

flags. The use of classical and Byzantine motifs conveys timelessness, suggesting that the Dodecanese had always been a part of the Greek nation. The intention is to add a historical legitimacy to Greek claims to the islands:

> Daughters of the Aegean who mourn as if a daughter is dead
> And are Enslaved and struggle against the dark Ocean
> Rejoice, and say give us
> our embittered Mother's holy embrace.

The poet maintains there is hope of redemption, and he encourages the lost children of the Aegean to seek out their 'Mother Hellas'. Other works could relate this feeling of disappointment in more vulgar terms. The following poem, which was written some time after Italy's victory in Ethiopia, uses racist references to project a feeling of anger:

> We are not Ethiopians naked, deprived!
> We are Greeks, Masculine, Blessed!
>
> . . . .
> Resurrect Oh Dodecanese! Liberty is Near.
>
> . . . .
> Nisyros, Astypalea, Kalymnos, Simi and Halki,
> Leros and Tilos and Lipsos, awake from your sleep![30]

This poet regards the Italians as unworthy because they can only defeat African 'savages', and since the islanders are considered superior to the darker 'races', he encourages them to fulfil their potential. An underlying source of frustration of all *morfoméni* was that Dodecanesians did not fight like the warrior bandits of the Greek War of Independence. The poet suggests that if only the islanders could reclaim that lost heroic spirit they might be able to drive the Italians out.

The written tradition includes many genres, from history to poetry, all of which exhort love for country and hatred for its adversaries. Yet this tradition tells us very little about the Italians, except that they were cruel and oppressive. The metaphors and allusions employed to characterise the Italians could just as easily be used to describe other occupiers like the Turks, Germans or Bulgarians, and when specific references to Italians are made, they often come in the form of well known stereotypes, such as the Italians as 'womanisers', 'poor soldiers' or as Fascists. The written tradition therefore has very little substance, but its political and social function deserves attention, for the act of writing on patriotic themes was regarded as an important form of 'struggle'.

This was especially true among Dodecanesian expatriates, who, from the safety of Athens, Alexandria and elsewhere, carried on the good fight throughout the occupation by composing poems and diatribes. Expatriates spilled much ink and went to great expense to publish their own works. Their expected audience, to be sure, was fellow expatriates, for anti-Italian literature could hardly be circulated in the Dodecanese, but the circulation of these writings in the diaspora helped confirm the existence of a general will, as if the flame of Hellenism was kept alight. Through writing, expatriates could 'show' their patriotic fervour and dissent, even though they were only really 'showing' each other. 'Showing' one's patriotism in print was considered a legitimate way of maintaining personal honour and reputation, for the more one 'showed' one's passion in print, the more one looked like a 'great patriot'.[31] Expatriates did perform some practical services. Most notably they raised funds for Greek schools in the Dodecanese and informed the western press about any Italian excesses. But writing patriotic prose and verse constituted their main activity, and overall, their record suggested they favoured form over substance. This predilection was to characterise the nature of the patriotic response to Italian rule and explain its ineffectiveness.

Most of our Greek written sources from the Italian period were produced in the diaspora. Among the numerous periodicals in which the poetics of 'struggle' was carried out were: *Avgí Dodekanisiakí*, which was published consistently between 1914 and 1941, *I Dodekanisiakí*, the *Dodekanisiakón Imerológion* (1924–32), and the short-lived *Foní tis Dodekanísou*, with 48 issues between 1922 and 1924. Newsletters for expatriate communities from specific islands included the *Foní tis Kásou*, which began publication in 1924 at Port Said, and *Simiakó Víma*, which was started in Athens in 1937. Many individual expatriates wrote a number of tomes on the great tragedy of the 'Italian-hostaged Dodecanese' (ta Italokratoúmena Dodekánisa), and most prominent among these writers was Skevos Zervos, who, along with his many propaganda tracts he produced during the Paris Peace Conferences, wrote a history of the Dodecanese, a study of Rhodian customs, and a long ode to the enslaved islanders. Another prolific writer, based in the United States, was Iakovos Casavis who, like Zervos, had his many writings translated into French and English.[32] Because of their immense output, Zervos and Casavis were considered by fellow *morfoméni* as 'great patriots'.

Expatriate *morfoméni* were free to express their enmity towards Italian rule with unbridled hostility, but how substantial was the patriotism of *morfoméni* who had remained in the Dodecanese? In what ways did they try to challenge Italian authority? During the first decade of the occupation, Dodecanesian elites had also voiced their nationalist sympathies quite openly, though their rhetoric was naturally more restrained. Their 'resistance' was effectively limited to politely disputing the legitimacy of Italian rule with their occupiers and the Great Powers. What will become evident from the following analysis is that Greek nationalism, while providing enormous inspiration for its patriots, did not really offer any practical advice for challenging foreign rule. Whilst local elites did much to 'show' their passion for Hellas and their outrage against Italian rule, their struggle had very little impact.

'GREAT PATRIOTS' AND HIGH POLITICS 1912–23

During the first decade of the Italian occupation, nationalist protests were orchestrated and led by local elites. Common folk participated in these pro-Hellenic demonstrations, but they knew they were mere pawns in a game of high politics. Their social superiors kept the limelight in this period, one which local historiography has presented as an age of 'great patriots'. Each island could boast its own 'great patriots', men like M.G. Minachoulis, G. Sakellis, K. Sakellis and N. Papadopoulos of Kasos, and A. Papadakis and A. Diamantis of Halki, who promulgated that, 'As one man, we will rise under the protection of the cross and the Greek flag to live free or to die.'[33] There were others like B.E. Kontos and Ilias Ftiaras of Kastellorizo, who claimed to have 'struggled' for the liberation of their island. Their 'struggle' included sending petitions to General Ameglio, in which the national allegiances of the people of Kastellorizo were demonstrated. A.K. Kouremetis, Kleanthis Zervos, Mikhail Manglis and Antonios Mailis did the same for the people of Kalymnos, and their aspirations were noted in proclamations which reached Paris and London.[34]

Italy's weak hold on the Dodecanese provided some scope for patriotic agitation of this kind. The occupied demonstrated in the streets and proclaimed their pro-Hellenic sentiments openly, for throughout the period of 'temporary' occupation, the Italians remained sensitive to Great Power opinion and were reluctant to retaliate against local political agitation. They tried to avoid situations like 'The Bloody Easter of 1919', which Great Power leaders were eager to use against them. Local notables were also keen to exploit these conditions, not only to promote unification with 'Mother Hellas', but to enhance their own reputations as 'great patriots'.

The 'great patriots' came from the highest echelons of Dodecanesian society. They were often major landholders and entrepreneurs, men who had capitalised most on economic expansion in the decades leading up to the First World War. They were often university graduates (epistímones), the most educated of *morfoméni*, and had studied French, the language of diplomacy. A brief prosopography of the Rhodian *demarchía* of 1912–13 will illustrate the socio-economic milieu of the 'great patriots'. The *démarchos* of Rhodes in this period was Savas Pavlidis, commonly known as 'Savas Efendi' (Savas the Master). Pavlidis was born in the village of Gennadi in 1860, the son of a merchant. He began his career as a clerk in the Ottoman bureaucracy in Rhodes Town, and later achieved prominence in the Rhodian law courts. In 1903 he was accused of corruption by the Ottoman authorities and was exiled to Constantinople. He spent his time there profitably, studying law and obtaining a degree. After returning to Rhodes, he entered local government and was elected *démarchos* in 1911.[35] His supporting councillors included Giorgos Giorgiadis, an author and a successful lawyer, who obtained degrees from Athens and Constantinople,[36] Giorgos Konstantinidis, a medical graduate from the University of Athens and former representative of Rhodes in the Young Turk parliament,[37] and Dimitrios Athanasiadis, highly respected schoolmaster who completed a degree in philology at Athens.[38] Other councillors came from distinguished families, including Theodoros Frangakis, son of a powerful merchant, and Pangiotis Agiakatsikas and Nikolaos Georgalidis, members of the Rhodian landed gentry.[39]

In leading the charge for unification with Greece, the 'great patriots' had two basic role models to follow. Greek nationalist iconography commemorates the warrior bandits as those who fought for Greek independence, men like Kolokotrones and Kanaris, yet just as many portraits can be found of those who weilded the pen, of men like the intellectual Adamantios Korais, the poet Rhigas Pharaios, and the statesmen Ioannis Kapodistrias. For the distinguished notables of the Dodecanese, the latter group served as more appropriate role models. Lobbying the Great Powers made them feel they were participating in high politics, and there was nothing more honourable than being involved in international politics and leading the struggle for unification. High politics also suited their social status, as shown by numerous photographic portraits which show the 'great patriots' in statesmen-like pose and conveying aristocratic pretension. This pretension was shown in their apparel; fine silk shirts, suits, ties, cuff links and velvet gloves, and some wore long tails and overcoats. Unlike commonfolk, most had a definite hairstyle, some with brilliantined hair. Moustaches were often thin and finely trimmed. Paris Rousos of Leros had medals on his smoking jacket and sported an elegant white bow-tie.[40] Such attire was more at home in the salons of Europe than in backwaters like Leros and Karpathos, but the intention of projecting these self-images was to accentuate their social superiority. So too did their manner of speaking and educational backgrounds. Only *morfoméni* of such high social standing had the ability and skill to draft letters to foreign statesmen in French or in high Greek, or 'katharevousa'. When dealing with Europe, the Dodecanese needed representatives who had adopted European high culture, and who gave Greek nationalism a respectable face.

In keeping with their high culture, official dealings with the Italians were conducted with considerable decorum. In 1912, the professed aim of the Rhodian *demarchía* was to realise 'the perennial desire for the unification of the island with its Mother, Greece'.[41] In April, local leaders greeted General Ameglio with an official welcome, and followed this with formal representations in which they communicated Rhodian aspirations for unification with Greece.[42] In August, the *demarchía* lodged a formal protest against Italy's rumoured plans to return the islands to the Ottoman Empire.[43] In September, the 'great patriots' organised a plebiscite, the results of which were sent to Giolitti, Sir Edward Grey and Venizelos in December.[44] By 12 February 1913, after more 'official' manoeuvrings, Ameglio had two councillors dismissed (Anthanasiadis and Giorgiadis). Savas 'Efendi' Pavlidis was dismissed four days later.[45]

Most of the other Dodecanesian *demarchíes* followed what appeared to be formal conventions, but there was also room for passion, as shown in the 'struggle' of Antonios Ioannidis, who was *démarchos* of Kos Town between 1919 and 1922. When news had

arrived of the disastrous defeat of Greek forces in Asia Minor in 1922,
Ioannidis was said to have suffered an emotional trauma. His godson,
Christoforos Fournaris, claimed that the people of Kos were touched
by Ioannidis's emotional reaction:

> He heard about the great catastrophe in the East. The horizon
> over the Anatolian coast was red; red with the blood of
> slaughtered Christians. He retreated heartbroken into his study,
> and he was so upset that he did not emerge for two whole days.
> He ate and drank nothing. His family pleaded with him to come
> out, but he would not come out.[46]

Ioannidis was a lawyer, a major landholder, and regarded by his
contemporaries as a tireless patriot. As *démarchos* he performed all
the conventional tasks. For example, he launched an impassioned
protest against Italy's violations of the Treaty of Sèvres in 1921. As
with his *démarchos* predecessor Partheniadis, who died because the
Italians planned never to leave, Ioannidis's despair over the disaster in
Asia Minor indicated the depth of his patriotism. To be sure, the
passion displayed by the 'great patriots' also reflected the exciting
international developments between 1912 and 1923. In 1912 and
1913, Epiros, southern Macedonia, Crete and the Eastern Sporades
were incorporated into the Greek state, and from 1919 and 1922,
Greek irredentism had reached its apex when the Greek army
invaded Anatolia. It seemed as if the Dodecanese would also be
redeemed, and the 'great patriots' heard their calling. Never before
had so many island notables shown such earnest civic-mindedness.
The Church, the *demarchies* and all eminent Dodecanesians seemed to
be involved in 'the struggle'.

But their passion could not be matched by substance. With luck,
lobbying Great Power support could produce some beneficial
outcomes, but even in playing the games of high politics, the 'great
patriots' were clearly out of their depth. Local historians flatter their
heroes by mentioning them in the same breath as Lloyd George,
Edward Grey, Poincaré, Clemenceau, a form of aggrandisement
through association. Admittedly, the 'great patriots' had few
practical options open to them in their pursuit of unification with
Greece, but their 'greatness' was more related to their social status at
home than their deeds in the international arena. 'Showing' their
patriotism might have raised local morale, but in the final analysis,
their efforts produced few practical results. After 1923, even 'showing'
patriotism was no longer possible. The Treaty of Lausanne effectively

gave the Italians licence to suppress all forms of patriotic expression. Most of the 'great patriots' withdrew into the safety of their private lives, knowing they had much to lose by 'showing' their patriotism any further. Of Ioannidis, for instance, nothing is heard until his death in 1933. The same could be said for most of his 'great patriot' counterparts throughout the Dodecanese.[47]

Greek historiography regards the first decade of the Italian Occupation as the most important phase because it offers suitable material for writing History. Apart from street demonstrations and flag waving, the period offers ample pro-Hellenic proclamations and other documentation which supposedly conveyed the deeply-felt nationalist aspirations of the Dodecanesian people. Faced with this comparative wealth of written sources, and inspired by its pro-Hellenic content, local historians have made the period 1912 to 1923 their favourite. It is presented as a golden age of Dodecanesian Greek nationalism, one which featured a distinguished array of 'great patriots' who are presented as local versions of Kapodistrias or Venizelos. Hence to a certain extent, the 'great patriots' are an invention of local historiography. The long forgotten 'struggle' of Antonios Ioannidis, for instance, was retrieved from obscurity by the conservative historian Hatsivasiliou.[48] In setting out to write his massive tome on the history of Kos, Hatsivasiliou had the responsibility of presenting his fellow Koans as worthy members of the Greek nation. Thus descriptions of Ioannidis's activities and patriotic resolve are intended to reflect upon the patriotism of the Koan people in general.[49]

PETTY BOURGEOIS PATRIOTS, 1923–42

From 1923, much more patriotic resolve was required than that displayed by the 'great patriots'. The *carabinieri* targeted the *morfoméni* for special attention, for Lago and De Vecchi would not brook any expression of Greek patriotism, and gaol and sometimes torture awaited those who were caught. In the wake of the Rock War, for instance, which was clearly a series of womens' protests, the *carabinieri* arrested thirty-one Kalymnian males, most of whom were *morfoméni*. They included two doctors, two dentists, seven teachers, two lawyers, one mechanic, one botanist, one tanner, five merchants, seven priests and three with no designated occupation.[50] In these repressive conditions, most of the 'great patriots' departed from public view, leaving a vacuum which was filled by *morfoméni* lower down the social scale. The patriots after 1923 were mainly teachers, learned priests, petty merchants and literate peasants. Another difference between these patriots and their 'great' predecessors was their closer ties with the community. While 'great patriots' were socially aloof and expected much deference from the lower classes, the new patriots were more like Gramscian 'organic intellectuals', providing leadership at the grass roots level. One could expect to find these *morfoméni* sitting with other menfolk in the café, reading aloud excerpts from newspapers for the benefit of the illiterate. These patriots would explain Italian policies to fellow villagers, advise parents not to allow their children to join the *Balilla*, and inculcate them with patriotic ideas. During De Vecchi's oppressive rule, it was these patriots who struggled more than most to combat the governor's assimilation policies and were largely responsible for the success of the 'secret school' movement.[51]

One of these *petit bourgeois* leaders was Apostolos Papaioannou, a deacon based in Rhodes Town. Between 1939 and 1940, Papaioannou, affectionately known by the diminutive 'the Diakaki' ('the Little Deacon'), made regular visits to every Rhodian village, where he often spoke to packed churches about 'Hellenism' and patriot duty. De Vecchi had his men follow him everywhere, but the deacon avoided arrest by giving his sermons in cryptic language. Frustrated by his inability to secure his arrest, De Vecchi allegedly told Bishop Apostolos Trifonos that he was quite aware of the craftiness of Orthodox clergymen, and alluded to the political machinations of the priesthood during the Byzantine Empire:

> Tell your deacon I am well read in Byzantine history, for I taught it in a seminary. He must be careful in future, for I'll tie him up and send him to that same seminary.[52]

De Vecchi eventually had him gaoled on trumped-up charges in August 1940. The Diakaki's social background was typical of Dodecanesian patriots in this period. He was born in 1917 into a lower-middle class family in Rhodes Town, and spent much of his youth as an altar boy, mingling with the higher clergy and other learned people. His father was a respected school-master who died in 1923, leaving behind a family of five children. The Church funded his education, as did his mother, who saved money by working as a seamstress in the evenings. In the mid-1930s he studied theology at a distinguished Orthodox college at 'Halki' in Istanbul. His first vocational appointment was as assistant to the Greek Patriarch of Alexandria in 1938, and while in Egypt, he was encouraged by Rhodian expatriates to return to his island and participate in the fight against Italian rule. When he returned to Rhodes, De Vecchi's assimilation laws were in full force. The Diakaki immediately began regular tours among the villages, pretending to give scripture lessons while giving Greek language and history classes, and preaching patriotic sermons from the pulpit. Supporting him were other *morfoméni* who posed as a travelling church choir.[53]

The Diakaki had firm ideas regarding patriotic duty, and in May 1940, he conveyed these ideas before a large congregation in the Rhodian village of Archangelos. He asserted:

We must never forget that a Greek is one who throughout his life is obliged to carry a basket full of goods, whose contents he never sells, as do other merchants, but he must never resist showing these goods to everyone; to children, to older people, to the young, to other Greeks, to Armenians, Turks, and to all other nationals who tread the soil of our country. These were goods which foreigners regarded with awe, and they returned to their homelands to copy and set their homes in order.... What are these goods? Certainly these are the attributes of Mother Greece, the altar and temple of Humanity, as well as the civilisation of Orthodoxy, the heroes of Greece,... the Hellenism upheld by priest and teacher despite centuries of efforts by foreigners to destroy it.[54]

His message implied that Rhodians were *not* behaving like good patriots. In the Diakaki's opinion, the Italians were not being 'shown' enough opposition, that Hellenism was not being expressed openly. The Diakaki believed, as many patriots did, that inactivity (*attendismo*) was just as shameful as collaboration. This was a view shared (though not necessarily practised) by most *morfoméni*. Nationalist morality asserted that true Greeks could not, justify inactivity, that every Hellene had an obligation to struggle. True Greeks had to show urgency, to evoke more passion, and suffer for the realisation of unification with 'Mother Hellas'. It was not always clear, however, in what ways a true Greek was supposed to 'struggle'. Nationalist ideology, if strictly applied, expected all patriots to rise up in armed revolt, just like the warrior bandits of 1821, yet everyone was aware that armed resistance was not a practical option in the Italian Dodecanese. Geography alone precluded this. The islands were thinly populated, small and very easily traversed by troops searching for partisans. All *morfoméni* were aware that armed revolt was not possible, but they could not think of an alternative strategy.

Morfoméni nevertheless agreed that they had to set an example to common folk and their children. All gestures of defiance, whatever their practical impact, had symbolic effect. Teachers, for instance, presented a number of ways of 'showing' defiance. Kostas of Gennadi, Rhodes, taught Greek language when he was supposed to teach Italian.[55] Antonios Karantonis of Antimachia, Kos, claimed he trivialised the Italian language during teaching hours with jokes; and Ioannis Halkias of Olymbos, Karpathos, one of the leaders of the protest against the census, mischievously sang anti-Italian songs in his local café in 1936.[56] Ioannis Gounaris proudly recalls in his memoirs how in 1922 he had his students sing patriotic songs as they marched by the *delegato*'s office in Kos Town.[57]

Such minor gestures of insolence could nevertheless provoke strong retribution. Halkias, for instance, served a prison sentence for his mischief. Others convicted of political crimes suffered torture and beatings (though none of the interviewees had heard of the use of castor oil).[58] Patriotism, if practised literally, was a high-risk activity. Teachers in particular were in an unenviable position because they were placed at the cutting edge of the political strategies of both Greek nationalism and Italian assimilation. All teachers were expected to serve the colonial government and, as will be shown in the case studies below, those who refused were victimised. Those who succumbed, however, were faced with profound moral dilemmas.[59]

The social and economic stability which characterised much of the Italian Occupation, especially Mario Lago's governorship (1923 to 1936), posed added difficulties for the *morfoméni*. These were times of economic development and high employment. Spreading patriotic ideas and cultivating anti-Italian feelings among common folk was much easier in times of crisis. *Morfoméni* were also enticed to accept the ruling order with attractive employment opportunities. Teachers had the option of working in Italian operated schools, which offered significantly better pay and working conditions. Those with families to feed were most vulnerable to such temptations, especially as the *demarchies* could only afford to give them very modest salaries. Ioannis Gounaris, for example, found he had to move from Kardamena to Antimachia during the school year 1927–28 because Kardamena, a much smaller village, could no longer afford to pay him his monthly minimum of 12 lire.[60] Teaching in an Italian-run school would mean stability and a higher standard of living, but 'true' patriots would have denounced this as a shameful option. It involved joining the Fascist Party and colluding in Italian policy. The conflicting demands of nationalist ideology and everyday needs was the matrix which produced a distinctive *morfoméni* experience of the Italian Occupation. Given the Italians had brought social and economic stability, and that the occupation now appeared permanent, it seemed sensible for a *morfoménos* to pursue a career in an Italian company or in an Italian school. But as community leaders, it was their duty to be exemplars of patriotic values. For *morfoméni*, living under foreign rule raised constant moral dilemmas.

Teachers had an especially important responsibility. Their particular patriotic task was to ensure the survival of the Greek language, and sabotaging compulsory Italian lessons was one of their related duties. Giorgos Koulianos, for instance, was remembered by his students at Asfendiou, Kos, for teaching his Greek lessons while standing on Italian textbooks. Giorgos Kastrounis, who taught in Embona, Rhodes, in the 1930s, also avoided teaching his Italian language classes. Mindful that his students might be interrogated by inspectors, he had them memorise set answers. One such student came to his rescue one particular afternoon when Kastrounis was accused of speaking Greek in class. Kastrounis recalled the following 'near thing' anecdote in his oral testimony:

I was detained after class one day in the classroom for teaching in Greek. The inspector said to me, '...we've spoken to you many times'. But I got away with it by claiming that I spoke to the children in Greek after three [3p.m., when school had finished], when it was not prohibited. I told them it was raining heavily and the children had to wait before they could run off home. Besides, I spoke to them only about religion. As the children waited for the rain to stop, they asked me to describe to them the Virgin birth in Greek. 'We don't understand it in Italian', they said. The inspector refused to believe me, and our argument was overheard in the café next door. Then one of my students,...the son of the man who betrayed me, came up to us and verified my story. His father was a collaborator from Leros. His uncle even fought for Italy in the war. It was a family which changed sides. [After the Italian occupation] they followed their stepmother home. Italy was a stepmother....[61]

Kastrounis believed his duty was to preserve the mother tongue, and the story of his encounter with the inspector was constructed to highlight the dangers involved in upholding this duty. The anecdote also confirms that there existed quite defined ideas about moral and immoral behaviour. A strict interpretation of patriotic duty would have it that to work in any capacity for the Italians was collaboration; it was as immoral as rejecting one's natural mother for a 'step-mother'. The following case studies give some idea of the kinds of choices and the travails faced by patriots who tried to apply the high standards of nationalism. They exemplified the difficulties of practising 'true' patriotism.

TWO PATRIOTS

Giorgos Koulianos was born in Kalymnos in 1905, the son of a shopkeeper. After completing secondary school, he went off to study accountancy at the University of Athens in 1924. Unfortunately, his financial resources were limited, and he only managed to complete his first year of studies. Koulianos then followed the path taken by many secondary school graduates and become a primary school teacher.[62] In 1927 he started his long teaching career at Asfendiou, then one of the largest villages in the Dodecanese. He soon married a local girl and received a house and a small parcel of land in the dowry settlement. Given their modest incomes, teachers often needed some land to supplement their income. By local standards, Koulianos had become a man to be respected and envied, for he was educated, a professional and had a family. But he seemed prepared to risk all of this for 'Hellenism'. In his oral testimony, Koulianos presented himself as if he had always been a patriot. As with the other patriot testimonies, his self-representation was an *identità senza sviluppo*, designed to reflect his indomitable and undying patriotism.[63] His oral testimony was focused almost exclusively on his record as an active patriot, and he used his self-portrait to confirm historiography's representation of Italian rule.

In July 1933, the people of Asfendiou prepared for their regular *demarchia* elections, unaware this time that the colonial regime had decided to appoint its own nominee. The new appointee was a tax farmer originally from Istanbul, an outsider whom everybody knew as 'the Politis' (which literally means the 'man from "the City",' i.e. Constantinople).[64] Soon after the announcement of

Politis's appointment, Koulianos and two other outraged *morfoméni*, Stamatis Kiapokas and Manolis Hatsinikolaou, called the villagers into the main square by ringing the church bells. The three patriots harangued the gathering crowd and then unfurled a Greek flag from the bell tower. Gabriel Kosaris related this incident in his testimony as proof of local patriotism. 'They made much trouble in the main square', he proudly recalled, 'raising the Greek flag on the tower and shouting "Long Live Greece" (Zíto i Ellás).'[65]

The incident gives some idea of the responsibilities carried by *morfoméni*. They believed that without their special guidance the common folk of Asfendiou might not have objected to Politis, thus bringing shame on the community. 'Showing' defiance kept the moral integrity of Asfendiou intact, and it was the role of patriots like Koulianos, as moral guardians, to lead. Unfortunately, someone informed the *carabinieri* of the incident, and Koulianos, Kiapokas and Hatsinikolaou were arrested, gaoled and beaten. Worse still, Koulianos was banned from teaching. (This was soon followed by great personal tragedy, as his wife died while giving birth.) He found work on a government farming estate, where, he claimed, he laboured in the fields from sunrise to sunset. Physical work was both hard and humiliating for the educated Koulianos. He remembered how a friend, who happened to be an Italian official, had recognised his sorry predicament and offered a solution:

> The Italian said to me while I was working: '*Maestro*, are you still here!'
>
> I said to him, 'I am not a worker.'
>
> He said, 'You must go from here, this is not for you.'
>
> I replied, 'But where?'.... Where could I go? 'They've taken me away from my job.'
>
> He took pity on me, working all day like a dog, so he helped me get a job. But where do you think? In Kattavia, at the other end of Rhodes![66]

That he had befriended an Italian official is only paradoxical if we literally accept his discourse of undying patriotism and anti-Italian sentiment. As with many of the patriotically minded interviewees, such friendships or any other positive reflections on the Italians were only related in passing and never allowed to qualify their negative representations of Italian rule.

With his Italian friend's help, Koulianos was given a teaching post at Kattavia at the southern extremity of Rhodes, which was a common destination for internal exiles. Koulianos settled there with his young child and eventually remarried, but his patriotic fervour again brought him into confrontation with the occupiers. He was dismissed from his post for not teaching Italian at the required time schedules. Once again he was forced to work with his hands, and through the mid-1930s, he gathered charcoal from the forests of northern Rhodes. Hard work again took its toll, and Koulianos suffered significant weight loss during this period. (According to his daughter, Koulianos had always been fat, though in this period his new wife had to continually reduce the size of his pants to meet his falling weight.)[67]

After carrying an injured Italian officer out of the woods, Koulianos was rewarded with another teaching post, this time on the island of Kasos. Many internal exiles were confined on this isolated outpost, though now Koulianos had agreed to teach Italian properly. He refused, however, to advise parents to have their children signed up for the *Balilla*. He recalled:

> In Kasos there was another teacher with me. He said to me, 'We must go around to all their [students'] homes and have their parents sign them up for the *Balilla*.' They tried to make me 'sign up' the children. This I couldn't do.... I just couldn't do it.... They then reported me as an anti-Italian.[68]

'True' patriotism often meant real suffering. Koulianos was reprimanded with a cut in pay, and as teachers were sometimes poorer than peasants, the impact of pay cuts could be excessive. The colonial regime exploited the financial vulnerability of unco-operative teachers with tough penalties and the threat of dismissal.

During the war, Koulianos was allowed to return to Asfendiou, where his family could live off land secured in his first dowry settlement. After unification with Greece in 1947, he settled permanently in Lakki, Leros, but his patriotic zeal again called him to action. He raised a storm when he publicly admonished locals for continuing to use Italian words and phrases in everyday conversation. He claimed it was unbecoming for Greeks to pervert their language.[69]

In his oral testimony, Koulianos conveyed no nostalgia for the Italian period. The primary aim of his autobiographical sketch was to show that Italian rule was oppressive and to explain that patriotic struggle was necessary. 'Irrelevant' personal details, like the death of his first wife, were related to me by members of his family. In patriotic terms, Koulianos's record during the occupation appeared impeccable, but his account did show inconsistencies between his anti-Italian rhetoric and his testimony. After all, he did have Italian friends who managed to find him work, showing how even the most indomitable patriots could not avoid being implicated in some way with the Italians. Moreover, common folk did find faults in Koulianos's patriotic behaviour. He was prepared to jeopardise his familial interests for nationalism, an abstract ideology which most common folk barely understood. As Ioannis Alahiotis claimed after reflecting on the 'Politis' incident, Koulianos was a foolhardy Kalymnian who got into trouble because he was unnecessarily zealous:

> He was of the type who had to 'show them' [the Italians]... he couldn't control himself. He had to 'get up' (xesikothí) and shout and make a big fuss, then and there... [but] there is not much you could do if they lock you up? How will you work then?[70]

The story of Giorgos Kastrounis further illustrates the nature of the patriotic experience of Italian rule, and how common folk did not share in his patriotic urgency and anger against the occupiers. He was born in Simi in 1910, and moved to Rhodes Town at a very young age. Like Koulianos, Kastrounis presented a self-image of having 'always been a patriot', though he added his Simian background as a source of his antipathy for Italian rule. Simi was socio-economically identical to Kalymnos, and its community was accorded similar stereotypical qualities; hardiness, recklessness, and bravery – the attributes needed for sponge diving and 'true' patriotism. Kastrounis believed his background had much to do with his career as a trouble-making teacher. He boasted:

> Simians are enterprising, lively, much tougher people. We are also miserly. That is why Simi became rich.... But the Rhodians (people of Rhodes Town), they are soft and placid. We Simians invigorated this place. We and the villagers (of Rhodes).... We came here and toughened the place up.[71]

He buttressed his point by alluding to the alleged sexual prowess of Simian men, as opposed to the allegedly impotent males of Rhodes Town. He recited a popular proverb in his testimony which warned that men from Simi and the Rhodian village of Archangelos should not be allowed near another man's wife of daughters. (Simiakó ke Archangelíti, min ton físis mes sto spíti.)[72] Virile Simians despised the apathetic Rhodians, whom he claimed were guilty of *attendismo*. In relating his own experiences under Italian rule, he presented a paradigm for how Rhodians should have behaved.

By the age of 17, Kastrounis had completed most of his secondary schooling in Rhodes Town. He decided his future lay in Greece, where he had hopes of becoming an officer in the Greek Army. When he applied for an exit visa, Kastrounis claimed the Italian officials mistook him for his distant cousin, Pantelis Kastrounis, an anti-Italian propagandist based in Egypt.[73] Security officials soon recognised he was not the man they were looking for, but they chose to incarcerate Giorgos regardless. He spent thirteen days in a dark cell where he was beaten and tortured, which included having his toe-nails pulled out. After three days without food he was given sardines and dry bread, but no water. Suffering from thirst he resorted to drinking his own urine. A Franco-Levantine guard later took pity on Kastrounis and gave him some food and water, as well as a few cigarettes. (He claimed it was the beginning of a life-long smoking habit.) He modestly claimed that the mere fact he was tortured did not necessarily make him a patriot, but the experience did generate in him an implacable hatred of Italian rule:

> It wasn't me [they wanted]. I could not have regarded myself as a hero...at 17 no less. But I was not the one. If I was a donkey I could have died [laughs]. I just had to bear it all. To cry? What for?! To satisfy them![74]

Modesty was a common attribute of patriotic interviewees. Kastrounis claimed he did not regard himself a hero, though his sufferings were still meant to be interpreted as patriotic sacrifice. For patriots, presenting their record in a modest fashion was supposed to have the effect of making their testimonies more believable.

After he was released from gaol, Kastrounis immediately went to the Greek consulate to seek permission to enter Greece. The consulate in Rhodes Town received many such requests from young *morfoméni*, but it encouraged most of them to remain. Their reasoning was thus: if all the *morfoméni* departed, common folk would be deprived of leadership. As Kastrounis recalled:

> I went to the consulate...they told me that 'you Greeks who love Hellenism must stay and teach. If people like you go, there will be no more 'káli méra' ['good morning' in Greek]. We need teachers....'[75]

Kastrounis took up the consulate's advice and began teaching at Embona, a large village about 55 km south-west of Rhodes Town. Between 1928 and 1937, Kastrounis boasted that under his tutelage his students learned very poor Italian, but this did not escape the attention of the authorities. The following anecdote again shows the special scrutiny which teachers incurred. Kastrounis was expected like other members in his profession to set an example by contributing money to the Italian war effort in Ethiopia. He refused, and in his testimony, he recalled the confrontation he had with his supervisor:

A telephone call came through to the village. <<*Maestro, telefono*>>. 'Teacher they're calling you on the telephone.' I won't say who called me because he is still alive. He was the head of our local area, a Greek, but he spoke in Italian! He was Dodecanesian, from Astypalea! .... He said to me:

'Do you know you shame me! You are the only teacher who has not made a contribution.'

I replied, 'That is not true, I know of many who have not.'

'I only know of you!'

'But I don't have any gold'.

'You should have'.

'But I only earn 9 lire a day. You earn six times that much because you are an Italian now.'

'If you do not pay I'll demote you.'

'Should I cut off the fingers of my dead parents and give you their rings?'

'Yes, you should.'

'Then I'll cut your head off!!'

I lost my temper. I then thought better of it. He was a traitor, and he would have surely reported me. So I gave what I could. I scraped some money up. What could I do.[76]

Despite this capitulation, Kastrounis was identified by the Italians as a troublemaker and was eventually sent into internal exile. His destination was Kastellorizo, 116 km east of Rhodes and the most remote corner of the island group. He settled, married a local girl and started a family. His deep sense of patriotism, however, put all this at risk. He continued to defy the authorities by teaching in Greek. Eventually he came under the scrutiny of a school inspector from Rhodes. Kastrounis's refusal to comply with Italian demands earned him a penalty of four months without pay. The inspector told him in front of his pupils that he was an appalling teacher, and read out his aptitude score as 'zero zero cinque (.005)'. In response, Kastrounis claimed he said:

> 'Thank you, you've made me a hero. Now you should sack me! In my terms this really means I am a good teacher. I would like my poor score confirmed in writing.'
>
> He said no because it would make me a martyr. I replied, 'Then you are not a real man, you are "unmanly" (ánandros). You [Italians] are men only when you hold guns.'[77]

In his testimony, he showed distinct pride in recollecting his 'show' of defiance, but he conceded it was a costly encounter. He was suspended and survived the next four months by tutoring children secretly at night. Before every tutorial he bartered his services for food: olives, oil, wheat, fruit, much of it smuggled in from nearby Turkey. Secret tutoring became his family's prime source of sustenance, especially in the early 1940s, when war in Europe brought strict rationing and rampant inflation. The poverty of teachers was never more shown than during the war, when, like most of the common folk, teachers and their families went hungry. Kastrounis claimed he could barely feed his wife and four children, and as he refused to join the Fascist Party, he could not expect any support from the colonial regime. 1943 especially was a year of dearth, and things grew quite desperate:

> One day, tired from teaching and weak from lack of food, I sat in the café. I allowed someone to buy me a coffee. The *demarchía* then paid me my monthly salary, but it was only 1200 lire. At the time it was enough to buy a kilo of bread. I had four children and a wife to feed.[78]

He spent almost half of his pay on a bag of wild corn husks, which his wife grated, fried and fed to the children. The meal gave them a mild case of food poisoning.

Had he been an illiterate peasant, Kastrounis might have fared better during the occupation. Because of their supposed 'ignorance', common folk could sit out the occupation without being expected to 'show' defiance. *Morfoméni* like Kastrounis felt they had no such choice. He believed it was his duty to uphold patriotism's exacting standards, and set an example for others. His prescribed role in society, as *morfoménos* and patriot, determined that he would have a distinct experience of Italian rule.

Every 'true' Greek was supposed to suffer as Kastrounis and Koulianos did, but many *morfoméni* refused to suffer. The following case studies will show how, faced with the realities of Italian rule, many *morfoméni* accepted work in the Italian bureaucracy and education system, and thus strayed into a morally dangerous area. Rather than discard their patriotic values, they chose to re-evaluate their understanding of nationalism's demands. In these case studies I am not concerned with those who actually identified with Fascist Italy and her interests, who donned the *camicia nera* and betrayed their fellow islanders. Rather, I will focus on those *morfoméni* who, unlike Koulianos and Kastrounis, entered the employ of the Italians because they put their personal and familial interests first.

LESSER PATRIOTS OR COLLABORATORS?

Giorgos Sakellaridis was one of many *morfoméni* who worked in the Italian colonial bureaucracy, and yet who maintained that he had always been a true patriot. His testimony challenged the view that the patriotic experience of Italian rule was necessarily one of undying enmity towards the occupiers. As an employee of TEMI, the colonial regime's tobacco monopoly, Sakellaridis was entrusted with the hapless task of introducing the monopoly to Kalymnos. He arrived there in April 1938, and admitted to having received a cold reception from the locals. In his oral testimony, Sakellaridis conceded that De Vecchi made membership of the Fascist Party compulsory for all public servants, but Sakellaridis insisted that he was exempted from wearing the Fascist insignia by his anti-Fascist supervisor.[79] He was quite aware, however, that many regarded him as a collaborator. The purpose of his oral testimony was to show that he was not a traitor, and that his patriotism was coveyed in quite subtle forms.

Born in Nisyros in 1915, Sakellaridis moved to Rhodes Town to attend secondary school. He had almost completed his studies when he decided to emigrate to Greece, but the Greek consulate convinced him that his patriotic duty was to remain in the Dodecanese. He claimed:

The consul said to me that if all the bright minds of the Dodecanese left, and all that remained were the *agrámmati* [the uneducated-ones], their scheme to Italianise the islands had a good chance of working. Who knows what would happen in the future.... I decided that I had to remain.[80]

Like Kastrounis, Sakellaridis was told by the Greek consulate that the Dodecanesian people needed leadership, which only the *morfoméni* were qualified to provide. In his oral testimony, however, he did not recall any confrontations with the occupiers, rather, Sakellaridis seemed busily consumed with his career at TEMI. His behaviour during the occupation might be described as *attendismo*, but in Sakellaridis's mind, the mere fact that he remained in the Dodecanese was an important patriotic gesture. After all, he followed the consulate's advice and put his personal interests aside. In a way, his mere presence constituted a modest contribution towards foiling Italy's wish to rid the Dodecanese of its potential leaders.

Sakellaridis settled in Kalymnos after the occupation, and later published many articles in local newspapers and journals, some of which were on the occupation itself. He wrote a short account of his problems in introducing the tobacco monopoly to Kalymnos, and of his many meetings with the *podestà*, one Antonio Ritelli. The relationship produced one of the more poignant moments in Sakellaridis's experience of Italian rule. He described Ritelli as a cultured and eloquent man, and Sakellaridis valued their friendship.[81] One day, Ritelli gave him a copy of Silvio Pellico's *Le mie prigioni*, about Pellico's captivity in a Habsburg prison in the 1830s. Though it is more a book about religious contemplation, Sakellaridis was meant to read it as a tract on political freedom. He was shocked when Ritelli asked him if the book gave him any inspiration for the plight of the occupied in the Dodecanese. Sakellaridis realised that the *podestà* was an anti-Fascist, and felt honoured that he had shared this secret with him:

> Then I heard the following words, which left me almost paralysed. <<perchè quanto scrive Pellico deve valere per gli Italiani e non per voi altri anche?>>....I was a stiff as bone. I lost track of time and space...truly I was stunned .... He was a man who rose above the environment of Fascism, which he was supposed to support. With difficulty and bravery [he upheld his convictions]. He noticed the true dissenting character of the Kalymnian people and had managed to love *irredentista Calino* [irredentist Kalymnos]....[82]

Sakellaridis described this meeting in an article called 'Antonio Ritelli', which was issued in the local journal, *The Kalymniaká Chroniká*, in a section entitled 'Pages on Resistance'.[83] In recording his emotional response to Ritelli's remarks, Sakellaridis tried to reveal to readers his undying, though discretely held, patriotism. The shrewd Ritelli had recognised that Sakellaridis had concealed his patriotism. In this subtle way, Sakellaridis tried to argue that one did not need to 'show' one's patriotism to be a patriot. The subtext of his article was that the patriotic experience was not simply a story of unyielding opposition to Italian rule.

In its Greek context, his is an unusually thoughtful study of foreign rule in that he addresses some of the ambiguities of Italo-Greek relations, far in excess of what local historiography would normally allow. The 'enemy' Ritelli is presented as having high moral worth, not a stereotypical foreign tyrant. In making this concession, Sakellaridis shares something in common with popular oral tradition. As will be shown in a later chapter on popular perceptions of Italians, the occupiers were stereotyped as having normal emotions and human concerns. Sakellaridis's representation of Italian rule was more balanced than those of either Koulianos or Kastrounis, for he was prepared to describe its more positive features. In his oral testimony, for instance, he talked at length about TEMI, which he boasted was a highly efficient and modern enterprise which employed hundreds of local workers. In presenting a more benign image of the occupation, Sakellaridis indicated that the Italians were not like the oppressive Turks, implying there was less need for heroic resistance.[84]

According to Greek nationalist strictures, Giorgos Papanikolaou also walked the fine line between patriotism and collaboration.[85] He was born in the Koan village of Kardamena in 1907, into a well-to-do peasant family. Like fellow-villager Heracles Karanastasis, Papanikolaou completed his secondary schooling in Kalymnos, and started his long teaching career in Kardamena in 1924. He attended the *Magistrale* in Rhodes in 1929, where all teachers received compulsory training in Italian, and he would later boast that he knew how to speak Italian better than the Italians. He became Kardamena's unofficial interpreter, and acted as a mediator between the villagers and the occupiers. He enjoyed the responsibility and power his language abilities had given him, as the following anecdote suggests:

A *carabiniero* (*sic*) from Antimachia turned up (in the café). We all stood up and saluted Fascist-style,... 'eh Mussolini'. He said, <<Perchè sedersi?>>. One person, an old man, remained seated and did not give the greeting.

'Why didn't he get up?' The Italian looked at me. I asked the man sitting, and he said to me in Greek, 'Today they rule, but tomorrow will come Greece.'

I was now in a difficult position... so I made up something. I translated this to the *carabiniero* (*sic*), 'Today I am an old man, tomorrow so will you be.' The Italian seemed very impressed with the answer. He said that from now on we won't salute.[86]

Difficult moments such as these seemed to justify Papanikolaou's chosen path. Though he claimed he did much good for his community, he was aware that some might stigmatise him as a traitor, as conveyed by the apologetic tone of his interview. At first sight his employment record reads like a classic case of collaboration. He became the school principal of Kardamena, served as a tax farmer, and supervised the local *finanza*. He could not have held any of these positions without joining the Fascist Party. After the occupation, he was officially denounced by the Greek government as a 'collaborator' and refused a state pension. But many of his fellow-villagers appreciated his assistance as a mediator. On one occasion he informed his neighbour, a tobacco smuggler, that the *carabinieri* were about to arrest him.[87] As Ioannis Alahiotis of Asfendiou noted in his testimony, the occupied did take some comfort if one of their own people worked among the Italians:

Sometimes, if he was our man, he could help us, and he would probably not abuse us like some of the Italians. He could pass us valuable information... warn us that the Italians were thinking this way or that way. Life was made easier if the man was trustworthy, one of ours.[88]

In his oral testimony, Papanikolaou maintained he was a true patriot, though when Greek was prohibited in the classroom, he claimed that he and his colleagues wanted to teach Greek, but they feared being betrayed. He confirmed that, 'We teachers – we were all patriots. We taught Italian, but we were always Greek.' He conveyed this concealed patriotism by recalling an incident in Rhodes during his studies at the *Magistrale* in 1929:

It was an Italian holiday and there were street parades. One of the groups marching past represented *Diagoras* [a Rhodian athletic club], and they were supposed to sing some Italian song, something... <<Siamo fratelli>>...something like that. Instead they sang 'Oh Greeks of the Mountains' [a Greek nationalist song]. We all took off our hats and started to cry. My 'hairs stand up' when I think about it.... The next day they shut *Diagoras* down.[89]

As with Sakellaridis, Papanikolaou was aware that if patriotic norms were strictly applied he could be seen as a collaborator. Kastrounis and Koulianos held steadfastly to the iron rule that those who worked in the employ of the Italians were collaborators. Most *morfoméni*, however, would privately concede that nationalism imposed rather unrealistic expectations, and they conveyed this through disemic responses. For example, Christoforos Fournaris proudly asserted in his testimony that only one per cent of Koans worked 'for the enemy'. He boasted that almost everyone in Kos remained a good patriot, and those who did not were scorned. He claimed: 'We would say to them, "What are you doing! Are you not ashamed? Shame on you!"' To appreciate Fournaris's advocacy of Koan patriotism, however, one must keep in mind the context of the interview. While speaking into the microphone, Fournaris was consciously speaking to outsiders. His testimony had to be carefully presented so as not to embarrass his community. Off the record, however, Fournaris gave a much more sympathetic view of 'collaboration'. With a more relaxed tone, Fournaris explained:

These were people who were not really tough enough to resist accepting the jobs the Italians were giving. They were not prepared to dig dirt and work hard and sweat, or emigrate to another country....None of them did any harm.... What could they do!?!....They had families to support like the rest of us. They had children. What could they do!?[90]

CONCLUSION

Morfoméni were expected to perform an onerous task during the occupation. Their class and educational background imposed on them the responsibility of setting an example of how patriots should behave, but as potential indigenous leaders, they suffered intense scrutiny from Italian authorities. Moreover, they were torn by the pressures of patriotic obligations on the one hand, and their personal and familial interests on the other. For many patriots, 'showing' defiance was one way of resolving the tension, for it involved low risk activity while maintaining their social status in the community.

Whatever their achievements, the most enduring legacy of the patriots was their hostile representation of the Italian Occupation, which has since dominated historical discourse. This representation is essentially a moral tale, a clash between the forces of good and evil, between Hellenism and its enemies. Yet even this black-and-white picture was not completely supported by patriotic testimonies. Sakellaridis and Papanikolaou, who did not quite uphold the heavy demands of patriotism, defended their reputations by drawing a more generous picture of Italians and Italian rule. Though a face-saving technique, their construction of a more positive picture was supported by less literate interviewees. The following chapters of this study will further explore the ambiguities found in Dodecanesian perceptions of Italian rule, and will discuss the reasons why ordinary Dodecanesians have retained feelings of nostalgia for Italians and Italian rule.

5 Colonialism and Modernity: Cultural Imperialism and Popular Memory

On 19 February 1933, the *Messaggero di Rodi*, the principal newspaper of the colony, celebrated the tenth anniversary of Mario Lago's tenure as governor. Normally a modest publication of four pages, the *Messagero* celebrated the occasion with a thirty-page bumper edition, adorned with a large portrait of Lago on the cover. The central theme of this special commemorative issue was the metamorphosis of Rhodes.[1] The *Messaggero* boasted:

> Since the Conference of Lausanne one can say the following of the Italian presence among these islands: it does not seem a presence of a mere ten years, but a century of change. . . . Rhodes of today has completely altered in appearance, in its life and in its activities.

Benevolent colonialism, so the claim went, transformed this oriental backwater into a paradigm of modernity. Once characterised by donkeys, primitive villages, and a main town which looked distinctly like a decaying middle eastern backwater, Rhodes now had a modern capital with boulevards and tall buildings, an international airport, hotels of the highest standard, bathing complexes, golfing, racing and other sporting facilities, and a modern bus system. The island had not merely become a modern tourist venue, for a discerning visitor could also notice serious programmes for economic development, including land reclamation, forestation, scientific research and mining. Moreover, radical improvements in medical facilities, public sanitation and education showed the regime was serious in pursuing a true 'civilising mission'. When Cesare De Vecchi, Mussolini's bombastic education minister, succeeded Lago in December 1936, the newspaper welcomed him as a suitable replacement, for he was a man of action, vision and experience. His record as a colonial governor in Africa showed how, despite formidable obstacles,

125

including hostile warrior tribesmen, De Vecchi turned Italian Somalia into '*un colonia organizzata, florida e produttiva*'.[2]

As the age of imperialism drew to a close, Europe's colonial powers desperately sought to justify keeping their empires on moral grounds which mid-twentieth century opinion would find convincing. As with their more successful counterparts, Italy sought legitimacy through colonial development, through bestowing the benefits of western civilisation on the savage or backward. Lago and De Vecchi shared the imperative to modernise along with the other Italian colonial governors, including the Duke Amadeo of Aosta, viceroy of the East African Empire. During most of its short existence, the Duke spent much of his time on infrastructural development programmes, ostensibly in order to improve the lot of the indigenous.[3] In Libya, Italo Balbo tried to emulate the legendary and flamboyant governor of French Morocco, Hubert Lyautey, founder of modern Rabat and Casablanca. Balbo tried to do much the same with Tripoli and Benghazi, transforming them into model garden towns, which he connected with the most ambitious road construction project in the entire colonial world: the *Littoranea Libica*.[4]

Development not only sustained new platitudes for the legitimacy of empire, but the colonial powers also hoped their overseas territories would become more profitable and financially self sufficient. 'Blessing' the natives with the fruits of western civilisation was perceived as an investment. Such levels of achievement continued to be a test of each colonial power's moral worth.[5] Fascist Italy, anxious to upgrade her flagging international standing, claimed moral superiority over Britain and France because her empire was not based on 'egoism' and exploitation, but on social justice and sacrifice.[6] The Italians took great pride in their colonial achievements; their model towns, hospitals and roads were held as proof that their nation was a credible world power and ruling culture.

Historians have rarely treated Italy's colonial experience seriously. Interest has been centred on those aspects of colonialism which reflect Mussolini's regime and its inadequacies, hence scholars have been fixated on colonialism's more negative aspects: its brutalities, corruption and pretention.[7] Indeed, of all the colonial powers, Italy is considered uniquely wicked, and her colonial administrations hopelessly deficient and bankrupt. Denis Mack Smith, a major exponent of this view, characterises Mussolini's empire as a chronicle of administrative bunglings and ineptitude, of pretentiously grandiose schemes, ill-conceived projects, racial discrimination, massacres and bureaucratic confusion. Mack Smith does admit, however, that some governors did do a 'good job'.[8] Alberto Sbacchi's picture of Italian Ethiopia is similarly bleak. He concedes the Duke of Aosta was an exceptional viceroy, though he is shown to have presided over endemic corruption and administrative incompetence.[9]

While historians of Italian colonialism have been justifiably critical of its record, and have gone far towards correcting popular myths, some have briefly noted that colonial subjects found much to admire in the colonisers. As Claudio Segrè has pointed out, many Libyans still hold fond memories of Balbo because he initiated significant development programmes in their country.[10] The Duke of Aosta maintained a popular reputation in post-colonial Ethiopia, where he received generous praise from the restored emperor, Haile Selassie, and from national hero Abebe Aragai.[11] During the occupation, the Duke was affectionately known as *in gamba*, meaning one who is efficient and clever.[12] These perceptions of Italian rule, which has otherwise been characterised as barbarous, corrupt and incompetent, suggest that a whole dimension of Italian colonialism remains neglected. Historians have been criticised for ignoring African experiences, discussing the conquest of Ethiopia, for instance, with little reference to Ethiopian political, economic and social contexts.[13] Fond memories of Balbo and Aosta do not necessarily contradict the black image of Italian colonialism, but they do suggest that Africans did not simply remember those times in terms of resistance and oppression. It seems that some aspects of Italian rule resonated with locals, or prompted reflection on indigenous cultural, social and political issues.

This is certainly true of the Dodecanese, where oral sources allow for a detailed investigation into perceptions of Italian rule and shed light on local issues of fundamental importance. The islanders were quite aware that public works programmes were designed to serve Italian military and economic interests, and the fact that many suffered from land expropriation, government monopolies and assimilation policy has not been forgotten. More than often, however, the islanders talk of their Italian legacy in appreciative terms. Most of the islanders resented the brutish nature of De Vecchi's governance, but his 'Fascist rule' was considered a brief phase within a period of great progress. The oral testimonies present the colonial period as a time when everyone 'lived well' (pernoúsame kalá), when administration was efficient and conscientious, and when the islands were bustling with building activity. Italian publications boasted that the islands had benefited greatly from Italy's benevolence, and to a considerable extent the occupied genuinely concurred. Stamatios Athanasiadis assumed, like most other Dodecanesians, that the Italians had invested a fortune in the development of their islands: 'They did a lot of work here. A lot! They emptied their treasury. They emptied their treasury!'[14] It was not merely the material benefits which Dodecanesians appreciated. They also sensed a convergence of interests, for as will be shown below, Italian administration, public order and economic development appealed to local attitudes on the role of government, on civic responsibilities, and on notions of progress (próodos).

Such positive responses to Italian rule, however, raise questions regarding the extent to which the indigenous were implicated in the colonial power's propaganda. How far were the Greeks of the Dodecanese influenced by Italy's 'civilising mission'? What did this disclose about the nature of the occupied–occupier relationship? All colonial powers of the interwar period sought to secure some degree of local consent for colonial rule. By introducing electricity, roads, railways, aircraft, automobiles, dams, new cities and grand monuments, the ruling powers tried to colonise the minds of the indigenous, to convince them of the advantages of foreign rule. In his family history, *Punjabi Century*, Prakash Tandon explained that while his generation found school textbooks describing the 'blessings' of the British Raj highly amusing, he admitted his grandfather's generation took such ideas quite seriously. For them, British law and order, and achievements in irrigation, roads and education were indeed regarded as blessings.[15]

To be sure, the introduction of efficient administration, modern engineering and modern technology were essentially meant to increase the exploitative potential of the colonial power. The extent to which the colonised recognised the political motives behind the new colonialism of the interwar period, and how far the indigenous resisted and negotiated the coloniser's political, economic and cultural influences, has yet to receive much attention from historians of European expansion. This chapter will analyse how far ordinary Greeks were implicated in Italian colonial policy, and what their memories of Italian governance and economic development reveal about the experience of occupation. In contrast to local historiography, in which Italian rule is characterised as oppressive and brutal, oral sources present the Italian period as a paragon of benevolent and progressive government. The occupation has also become a myth about positive civic values, which the islanders recall for critical commentaries on the present. One of the purposes of this chapter will be to qualify and assess the significance of their idealistic characterisations of Italian rule, and shed further light on the function of nostalgia in everyday life and political discourse.

PUBLIC ORDER

The phrase 'the Italians had laws' recurred quite frequently in the oral testimonies. Of course, the islanders have always had laws to abide by, including those of the Ottomans, the Orthodox Church, and the Greek state, but the Italians were remembered as being the most resolute in enforcing their laws. As Kalliope Harapas of Kos Town claimed, the Italians were 'good people' because, 'they were very serious with their laws. They'd say "you must not do it", so you did not do it.' Colonial governors issued many unpopular decrees, some of which offended patriotic sensibilities, but like many of her compatriots, Harapas could still admire Italian assiduity:

When they did something it was according to the law. They'd say, 'Sir don't do this, I don't want you to have your [Greek] flag in your house. Why then do you have it? It is illegal, isn't it?'. . . . They told us you cannot have Greek flags, you can't wear a blue and white skirt, that was that. . . .[16]

It was not uncommon among subject peoples to appreciate the stability and order enforced by their foreign overlords. Prakash Tandon, for example, claimed his grandfather's generation were grateful that British rule had finally brought peace to the Punjab.[17] In the Dodecanese, the occupied generally appreciated the introduction of Italian administrative structures, for unlike their Ottoman counterparts, these structures attended to many local needs and were thought to have operated effectively. The colonial regime presided over almost every aspect of public life, and for the first time in popular memory, the islanders were obliged to conform strictly to rules and regulations. There were now traffic rules, hygiene and sanitation standards, night curfews, surveillance of prices, building regulations, permits required for certain trades and vehicles, laws regarding wood-burning and rules on noise levels. One could no longer do as one pleased, and the interviewees often conceded that this was a good thing. Dodecanesians believed that public order was necessary for communities to progress, and they acknowledged that authorities needed to implement coercive practices to ensure the interests of the community were upheld.

The Ottomans had failed to promote such values. The contrast between Ottoman and Italian rule is stark, and its refractions in popular memory are illuminating. Ottoman rule is remembered as a time of lawlessness in many parts of Greece, especially where the Ottoman presence was thin. A recent study conducted among villages in central Greece shows that locals associated the Turkish period (pre-1821) with lawlessness and freedom, when villagers were free of the heavy hand of the state.[18] As shown earlier in Chapter 3, the autonomous 'Privileged Islanders', who had enjoyed quite significant tax exemptions during the Ottoman period, would protest vigorously against Italian intrusion into their affairs. The people of Rhodes and Kos, on the other hand, regarded the Ottoman Empire as a tribute-gathering system which performed few public duties; peasants paid tax and received almost nothing in return. In order to convey the essence of Ottoman governance, Ioannis Alahiotis recalled a story of when his father and other villagers were arrested and locked up by Ottoman troops. 'They grabbed my father and some other villagers', he claimed, 'and locked them all up':

> They all made a lot of noise in the gaolhouse. So a big Turkish officer came in to see what all the fuss was about. He asked what these Greek peasants were doing in the gaolhouse. So my father told him [the officer] that if they were not released they would not be able to harvest their crops and pay their taxes. So he said 'Throw them out, quickly! How are they going to pay their taxes if we keep them in here.' [Alahiotis laughs]. You see. That is what the Turks were like. All they wanted was tax. Otherwise we hardly saw them. . . .[19]

Ottoman priorities were revealed by the officer's instinctive and *ad hoc* decision. Alahiotis's father had broken the law, but the law meant nothing if it jeopardised his ability to pay his taxes.

Despite decades of trying to reform the empire's administrative structures, the Ottomans were still lax in the enforcement of provincial law and order, and they continued to neglect public amenities and other responsibilities. The *demarchíes* sometimes filled the vacuum, but their ability to carry such responsibilities depended on the community's level of autonomy, wealth and stability.

Kalymnos and Simi were exemplary models of responsible and enterprising local government, but most village communities were usually too poor to fund their own public amenities, and, moreover, most did not enjoy Kalymnos's or Simi's civic traditions. Greek society has not been known for its civic values, and modern ethnographic studies have confirmed how the alleged factiousness of 'the Greek' has been a popular topic of social discourse. Widely known phrases like, 'Twelve Greeks, thirteen captains', have either been used to praise Greek individuality, or to lament Greek divisiveness.[20] The interviewees claimed that public order was one of the significant achievements of Italian rule, for these occupiers were accredited with having disciplined the unruly 'Greek'.

Internal disharmony is considered shameful in Greek community life, especially when disunity is revealed to outsiders. Local historians have therefore tended not to write on intra-community conflict, but there is one unique study which indicates that local government instability had been a prevalent problem before the coming of the Italians. This study recounts the career of a successful *démarchos* of Mandraki, Nisyros, named Giorgos Kammas, and to highlight his achievement, the author, Kostas Sakellaridis, had to relate the many obstacles put up by the unruly constituents. After a series of troubled and short-lived administrations, Kammas was elected *démarchos* in January 1916. He introduced efficient record keeping and an accounting system, and in order to balance the budget, service *demarchia* debts, and continue important public works, he forced all community members to pay their rates, and did not hesitate using the *carabinieri* to help him enforce such measures. With food shortages looming in the latter years of the First World War, Kammas instituted an austere food rationing system. He also raided the private stockpiles of rich Nisyriotes, and forced local merchants and fishermen to sell their catch at set prices. Through his efforts, the people of Mandraki did not go hungry as did other islanders. His reputation had spread to nearby islands, including his native Tilos, which begged him to return and continue the good work in his own *patrida*.[21]

However, when the next free elections were held in September 1920, Kammas was rejected by 160 of the 186 eligible voters.[22] The moral of the story is a familiar one in modern Greek culture; that Greeks are an ungrateful lot; they are factious by nature and have to be forced to cooperate;[23] and that their divisiveness has inhibited the progress of Greek society. This piece of self-knowledge seemed to hold true in Kammas's story. The ungrateful voters rejected their conscientious and civic-minded *démarchos*, even though his good management kept them from starving. As will be shown below, the interviewees believed that governing bodies had the responsibility of ensuring that private and familial interests did not diminish community interests. Interviewees admitted that upholding the common interest necessitated the use of coercion against uncooperative constituents, which is what the Italian occupiers did. That the interviewees believed government should rule with a firm hand does not necessarily suggest fascist leanings in the Greek character, nor a yearning for Mussolini's Fascists or the Colonels' regime.[24] Rather, such views constitute a grudging admission of the need for government to enforce its public responsibilities with real sanctions. Kammas used *carabinieri* to force compliance, but he used them to promote the public interest.

Interviewees were quite impressed with the standard of Italian policing. Though most recollections of the *carabinieri* and the *finanza* were conveyed by interviewees with a noticeable feeling of frustration, they grudgingly admired their efficiency. Locals felt that both *carabinieri* and *finanza* were omnipresent, waiting to pounce upon any infringement, always searching locals for illegal arms and contraband goods, and throwing people into gaol on the slightest pretext. The *Messaggero di Rodi* published regular lists of law-breakers arrested for various crimes and misdemeanours. Among the more popular categories were: disturbing the peace, traffic infringements, selling at black market prices and smoking contraband tobacco. The *Messaggero* reported a number of Lerians arrested for selling vegetables above the price set by the colonial government;[25] one 'Giovanni' of Asfendiou was arrested for drunkenness, while another named 'Antonio' was fined for carrying a passenger on his bicycle.[26] Authorities were particularly watchful of traffic infringements, a category in which, for unspecified reasons, members of the Turkish community were over-represented.[27]

Dodecanesians had been unaccustomed to such close supervision. Interviewees complained that the *carabinieri* were over-bearing, but they acknowledged that zealous policing had its benefits. In Kos Town, for instance, riding a horse, mule or donkey in certain streets was prohibited. For Kalliope Harapas, the strict enforcement of this regulation showed how far the Italians were sincere about the necessity for order. She did not necessarily like the law, but she applauded Italian stringency:

They did a lot of good things. And they had laws, . . . you could not ride your horse in these streets. 'Why do you ride your horse in Kos [Town], why do you do it?' And then they fined you. 'Don't do this', so you didn't.[28]

Such vigilance always ensured that traffic moved smoothly. Lefteris of Leros remembered how traffic on his native island was very orderly. 'They were Europeans', he pointed out, 'good people. Very genuine people . . . .They tried hard to please the people, you understand. I lived among them. When we travelled in the streets with, eh, you'd forgive me, our beasts, they made us travel in a line so we would not harm anybody.'[29] Archondoula Kanaris of Kos Town recalled an occasion when her husband, then her fiancé, was arrested for singing in public after the noise curfew:

My husband would sing for me because he loved me. In those days young men would sing for you from the street, there was none of the freedom to mingle in the evenings, as they do today. Then we heard outside; 'baam, boom, pung':
  <<Mascalzone, stupido, attento>>
He (her husband) said, <<ma scusatemi signore, ma vale niente>> (*sic*), I didn't do anything. <<Non e fare niente>> (*sic*)
  <<Perchè la cantare questa ora>> (*sic*), he asked. Why are you singing at this hour. . . . ., it is illegal.
  They took him to the gaol house, and the *maresciallo* asked them what he had done. <<Che cosa fate>>, he said, what did he do. The soldiers said that he made loud noises at an illegal time.[30]

The incident was no doubt a traumatic one, not least for her fiancé, who was humiliatingly abused and beaten, yet Kanaris chose to recall that incident to explain Italian commitment to law and order, and how this kept noise levels down.

When recalling such issues, interviewees often had present concerns in mind. In Dodecanesian towns today, mass tourism has seen the establishment of bars and discos which blast loud music into the early hours of the morning, and parents fear that the alleged loose morals and drug-taking habits of the tourists might have an influence on local youth. Interviewees claimed that such licentiousness would not have been possible under the Italian rule. Kanaris invoked memories of the Italian Occupation to complain about the apparent loss of morals among modern Dodecanesian youth:

This kind of 'whoreing around' that you see now, . . . if they [the Italians] heard a mere rumour that a girl was immoral, they'd quickly take her away. They'd say, 'if you want to act bad we'll lock you up'. . . . They were very law-minded. If you didn't do anything wrong they'd never touch you.[31]

As Natalie Zemon Davis and Randolph Starn have warned: 'If we call on memory to inform or confirm present convictions, it may become an all too obliging mirror.'[32] David Lowenthal has also warned that nostalgia is a symptom of current malaise, or perceived malaise.[33] Certainly, one often finds the good old days were not so good, but in the Dodecanese, local nostalgia for Italian rule has a firm historical basis. This is a case study of nostalgia derived from lived experience, where locals have resisted moral pressure to adopt the Greek nationalist version of the Italian Occupation because they remember things differently.

To be sure, perceptions of current malaise did seem to influence the kinds of themes discussed by interviewees. Sevasti Kortesi of Kalymnos, for instance, lauded the high standards of cleanliness which the regime demanded of shopkeepers. She also remembered the benefits of government controls on pricing, as she was clearly irritated with current inflation and the pricing practices of shopkeepers. 'Back then', she asserted, 'you'd never find prices different from one shop to another. The shopkeeper was given a fine! And bakeries, they had to be clean!. . . . And the shops, there were standards, high standards!':

> The Italians had laws, strict laws. I tell you, this was a good thing. Because there were standards. Not like now. You go to a shop and they sell something to you for 'this much', the next day they'd sell it to you for 'that much'. For what reason?[34]

Kalliope Harapas claimed the Italians would never have allowed Kos Town's current car parking problems to get out of control. Car ownership in the Dodecanese has risen dramatically since the early 1980s, and, despite the fact that Kos Town has wider streets than most Dodecanesian centres, the town has often experienced traffic congestion and parking problems. 'If the Italians were here today', she said, 'we would not see such a mess, this parking on footpaths. If the Italians said, "Sir, you cannot park your car in such a narrow road", then you didn't.'[35]

Memories of 'the Italians' are also invoked in response to current environmental problems. Forest degradation is a running concern among Rhodian villagers, though similar problems were experienced prior to the Italian occupation, when peasant wood-burning ruined the woodlands of Rhodes, Karpathos and Kos. The Italians designated large parts of these islands as forestal zones – nearly one-fifth of Rhodes was so designated.[36] The results were impressive. As J.L. Myres reported in 1941, the Italians had gone far towards redressing the problem of deforestation, for by 1938, Rhodes and Karpathos could produce 21 000 cubic metres of timber.[37] Reforestation did inflict hardships on the local peasants, who were denied access to wood and game. Isabelle and C.D. Booth noted the frustration of Rhodian peasants, and their fear of being arrested by the *finanza* for such basic activities as collecting wood.[38] Philipos Sofos of Asklepion, Rhodes, related memories of his own frustration: 'There were laws on when to burn, when to do this, when to do that':

> They wanted to make all of Rhodes into a forest, so Rhodes would become a tourist centre. All forest, all forest!! This of course threatened farming. But they believed there would be an influx of tourists. . . . They gave us farmers a hard time.[39]

And yet during his oral testimony, which was conducted in a crowded village café, Sofos agreed with his fellow villagers that protecting the forests was indeed good for Rhodes. In light of recent devastating bush fires, and the inadequate response by Greek authorities, the Italians were thought to have taken the appropriate steps:

> they were strict, but that was good. We would say back then that they [the laws] were barbaric, but they were good for us!! . . . Now there are no laws . . . .
>   We didn't like it then. But now when we see these things, with all of Rhodes almost burnt . . . what can you do. . . .[40]

AN EFFICIENT REGIME – EARTHQUAKE IN KOS, 1933

Another recurrent theme in the oral testimonies is Italian administrative efficiency. The Italians were not just admired for the sophistication of their organisational structures, but also the way in which formal procedures were applied to the letter, and how most tasks were carried out quickly and effectively. Colonial personnel were regarded as punctual, conscientious and invulnerable, and Italian administration in general was remembered as paradigm of efficiency. To be sure, this rather idealistic image is often recalled by Dodecanesians when exasperated with contemporary Greek bureaucracy. The occupation is contrasted as a time when administration functioned smoothly, and when bribes or personal 'connections' (méson) were not necessary to get the wheels of bureaucracy moving. Interviewees insisted that it was a time when things got done.

Civic values and efficiency are rarely associated with contemporary Italian bureaucracy and public life, indeed quite the contrary. As Jonathan Steinberg has recently remarked, 'no sane person' who has travelled on a German bus or used a German post office would prefer the Italian alternatives.[41] From the highest levels of government in Rome down to the local post office, Italian public life has long been stereotyped as chaotic and cumbersome. As mentioned earlier, historians of Italian colonialism have assumed that colonial administrations were hoplessly inept and corrupt, and there is little doubt that such assessments were influenced by stereotypical images of Italian bureaucracy. Dodecanesian perceptions therefore seem paradoxical, though when contextualised in the history of European colonialism, these perceptions have a plausible basis. As D.K. Fieldhouse once pointed out, colonial administrations world-wide, particularly in the interwar period, functioned in the best traditions of civil service. Colonial personnel exemplified duty and purpose, values needed in order to improve the lot of the 'natives'. It was such colonial personnel, idealistic young men serving both empire and the indigenous peoples, who believed more than most in paternalist notions of 'trusteeships' and 'the white man's burden'.[42] The Italian colonial service was no different. Remarkable achievements in public works in Italian east Africa could not have been achieved by colonial administrations weighed down by *menefreghismo* ('I-could-not-care-less-isms') and *la bustarella* (endemic corruption).[43]

Dodecanesian oral sources confirm a very positive picture of Italian bureaucracy, perhaps too positive. When faced with the frustrating practices of their own Greek civil service, with its reputation for rudeness, obduracy, imperiousness and corruption, elderly Dodecanesians yearn for the 'good old days' of Italian administration.[44] Conditions in a Greek bank or post office are similar to those in contemporary Italy, and, as is the case in both countries, having friends or family in important positions is widely believed to be the only way of getting things done.

Elderly Dodecanesians, however, would insist that Italian colonial personnel were officious yet polite, and that the Italians did things properly and efficiently. In his testimony, Antonis Stergalas recalled what usually happened when one entered an Italian administrative office:

> If you didn't know the language and you went to an office, for a licence or something, they'd say <<Parlate Italiano?>>, 'Do you speak Italian?' If you said 'no', then they'd shout <<Fuori!!>>, 'Out, Out!!' But if you said <<Si>>, they'd say <<entrate, come va? come sta?>>, How have you been? <<Che cosa mangare?>> (*sic*), have you eaten, <<Com'è la vita?>> [laughs], ... these things I know. . . . I knew enough [Italian] from my work.[45]

The same story was also given by four other interviewees, all of whom used it to convey the benefits of Italian practices.[46] While the islanders resented having to speak Italian when dealing with officialdom, they applauded the enforcement of forms and procedures, which made for greater efficiency. As with the stringent application of rules and regulations, the islanders appreciated the attention which Italian public servants paid to attire, conduct and etiquette. Locals continue to maintain that the Italian bureaucracy was, both in form and in substance, a suitable model for modern Greeks to emulate.

Interviewees singled out a number of ways in which Italian colonial bureaucracy was better than its modern Greek counterpart, though in each case the Italians were characterised as perfect. Mehmet Meerzam claimed that Italian bureaucracy did not suffer from 'red tape'. He compared Greek and Italian ways of dealing with building construction regulations and related permits. 'There was an enormous difference', he claimed. 'They [the Italians] did a cleaner job. These days you have all that trouble and time wasting. Back then they virtually came up to you to give a permit.'[47] Interviewees also idealised Italian administration as incorruptible, which left no room for bribes or the need for personal 'connections'. To counter corruption, Ioannis Alahiotis claimed the Italians had perfected a system of checks and balances. 'They had numerous people working for them', he explained, 'They were not only craftsmen, they were *morfoméni*!':

They monitored everything. You might have someone building for you, and if he was corrupt, and your piping didn't work, they had people supervising everything, and they watched everything that was done. They looked at the structure, the quality of your cement. The builder didn't have to contend with me, but with an official. He [the official] had the force of law. Nowadays you have to bribe them. . . . There were laws back then, and these things could not happen. If an official tried this [accept a bribe], there was another official to contend with. . . . Could a builder have it good with so many officials?!. . . They showed much attention to these things.[48]

For many interviewees, Italian efficiency and organisation was exemplified by the *Ordinamento Fondiario*, which saw the introduction of a modern cadastre. Thorough surveys were carried out on Rhodes between 1925 and 1933, and Kos between 1927 and 1931, as were zones designated for military use on Leros.[49] Most Rhodian and Koan land owners saw property registration as a progressive measure, for the Ottoman system, which was based on oral traditions and operated without titles, left considerable room for confusion and conflict. Locals were quite aware that the colonial government introduced the *Ordinamento Fondiario* to expropriate land in a 'legal' manner. Nevertheless, the innovation was welcomed because it reduced uncertainty over land ownership and diminished the scope for intra-familial and intra-community conflict. All relevant details such as ownership, location, size and original value were now documented and held in an official registry. Mikhail Hatsinikolaou pointed out in his testimony that the colonial government had mischievously undervalued land which it sought to appropriate, but he still considered the *Ordinamento* a progressive measure because it introduced order and security of ownership:

The survey (ktimatológio), I must say, was a commendable achievement, one which you cannot find anywhere else, even in other parts of Greece . . . the system we have here is excellent.[50]

The complex and wide-ranging structure of the colonial government has already been outlined in Chapter 3, including its numerous departments and sub-departments which were designed to cover every conceivable area of public interest. Thus the colonial government paid considerable attention to excavation and maintenance of antiquities, particularly monuments which could be categorised as Italian heritage, like Roman ruins and Venetian castles. Forestation and land reclamation received exclusive attention by specialists of *L'Azienda Speciale Foreste Demaniali*, while the *Servizio Agricultura, Lavoro, e Sperimentazione Agraria* promoted new farming techniques and ways to eradicate pests. The latter also conducted regular meteorological tests and other forms of scientific experimentation.[51] These two departments did much to promote Italian modernity in Kos Town, as the following example shows. The Italians drained the swamps north of Kos Town to plant vineyards and orchards, and locals were encouraged to come and witness new farming techniques and the use of fertilisers. One of the myths associated with this model plantation was that it could produce huge vegetables. 'Once they weighed an onion', recalled Pantelis Tripolitis, 'at one and a half kilos! Do you believe it. One and a half . . . they planted vegetables, fruit trees, melons, everything you could think of.'[52] The story of the 'one and a half kilo onion' was told by five of the interviewees, most of whom insisted they actually saw it on display.[53] For them, the onion exemplified the high standards of Italian technology and innovation.

Natural disasters represent the ultimate test of government competence and organisation. In 1908, a major revolt on Crete saw the displacement of the island's Muslim inhabitants, creating a massive refugee problem for the Ottomans. Many of these refugees were re-settled in new neighbourhoods on the fringes of Rhodes Town and Kos Town, which were subsequently called 'the Kritiká' ('the Cretan Homes'). According to Ioannis Alahiotis, however, 'the Kritiká' showed how the Ottomans could not even take care of their own people:

> They came here, but they were not given homes. The Turkish government tried to shelter these people, and built for them these so-called 'Kritika'. There were quite a few of them [the refugees], maybe even a thousand. They came with their families, but in them [the new homes] they tried to fit two families . . . and each house was very small, one room each. . . . And this was the 'benevolence' of the Turkish government. This is what they did out of 'patriotic' feeling.[54]

'The Kritika' represented an inadequate response to a serious refugee problem. A significant contrast was set twenty-five years later, when the Italian colonial government was put to the test. The earthquake which devastated Kos Town in 1933 is worth recalling in some detail, partly because the reconstruction showed the Italian efficiency in its element, and partly because Italian relief efforts left a deep imprint in local popular memory.

The earthquake struck on 23 April, at 8 o'clock on a Sunday morning. As is often the case in these circumstances, most people vividly remember what they were doing when the tremors began. Archondoula Kanaris recalled trying to finish her house duties before going off to church. She stopped momentarily to chat with a neighbour who happened to be walking by, who claimed she dreamt of a bad omen the night before. At that moment, Kanaris claimed the earth suddenly started to move:

> A Jewish woman came past our house and told us she had had a dream about me. She put down her basket at our doorstep, and as she began to talk the earth started to move. 'Boom', 'boom', 'boom', 'boom'. It was like you were dancing. . . . We had lots of copper-ware. It all fell down, 'Paaaam', 'paaam'. . . . The earth was dancing.[55]

Many had already gone to church. The 23rd of April happened to be a special day in the Orthodox liturgical calendar. It was both St Thomas's and St George's Day, so church attendances were higher than usual. Divine Providence seemed to favour the more punctual faithful, as the two main churches, St Nicholas' and St Paraskevi's, withstood the impact of the earthquake and remained largely intact. Kalliroi Dimitriadis had promptly arrived at St Paraskevi's when the doors had just been opened. When the earthquake struck, she recalled how some parishioners panicked and took flight, only to be crushed by a collapsing wall outside. As Dimitriadis recalls, as Kos Town seemed to be falling apart, church served as a true sanctuary:

> I tell you, . . . it was like trees were being uprooted. 'Crrrack, crrrack, crrrack'. The ground moved around, it was all happening from underneath, you see, as if trees were being pulled out. Inside the church, of course, the building was fine. It had just been built by the Italians, and it was strong. But everything outside had fallen down. . . .[56]

The vast majority of the townspeople were left homeless, and only a small section of the old town remained substantially intact. The injury toll was rather high for such a small town, with some 150 dead and another 600 wounded.[57] Most families suffered at least one loss. Over one-third of the dead were aged under fifteen, and thirty-nine were under the age of ten. Some families suffered more than most; Pantelis and Ourania Samaras lost two daughters, aged four and three, while the respected doctor Giorgos Loukidis lost his wife and three children.[58] What made the earthquake particularly tragic for locals was that all the dead, whose bodies were quickly dumped in a mass grave, were familiar. The following is an excerpt from a local poem:

> Some wail for their husbands, and others their children,
>   which so suddenly were torn from their arms.
>   The walls fall and kill anyone below,
> and the soldiers begin immediately to unearth them.
>   They find some alive and others dead,
>   and the hospitals fill with the wounded.[59]

It is noteworthy that the soldiers rate a mention. Given the extent of the tragedy, it is significant that the efficiency of Italian relief work is also given much emphasis in oral tradition. The testimonies give the impression that Italian relief work and reconstruction were exemplary, far better than the locals could have hoped. The colonial government had already tested its skills in relief work in February 1926, when a minor earthquake damaged Kastellorizo and the Koan village of Antimachia, and in both places the Italians left a good impression.[60] Kalliroi Dimitriadis remembered how quickly the Italians responded to the disaster in Kos Town:

> The Italians ran, they ran. They helped. Yes they helped! They were almost naked when they ran out of the barracks to help everyone. They went to everyone and asked if they needed help, they asked where your family was, if anyone was caught [under rubble] anywhere.[61]

The key image in the above excerpt is, 'the Italians ran'. As with other Koan interviewees, Paraskevi Angopian used the verb 'running' consistently to emphasise the urgency shown by the Italians during the crisis. 'Everything went dark', she recalled, 'The Italians, *they ran* with their shovels and picks, and they dug up to find the people. . . .'[62] Locals were appreciative of how well organised the Italians were. Soldiers and *carabinieri* quickly ushered people into the harbour, from where they were transported to open country. Ample food, clothing and shelter were later provided.[63] In her testimony, Archondoula Kanaris indicated how confident most felt in the colonial regime's relief operations:

anyhow, when it all stopped [the tremors], then the soldiers came running. Everyone was shouting, <<aiuto, aiuto>>, 'help', 'help', everyone was shouting. They rounded up everyone and brought them to the harbour. They then put us into trucks and sent us out into the fields, you know, because it was very open . . . quickly they brought us tents, and we slept. . . . It was raining heavily, lightning, thunder. . . .[64]

The Italians were keen to show they had mastered the crisis. Boats arriving with food and clothing from Kalymnos were permitted entry to Kos harbour, but relief vessels sponsored by Dodecanesian expatriates, the Greek Archdiocese in Athens, and the Greek government were all refused access by Italian authorities.[65] The Greek press reported this as evidence of Italian barbarity, but the colonial government simply wished to show it didn't need any help. Italian pride in relief work did not go unnoticed among people in Kos. 'Then came ships from everywhere', recalls Archondoula, 'from every country. But they didn't let them in. They [the Italians] were very proud. They came around every Friday to pass around new blankets, they made sure we were well fed.'[66]

The colonial regime also offered sympathetic gestures. Lago and his wife Octavia were in Rome on official business when news of the tragedy reached them. Both returned to the Aegean immediately, and the *Messaggero di Rodi* reported this as a 'simpatico gesto del Capo Possedimento e prova fraterna che lo unisce, nella buona come nell'avversa fortuna, alla popolazione. . . .'[67] When inspecting the damaged dome of the Church of St Nicholas, Greek sources reported that Lago had shown some emotion.[68] Generous donations for reconstruction soon followed. Achille Starace donated 50 000 lire on behalf of the Fascist Party. The King followed with 30 000, Mario and Octavia Lago gave 4000, while personnel in the Dodecanesian branch of the *Banca di Sicilia* pooled their resources and donated 245. Donations were also forthcoming from Italian companies like TEMI and *Compagnia Commerciale Italiana per l'Egeo*, from the *Messaggero di Rodi*, and the Alhadeff banking family of Rhodes.[69]

Italian reputation for efficiency was further exemplified by the reconstruction of Kos Town. Over 150 units of housing were provided for common folk at quite affordable rates, with rent varying from 15 lire a month for one bedroom homes, to 35 lire for three bedrooms.[70] Others who could afford to buy were encouraged to do so. Loans were offered at 3 per cent interest, and were to be re-paid over a fifty-year period.[71] Cheap finance was also granted to others whose homes had suffered significant damage.[72] Locals were also amazed by the speed of the rebuilding process, as conveyed in another popular saying which held that 'the Italians rebuilt Kos in three years!'[73]. Antonis Stergalas's appraisal was typical:

> I was here during the earthquake. . . . There were about 180 killed . . . eh, up to 200. Here houses fell down. You know why? They were all stuck together and made of mud. One would fall, dragging down the other [Stergalas laughs]. . . . But they [the Italians] had programmes. In three years, 1933 was when the earthquake happened, and in 1936 people were living in homes! They rebuilt Kos in three years![74]

In light of the Greek government's much criticised tardiness in reconstructing Kalamata (Peloponnese) after a serious earthquake in 1986, Kalliope Harapas reflected upon the good example set by the Italians. She asserted that no one has been able to match them since:

> The Italians, to try and rebuild Kos, made a big attempt, and I must say, they did it without being asked to do it. . . . Since then, as I have grown older, I've heard of many earthquakes all over the world and no one else was put back into their homes faster than we were.[75]

PUBLIC WORKS

The reconstruction of Kos Town provided a chance for the Italians to demonstrate their modernity. Prior to the earthquake, the town had many 'pre-modern' characteristics; it had dark, narrow streets, it was densely populated and it had no sewerage system. By 1936, Kos Town had become a model garden town, a paradigm of space and order, with wide, tree-lined streets, piazzas and esplanades, and homes with private gardens. For locals the transformation was quite stunning. They were not merely exposed to things 'modern', but were also left with a permanent reminder of Italian ingenuity.

Even the most ardent critics of Italian colonialism have praised its record of development projects. Denis Mack Smith admits that Italy did many things for her empire, 'spending a great deal of money there and leaving behind some notable public works'.[76] In his otherwise damning study of the conquest of Ethiopia, Angelo Del Boca praises

Italy for having provided the vanquished with hospitals, schools and factories. Haile Selassie himself told Del Boca that the Italians had a 'genius for constructing'.[77] Selassie's sentiments were not uncommon in the colonial aftermath, particularly as Italian public works were tangible legacies, very useful indeed for emerging post-colonial nations. In the Dodecanese, the Italians are remembered as a progressive, enterprising and skilful (prokoméni) people. The interviewees remembered the high period of the occupation as one of great activity, of major projects and a seemingly endless reservoir of finances to fund them. Admittedly, military and economic interests made the Italians concentrate on three islands, Rhodes, Kos and Leros, but the belief that Italian rule was 'progressive' was held throughout the island group.

The reconstruction of Kos Town was a case in point. Prior to the earthquake, Kos Town consisted of three neighbourhoods, 'Hora', 'Aspa' and 'the Kritika'. Hora, the largest of these neighbourhoods, had been completely devastated, while the other sections had also been substantially destroyed. The new town was planned on a modern grid pattern, characterised by wide, rectilinear avenues. An old section of Aspa which had survived the earthquake was left intact, as if to accentuate the new town's modernity. Thus the old quarter, with its narrow and winding streets, was juxtaposed with the new, Italian-built sections. It was the new sections with which the inhabitants of Kos Town began to identify.[78] Koan interviewees often associated narrow streets with backwardness and Ottoman rule. 'Before the streets were narrow . . . narrow', explains Kalliroi Dimitriadis of old Hora, 'in some places a donkey carrying baskets could not get through.'[79] According to Archondoula Kanaris, the Italians had upgraded their town from its embarrassingly backward state. 'Before the earthquake we never had streets', she claimed.

> You know what our houses were like?! Your house was here, mine was there. A car could not pass through. And they were made of rocks, not cement, but little tiny stones. But when the earthquake happened, Kos [Town] was changed. They put in trees, they put in streets. . . . [80]

The reconstructed town gave locals considerable civic pride because it became a showpiece for passing visitors. 'Who would have thought', remarked Antonis Stergalas, 'that we would have tourists and so many people here!'[81] Ioannis Petalas, who worked on building sites during the reconstruction, was unreserved in his praise of the Italians.

He explained, while looking around from the centre of the main piazza, that 'for us who witnessed all these things being built around us, we all believed it was like a miracle. . . don't you think'.[82]

Similar sentiments were expressed by interviewees regarding the construction of new towns in Rhodes and Leros. The pride of Leros was Lakki, the Italian naval base. Like Kos Town, Lakki had been designed as a garden town, with wide streets and modern buildings. As Argyro Papadopoulos boasted, Italian politicians and even royalty came to see Lakki:

> And through Leros passed all the important politicians of Italy, to see all the great works they did here. Even Vittorio Manuele (*sic*) came. . . . He was very short, always very short. He would pass by our house to go for a swim. They all passed by our house. They all walked past. They put flowers on every balcony which he passed. . . . One of Mussolini's sons came to Leros, and a many, many other Italian politicians.[83]

The interviewees often raised notions of 'Europe' to convey how 'progressive' the Italian impact was. In forging its national identity, Greece has identified with an idealised Europe (i.e. western Europe), which has served as a generic model for the nation's political, economic, social and cultural development. Ethnographic studies of rural Greece have also shown that 'Europe' has been a symbol of high culture and modernity at a popular level. Therefore, just as narrow streets symbolised 'Turkishness' and 'backwardness', so wide, tree-lined streets symbolised 'Europe'. 'Europe' and 'the Turks' have served as binary opposites in Greek social discourse, and in the Dodecanese, the Italians were thanked for having taken the islands closer to the former.[84] Hence when Lefteris of Leros sought to describe the garden town of Lakki during the Italian Occupation, he invoked 'Paris'. He remembered the town as bustling and exciting, with its grand and elegant buildings, and its modern features:

> There were 35 000 Italians here. There were army, navy, airforce personnel, there were many hydroplanes. Big things . . . Lakki was like a Paris. There was much movement, 500, 600 people in the street. . . . In Lakki . . . there was a cinema with 1900 light bulbs![85]

The islanders generally take great pride in Italian achievements, and the fact that the Italians were foreign occupiers seems inconsequential. This phenomenon has a cultural explanation. As Rudolph Bell shows in regard to Italian village life, community space, landmarks and environmental features informed the rhetoric of *campanilismo*.[86] This was also to be found in Greek inter-village or inter-island rivalries, where, for instance, the inhabitants of fertile Rhodes and Kos have long claimed an advantage over communities living on the more barren islands. Italian development was welcomed by the islanders because it 'Europeanised' or modernised local space. Thus Argyro Papadopoulos and 'Lefteris' took pride in Italian achievements in Lakki because Leros was now worthy enough to attract the interest of royalty. Whether in the form of new towns or agricultural development programmes, the Italians were seen to be upgrading the symbolic value of their locality.

People throughout Rhodes took exceptional pride in what the Italians did with their main town. Since the 1950s, Rhodes has arguably been the most popular resort for Greek tourists, and locals acknowledge that this has had much to do with the island's Italian legacy, for the colonial regime saw much importance in its cultural *funzione*.[87] Outside the walls of the medieval town, the Italians built a modern section with wide thoroughfares, piazzas, a market complex, and many other ornate public buildings. The political and symbolic function of these innovations will be dealt with further below, suffice to say that the new section, combined with the painstakingly restored medieval section, became the colonial regime's premier showpiece. Of Mandraki harbour, Philipos Sofos claimed, 'When they [the Italians] left, Rhodes had everything. Remember what Mandraki was like before! It was all mud . . . mud!'[88] Giorgos Sakellaridis remembered Rhodes Town as a bustling, cosmopolitan centre, and argued that foreigners were keen to come and marvel at Italian ingenuity.[89]

Italian-built towns were designed to be pleasing to the eye. They were also meant to smell better. Most interwar colonial administrations paid much attention to urban waste and sewerage as part of their new 'civilising mission'. Promoting better hygiene was another way in which colonial powers sought to project their modernity and cultural superiority, and in the Dodecanese, the occupied noticed a big difference in living conditions. Kos Town, for instance, did not have a hygienic sewerage system before the earthquake. As a peasant farmer who visited Kos Town regularly to sell his produce, Ioannis Alahiotis could appreciate the difference in smell before and after the earthquake. While villagers would use the woods for their convenience, until 1933 the townspeople were generally forced to use cesspits. These cesspits produced odours which visitors like Alahiotis found quite unbearable:

When you walked into a Koan home before the earthquake, it stank. Because toilets did not exist. . . . Even the 'sifoúni' (septic tanks) they did not know about. They just dug a deep hole in which everything was poured in. And the stench came out of the hole and into the street, and from there of course it moved everywhere. We who came down from the village [Asfendiou], we couldn't even sleep in a house owned by say a doctor. But that was the technical state of the times. . . . The Italians, they knew about such things, and they were able to introduce them to us. . . .[90]

Given the nature of the topic, the interviewees did not volunteer much information about hygiene practices and facilities, but since the new sewerage system flushed effluent out of town and into the sea, greatly reducing local discomfiture and the threat of disease, there is little doubt that locals welcomed the Italian innovation. 'Of course', explains Kalliroi Dimitriadis, 'we did not have a chain to flush things away. We poured water into the bowl. But before,' she adds with some discomfort, 'a man would come around – you'd pay him – and he would take "everything" away.'[91] For Kalliope Harapas, the sewerage system was a great source of civic pride:

The Italians had laws. They did many good things. We have gutters and sewerage drains, . . . you know what a difference that makes!? Today, there are places in [mainland] Greece where the filth is unbelievable. All this city [Kos Town] has an underground sewerage system. Before that we would empty our things in the streets. We had deep holes in our homes and used them as toilets. . . . It was a 'wee wee' carnival [laughs]. After 1933 we had cleanliness.[92]

Another innovation which affected many Koans was the quality of housing built after the earthquake. As mentioned earlier, the Ottomans resettled their Cretan refugees in one-room hovels with few basic amenities. In contrast, the Italians seemed to spare no expense when it came to home construction. For instance, they introduced what had only been available to the wealthy; homes with different rooms for different functions. Landed and merchant families lived in two-storey homes called 'archondika', with neo-classical facades and small courtyards. Inside they had separate kitchens, bedrooms, and rooms for dining and washing. Poorer folk usually lived in one- or two-roomed mud brick homes, which were poorly lit and ventilated. Moreover, these modest dwellings usually housed large, extended families, most of whom slept on floor mats. After the earthquake, the Italians made modern housing available to the displaced people of Kos Town, and each home had a kitchen, living room, bedrooms, bathroom and hallway, as well as a small yard.[93] Larger windows and doors improved ventilation and lighting. For women, whose lives were basically confined to the home, Italian-built homes were particularly welcome. Kalliope Harapas claimed the pre-earthquake homes could not compare. 'It's not worth discussing' (min ta sizitás), she scoffed. As she pointed towards one of the Italian-built homes, she explained:

> Don't you see here right in front of you. . . . There is a good example on the corner. Newly built, free standing, roomy [spacious], . . . they have bedrooms, hallways down the middle, and outside they had big backyards . . . if you walk into one you will find they are lovely.[94]

All Dodecanesians stood to benefit from Italian road construction. No colonial power in the interwar period could compare with Italy when it came to building roads,[95] and of all the islands, Rhodes benefited most. All forty-seven villages were connected by a large road network, which vastly improved the transportation of primary produce from the villages to the main town. Donkey tracks were replaced with 300 miles of roads, a third of which were suitable for motor vehicles.[96] Public transport also made Rhodes Town much more accessible to the villagers. Giorgos Giorgalos of Asklepion complained that one needed to travel for two or three days to get to Rhodes Town from his village (47 km), and this usually involved an overnight stay at one of the villages en route.[97] Stamatis Athanasiadis lived in the village of Paradisi, which was closer to Rhodes Town (15 km), but he too found travelling an ordeal:

> Paridisi to Rhodes on a beast took two hours. Everything went on the back of animals . . . we got, after a while, the buses, you know, the 'buses' [in English]. They brought buses and these covered all the islands. Yes, they made things easier. They [the Italians] didn't leave things as they found them. They fixed things, they spent billions of Italian lire. . . .[98]

Athanasiadis asserted that the Italians 'fixed' much of Rhodes. In Greek, 'to fix' (na fiáxis) can mean to improve, to add value, as well as to build. Unlike the Ottomans, the Italians were regarded as an enterprising and constructive people, and the testimonies are full of recitations of things 'fixed'. Thus:

> They fixed things here in Rhodes; the harbours, buildings, they made roads. The roads . . . you could not move on them before . . . there were pot holes, pot holes there, puddles here, puddles there. . . . They put asphalt on all of them. They made new roads. In all they spent billions of Italian francs [lire] to fix Rhodes.[99]

To be sure, only Rhodes, Kos and Leros enjoyed substantial Italian attention, and consequently, other islanders felt rather aggrieved that had they missed out. Marigo Katris of Astypalea complained that her island was unfairly disadvantaged:

> They made roads for us but not paved roads . . . dirt roads. Only dirt roads. Buildings? What buildings? They built the barracks and . . . eh . . . no they didn't build anything. Except for the church, because they wanted us to go to an Italian church. But what were we supposed to do with that? We never wanted it.[100]

Basil Galettis of Kastellorizo postulated that the attention paid to Rhodes and Kos was at Kastellorizo's expense, but he did admit later in his testimony that the colonial government did erect some buildings on the island, and he spoke of these with considerable pride. 'They fixed many things here', he explained. 'The administrative office, the barracks . . . they did good things in Kastellorizo.'[101] Given that the Kalymnians have prided themselves as being the most anti-Italian Dodecanesian community, they have managed to use the apparent Italian 'neglect' of their island to their moral advantage. When asked why the Italians did not build much on their island, Kalymnians often reply with the set answer, 'We didn't let them' (then tous fisame). Such boasts, however, are often accompanied by disemic responses which concede their envy for the generous attention which Kos Town received. When asked what they thought of Kos Town, Kalymnians express their admiration by asserting with such typically unkind responses as, 'Lucky the Italians built it for them', suggesting Koans were not capable of building such wonders themselves.

ARCHITECTURE AND EMPIRE

Whether in the form of official attire or in town planning, Italian colonialism tried to uphold high standards of taste, and when it came to 'fixing' things, the Italians were just as concerned to promote aesthetic quality as they were to project power. As Jonathan Steinberg points out, one of the cultural realities of Italy is the importance accorded to forms and appearance, in the 'proper' performance of tasks, and their 'proper' presentation: *fare una bella figura*.[102] Development projects in the Dodecanese seemed to suggest the Italians were not prepared to compromise when it came to the quality of materials or in aesthetic considerations. The interviewees regarded this aspect of Italian rule as another progressive feature of the period. The most manifest expression of Italian 'civilisation' in the Dodecanese was architecture, which will be the focus of this section. Dodecanesians regarded Italian buildings as *oréa pràmata*, meaning 'beautiful things', or things which are well produced and presented.[103] In architecture, much as in administration, civic government and economic development, the Italians seemed to show the way forward.

The sterile simplicity of Greek architectural forms since the war, as exemplified by modern Athens and the newer sections of Rhodes Town, have served to confirm the high quality of Italian architecture. The contemporary urban landscape, with its dusty concrete buildings, large aluminium antennas, exposed iron girders and inornate balconies, lacks the kind of charm which tourists tend to expect of the land of Homer, Aristophanes and Sappho. In the Dodecanese, cheap, simple and functional structures also prevailed before the Italian Occupation, as most of the islanders lived in modest, mud-brick, white-washed cottages. The wealthier classes could afford neo-classical facades and balconies, but in general Dodecanesian architecture was dictated by poverty and meagre resources. The Italians transformed the panorama of Dodecanesian architecture with a variety of architectural styles, and with buildings which towered over almost all pre-existing structures.

Much has already been written on the politics of European colonial architecture. Scholars have noted how size, strategic location and style has served to symbolise the power relationship between the coloniser and colonised. As architectural historian Diane Ghirardo has pointed out, 'any government architecture has a rhetorical function', and that architecture tells us 'what the regime wants us to believe of its nature'.[104] The Italians had also prescribed a role for architecture in promoting their imperial destiny. In their Dodecanesian context, Italian buildings seemed larger than life, and were only exceeded in magnitude by the monuments built by the Knights of St John. However, the Italians were just as concerned to *fare una bella figura*, which meant putting as much emphasis on aesthetic as on political considerations. The result was a colonial building scheme which seemed to lack a comprehensive strategy.

Architecture in the Aegean 'possessions' reflected trends in the metropolis. Scholars agree there was no distinct 'Fascist' style, though certain architectural movements did compete for the Fascist label. Put simply, Rationalism, the dominant radical movement, was pitted against the more established and conservative neo-classical movement. The Rationalists sought to evoke Fascism's radicalism and modernism, while the neo-classicists looked more to the past, seeking to legitimise Fascism by linking it to Italy's glorious past, particularly Imperial Rome. The competition helped give the impression that Fascism suffered from a 'confusion' of styles,[105] and this apparent 'confusion' was evident in the Dodecanese.[106] In Lakki, for instance, the market building has some of the hallmarks of the Rationalist movement. With its elliptical shape, its rounded corners, and its roof, which consisted of layers of concentric circles, the market exemplified Rationalism's emphasis on functionality and simplicity. Only a small distance away, however, were the monumental and rather austere buildings used by the military. While these structures were essentially neo-classical, they did not have columns or any other motifs which could be construed as 'Hellenic'. If there was a dominant architectural style in the Dodecanese, it was a peculiar combination promoted by Mario Lago himself. It too was a decidedly un-Hellenic combination; a mixture of Venetian, Gothic, Baroque and Islamic elements, with ochre as the dominant colour, often accompanied by maroon. The most pronounced example of this eclectic style was the Palazzo del Governo in Rhodes Town. The Palazzo was built with Gothic windows, a mixture of Islamic and Baroque arches, curving Islamic parapets, and a very long Venetian colonnade. The Palazzo was one of many major buildings erected around the Foro Italico, the main thoroughfare of Rhodes Town. These buildings, which included the Banca d'Italia and the Circolo Italia, were radically different from the Palazzo, but they served to display the richness of, rather than the 'confusion' in, Italian architecture under Fascism.

The Italians also followed standard guidelines regarding the projection of imperial power through architecture. Thus large colonial structures, which were located within civic space and were prominently positioned, were often juxtaposed against smaller indigenous structures. Even in Kalymnos, where the occupier's impact was minimal, Italian buildings held the most commanding positions in the main harbour, and the same could be said of the other 'neglected' islands, like Simi and Kastellorizo.

So what did the indigenous make of all this? Were they daunted by symbolic projections of Italian power? Dodecanesian writers have consistently argued that Italian colonial architecture was part of a grand political design to overawe and Italianise the Greek people. In 1946, Simian writer Sotiris Agapitidis claimed Italian public works must be viewed within the context of the colonial government's assimilationist programme.[107] Ten years later, the Rhodian writer Emmanuel Kariotis wrote an article which was ostensibly on Italian architecture, but his sole concern was its political function. He claimed that by building large and impressive structures, the Italians hoped to dupe the ignorant (i.e. common folk) and convert them into Italians.[108] Concern for the 'ignorant' was again raised in 1972 by Christodoulos Papachristodoulou, who claimed that only the *morfoméni* could resist the disarming charm of Italian architecture:

> In these buildings, full of pathos, the Italians . . . built these to unsettle the on-looker, to terrify the observer, to re-introduce the reign of the Hospitallers and rewrite history in their own way.[109]

In warning about the dangers posed by Italian architecture, Dodecanesian *morfoméni* conceded their deep admiration for it, but their fears for the common folk said more about the conceitedness of *morfoméni* than anything else. The oral testimonies show that the indigenous were certainly impressed by Italian architecture, but there is little indication that they were overawed by it. As will be shown in the following chapter on occupier–occupied social relations, Dodecanesians associated the Italians far more with culture and style, than with images of conquest and power. Italian rule did not command the kind of respect induced by fear, rather, architecture confirmed local views of Italians as craftsmen, as men of taste (me goústo) and enterprise. Architecture evoked *bella figura* rather than 'imperium'.

Whilst the islanders cherished Italian works for their functional and symbolic value, they also appreciated their aesthetic features. Of course, common folk could not be expected to understand the finer points of Rationalism or Lago's eclectic novelty, but they could recognise craftsmanship and a considered piece of art. Most popular were the more elaborate and ornate buildings, like the Palazzo del Governo, the Grande Albergo delle Rose, and the court house in Kos Town. These were considered *oréa prámata*, items to be treasured. For Antonis Stergalas, the artistic merit of Italian architecture in Kos Town gave him much civic pride. He provided an inaccurate description of architectural styles, but his estimation of their value was quite clear. 'You see, my son, arches everywhere', he boasted:

> Byzantine! Big windows, you see. . . . All the people here loved to look at these things. Tourists would come and take pictures, Greeks mainly. . . . Every Friday there came a boat passing by filled with tourists . . . they loved our city.[110]

Locals thought Kos Town had been blessed with treasures. Rhodian, Koan and Lerian interviewees often conveyed their pride by identifying many of these buildings by name or function. They often noted and discussed the merits of each of these structures, especially those who participated in the building process. Ioannis Petalas recalled which buildings were constructed before and after Kos Town's earthquake, and referred to them by current titles. Thus,

> Now, we'll begin with those built from 1925 to 1928, eh, before the earthquake. These were the *demarchía* with all the surrounding area, with the customs house etc, there was the *dikitírio* [*podesteria*], there was the *aktéon* [theatre], there was the [Church of the] Holy Annunciation, there were the schools, these are the first buildings which the Italians erected. . . . After the earthquake, . . . they did something which nobody expected . . . they built a new city. . . .[111]

Listing the names of Italian buildings was a common narrative technique employed by interviewees. In reciting the names of each building, the interviewees seemed to be counting their prized assets, hence evoking images of riches amassed. For instance, Rhodian interviewees, both in the villages and the main town, conveyed their pride by recalling the names of the Italian buildings which continue to dominate Mandraki harbour. As Philipos Sofos asserted, 'The best buildings in Rhodes [Town] were built by the Italians', as if this was an undisputed fact.[112] With the help of several fellow villagers, Sofos recited many of these structures by their current Greek titles, and as in the other testimonies, current Greek names were preferred to the old Italian names. Stamatis Athanasiadis of Paradisi worked on many buildings in Mandraki harbour, and therefore he was more capable than most of remembering their old Italian names:

> We worked 1924, 1925 . . . 1928, five years on the buildings . . . .
> First on the Vangelismós, then the Banco di Roma, which is now the National Bank [of Greece], then we worked on the new markets . . . then my father and I bought a small farm, but my brother continued to work on St Francesco. . . .[113]

While public and private interests have used Italian buildings for their symbolic value, and have replaced their original names with Greek names, the islanders never hide the fact that the Italians had built them. Indeed, the islanders have found it useful to remind themselves that these structures were built by a 'progressive' European power, for the cultural level of the Italian occupiers has formed a reference point from which Dodecanesians judge their own cultural level, and that of Greek society in general. Among the more notable structures in Kos Town was a large belltower which stood outside the main Catholic church, now the residence of the Orthodox bishop of Kos and Nisyros. Interviewees remembered how the bells could be heard throughout the town and beyond. Unfortunately the tower was pulled down by Greek soldiers soon after the Germans had withdrawn in early 1945. Many Koans disapproved of this act of 'barbarity', and Kalliroi Dimitriadis recalled this as a shameful event:

> Yes . . . the beautiful bell-tower, it was big and beautiful with large bells, it had a square base . . . and the bells were heard morning, midday and evening. Then came our 'cultured' lot [the Greeks] and as soon as they came they pulled the tower down. . . . 'Their brains for one lira' (ta mialá tous ke miá líra). They should have left it as a memorial. It was a beautiful tower, with great bells. They even played in harmony![114]

The interviewee's irritation with this act of vandalism was partly due to the sad loss of such a fine structure, and partly due to her disappointment that such a barbaric act was carried out by 'our cultured lot'. The event symbolised her disillusionment with aspects of Greek society.

When thinking of Italian craftsmanship, interviewees were just as concerned with quality as they were with style. The general consensus among Dodecanesians was that Italian structures were 'strong' (gerá). 'Strength' evoked the high level of building expertise as well as the quality materials. As mentioned earlier, Kalliroi Dimitriadis claimed she survived the earthquake in Kos because she took refuge in a church built by Italian hands.[115] St Paraskevi was erected according to standard building procedures and with standard materials, but Dodecanesians regarded all this as highly advanced. The Greeks had long been accustomed to using mud and limestone, and digging shallow foundations. The Italians, on the other hand, used cement, wire mesh, iron girders and bricks, materials which helped make buildings more resistant to earth tremors and quakes.

Each structure was closely supervised by master builders from various Italian firms, and the popular consensus was that these buildings were solid and sturdy. Men who laboured on these sites took particular pride in their workmanship. Mehmet Meerzam, who worked on many sites throughout the 1930s, emphasised that Italian buildings were 'strong'. 'All these were anti-seismic', he explained, 'that is why they are strong buildings. . . . Most of the pre-Italian stuff fell down. They were not for earthquakes.'[116] Having worked on many building sites in Rhodes Town, Stamatis Athanasiadis fondly recalled, 'We cut the stone . . . we made all the arches, all the sculpturing, the chain designs. We did fine work . . . what fine work! . . . what craftsmanship!'[117]

That the Italians were fine builders and architects is not contested in Dodecanesian social discourse. The islanders have often questioned whether they or Greeks in general would have been capable of emulating such ingenuity. These doubts were concealed in the subtexts of the oral sources, but they sometimes surface in open expositions of self-knowledge, as Dimitriadis showed in her telling of the 'belltower' story, or in well known jokes. As mentioned earlier, there is a popular joke in Kalymnos about the reconstruction of Kos after 1933, that 'lucky the Italians did it for them'. The joke does not merely question Koan building skills, but also their ability to organise themselves to meet such a massive task. Yet the same kind of joke has often been levelled by Dodecanesians against themselves and against their state. Until the tourist boom of the 1980s, which brought with it a windfall of capital and a massive growth in building activity, most Dodecanesians did not see any manifestations of 'Greek' innovation and expertise. And when the boom finally came, most of the islanders would concede that town planning has been ill-organised and buildings have lacked aesthetic merit. Their rich legacy of Italian architecture and town planning have served to expose Greek deficiencies in these areas.

WORK AND NORMALCY

During the governorship of Mario Lago, the Dodecanese enjoyed a sustained period of high employment based on Italian public works programmes and private investment. The impact of these developments on the indigenous population was profound. Long accustomed to seasonal and irregular work, thousands of Dodecanesians now found regular employment and a source of stability. One theme which local historiography has ignored, but which the interviewees dwelled on, was the theme of 'work'. If anything, the Italian Occupation is associated in popular memory with high employment, which made for stable or 'normal' conditions. The nexus between work and normalcy was crucial in Ulrich Herbert's oral history survey among Krupp steelworkers. The high period of National Socialism (1935–42), as with the decades of economic and social stability in postwar West Germany, were regarded by these steelworkers as 'normal times', for these periods were characterised by regular employment. German workers could therefore commit themselves to 'normal' pursuits like marriage and raising children. These certainties, the ability to raise a family and maintain a comfortable standard of living, were the basic preconditions for 'normal' times, even 'good' times. Equally, these steelworkers remembered the unstable Weimar years as their reference for what was *not* normal. Lack of job security and chronic economic instability made for conditions in which young German males could not commit themselves to 'normal' pursuits. Like the Fascists in Italy, the Nazis recognised that the best way to placate a troublesome working class was to guarantee 'work and bread'.[118] As Herbert's steelworkers testified, secure and steady employment allowed little time for politics and other secondary pre-occupations. They seemed willing to withdraw into their own private spheres, while leaving the Nazis to reign over the public domain.[119]

Dodecanesians also drew a connection between secure employment and normalcy, though unlike Herbert's German workers, most of the islanders did not have memories of an earlier 'golden age' to serve as a reference for normalcy. Some of the former 'Privileged' islanders could look back to their *belle époque* before 1912, when the sponge trade was at its height, but for the majority of Dodecanesians, life was described in terms of enduring poverty, and such feelings were evoked with fatalistic rhetoric. In *The Moral Basis of a Backward Society*, Edward Banfield remarked how poor peasants in Basilicata in the 1950s found that no matter how hard they struggled, they could not 'get ahead' and were fated to remain *indietro*. They described life as 'la miseria'.[120] Dodecanesians lamented about life in a similar fashion, having terms like 'the black life' (i mávri zoí) and 'wretched life' (palió zoí).[121] Dodecanesian folklore is full of poems and proverbs which evoke a bleak picture of everyday life. The following proverb is from Nisyros:

> The poor man dies every day,
> The rich die only once.

Small and often disparate plots of land, lack of capital, predatory usurers, a volatile market for local produce, burdensome taxes and an exploitative landed gentry class all seemed to conspire against the Dodecanesian poor. Some common folk resorted to more profitable work like sponge diving, but diving was profitable because it was fraught with mortal dangers. Much like Carlo Levi's peasants in *Christ Stopped at Eboli*, who believed the politicians in Rome did not want them to live 'like human beings', the islanders complained that there were too many factors stopping each person from living 'like a human' (na zísis san ánthropos).[122]

Such expressions presupposed a state of normalcy, a condition which was better and just. What most Dodecanesians craved for was security through gainful and regular employment. With steady incomes they could raise their families, pay for their children's education and provide their dowries. For many who could afford the option, emigration was the only chance of fulfilling such basic ambitions. Before the high period of Italian rule, one had to move to the Levant, Athens, and increasingly, to the United States to be able to 'live like a human'.

The employment opportunities provided by the Italians gave many islanders a much welcomed respite from the vicissitudes of 'the black life'. The colonial government required a vast pool of labour for its ambitious development projects. Buildings, roadworks, airports and land reclamation provided peasants and mariners with regular employment throughout the 'Italian' period, hence the tendency of male interviewees to describe the 'Italian' period as a time of 'work'. This was particularly true of interviewees from Leros, Rhodes and

Kos, where most of these development projects took place. As a young boy growing up in the 1930s, Epaminondas Diamandaras remembered Leros as an exciting centre which drew workers from Italy and from all over the Dodecanese. He claimed that high employment was the most distinctive characteristic of the occupation:

> The locals were busy with work. Everyone left their other jobs and were employed in public works. We had people from all over the Dodecanese; Koans, Rhodians Simians, . . . they all came here. It was all worth it, you know. There was a lot of work here. . . . There was no modern machinery. . . . My father, God rest his soul, worked with them for years, and I remember him telling me that they would smash stones with hammers. . . . The roads they made with sledge-hammers, there were no machines. . . .[123]

Diamandaras proudly claimed that the Italians gave his father 'years' of steady employment, and he noted that peasants would abandon their plots in order to find work on development projects. Gone was the insecurity of under-employment. Now, claimed 'Lefteris' of Leros, 'the people had work'. He described high employment as a blessing which exemplified the extent of Italian benevolence:

> There were many companies here. . . . Gennari . . . many were working on different things. Systematic things. They built Leros really. . . . For all these works, when there weren't enough of us to help out, they'd send out messages to other places for workers . . . people came from Rhodes, Kos, Lipsos, from many places. Because we didn't have the machinery we have today. We struggled with shovels. Work was done very systematically. . . the people had work. . . .[124]

Diamandaras and Lefteris noted that 'there were no machines'. The lack of mechanisation was regarded by some Dodecanesians as a curious oversight, given that Italy, in their estimation, was a modern, 'European' state. Locals nevertheless saw this as a fortuitous oversight, for there were more job opportunities as a result. It was a deliberate measure, for as Cesare Vannutelli points out, the Fascists often awarded public contracts to companies in Italy on the condition that they did not use new machinery in order to provide more jobs.[125] Ioannis Petalas, who worked on many construction sites during the reconstruction of Kos Town, argued that the Italians wanted to give work to everyone. Like 'Lefteris', he interpreted this as Italian benevolence:

> I'd like to say something on this. Wouldn't you think they had tools in Italy to do all this work? But they didn't bring any tools, just so that the people could work. . . . So people could work! There were also women working here, maybe thousands, working, smashing rocks. . . .

Like many other Dodecanesians, Petalas left his farming plot to find more profit and security in the employ of the Italians:

> Everyone was getting work. I had a small farm, but I decided instead that I'd go and work on building sites. My father too. We'd be sent off by my mother, with a boiled egg and some olives for lunch, and we'd work all day. . . .[126]

While the interviewees appreciated their chance to work, Dodecanesian historians have interpreted high employment in the Italian Dodecanese as colonial exploitation, and have argued that the Italians did not need to import machinery because they could take advantage of cheap labour. Much is made of the fact that Greek workers performed the most arduous tasks, and that they received less than half the pay of their Italian counterparts. (In Italian East Africa, the indigenous workers were sometimes paid less than a quarter of what their Italian counterparts earned.)[127] In his report on the Dodecanese, Sotiris Agapitidis claimed that Greek workers were forced to endure incredible suffering and humiliation in order to build facilities which served Italian military and economic interests.[128] But this is not the impression given by the workers themselves. Ordinary Dodecanesians were well aware of the fact that Italians were better paid, but they also noted that most of these Italians were skilled workers and professionals. Mehmet Meerzam provided a more balanced assessment of the differences in pay:

> During the Italian occupation I was a builder. I worked on all the buildings here. The Italians erected all of these buildings. . . . With the earthquake, there was much work. . . . The Italians who came from Italy were of course craftsmen. We used to get four to five lire daily, but they'd get ten to twelve [laughs], . . . because they came from Italy, you see. They of course had to pay rent, we already had homes . . . yes, there was work, work, . . . lots of work. . . .[129]

Discrepancy in pay was not nearly as important a consideration as the purchasing power of the lira (i lirétta), which was also called 'the frank' (to frángko). The lira was regarded by Dodecanesians as hard currency, or 'hard money' (gerá leftá). The 'Italian' period is remembered as a time when the cost of living was low and the currency was stable. For those who worked on building sites and roadworks, like Ioannis Petalas, pay rates were considered fair and much better than any local source could provide. He explained:

> Listen, listen, for that time, that time, it was good, and you got paid. Today you need two jobs to get by, but back then the one job was enough. And they paid you regularly. If you didn't turn up, they'd sack you. . . . You had to be capable of working, and you had to work hard for your living. . . . I worked for one company for nine to 10 years. . . . There existed an opportunity to build all this [Kos Town]. It was a time when all wanted to work. There were true workers then. There was a working system, a system, from the head office down to the dirt diggers. Do you understand!? . . .[130]

Getting paid regularly with 'hard money' provided many with the chance to 'live like humans'. Recollections of the 'Italian' period were devoid of fatalistic rhetoric, and were characterised instead by language which evoked progress. The testimonies speak of 'everyone' having the chance to work and get ahead. Throughout his testimony Meerzam, once a landless rural labourer, approvingly muttered the words, 'there was work, there was work' (íhe douliés, íhe douliés). Stamatis Athanasiadis of Paradisi, Rhodes, described the 'Italian' period as a time of personal development, during which he made the transition from a small peasant farmer to buying his own barber shop in Rhodes Town. Working on building sites in Mandraki Harbour in the 1920s and early 1930s gave Athanasiadis the chance to save money and set himself up in a more prestigious and profitable occupation. He claimed 'Italian rule' gave many Rhodians the chance to escape poverty:

> The people were poor, . . . they were poor. Most were, three-quarters were farmers. Others were shepherds, others builders, carpenters, ironmongers, the people now had a chance to work; they didn't live well before. There was little money around. After some time things changed. Everything changed in 19 . . . 1924.

The Italians began to construct buildings. . . . They made roads. . . . I worked on the buildings. I worked on the [Church of the] Evangelismó . . . I was a technician. We smashed the rocks. . . . I worked with my brother and my father. We earned good money. But we worked 10 hours a day. I earned 30 lire a day, so did my brother, and my father earned 40. . . .[131]

Not everyone participated in development projects, but many of these people benefited indirectly. 'Lefteris' of Leros operated a modest stall in the town of Agia Marina, but he was given an exclusive permit to operate his stall in Lakki, the centre of Italian development activity. His chance to conduct a 'normal' life was directly attributed to occupier benevolence:

I once had a little stall in Agia Marina, and I used to sell sweets, eh, . . . this and that . . . to soldiers and visitors. They [the Italians] stopped me from doing this because there were stores which were already selling these things. They said to me, sell off what you have in stock and stop trading. 'We will give you an occupation so you can live', do you understand. They gave me a job. [They] set me up in Lakki, and I was able to support my family, my mother, my sister and her child.

The Italians treated us better than our own. They didn't touch us at all. They didn't bully us, they gave us work. . . . I had a stall. . . . These people were Europeans, the real thing, and they looked after me. Someone else tried to do my job in Lakki and they got rid of him . . . they never gave anyone else a permit. . . .[132]

CONCLUSION

In order to define their Italian legacies, the interviewees found it useful to locate the occupiers on the symbolic scale between 'Europe' and 'the Orient', and apart from a few recalcitrant patriots, the islanders associated Italy and her achievements quite decisively with the former. This is similar to what Fascist propagandists had been preaching, that the Italians represented a modernising, western influence in the Levant. To a certain extent, Dodecanesians were implicated in this projection of Italian cultural imperialism, but they interpreted Italian achievements according to their own terms and derived their own meanings. There is little evidence to suggest the islanders were indoctrinated by Italian propaganda, nor were they 'over-awed' by stunning monuments, despite the fears of their own social elites. Certainly, the oral testimonies show the extent to which locals idealised Italian administration, order, technology, expertise, and culture, and how they associated these traits with 'progress' and 'modernity', but this reflected a convergence of interests and values rather than cultural imperialism.

When accounting for Dodecanesian nostalgia, however, the material and cultural benefits of the Italian presence were not the only factors influencing the minds of the colonised. Interviewees were equally keen to relate the nature of social relations, claiming that the Italians were very much like themselves, or that they were very civil, humane and good-humoured. The islanders felt they could co-exist quite comfortably with such people, and they constructed a stereotype of the Italian coloniser which corresponded with the Italian myth of 'brava gente'. This interest in Italian character might seem trivial when discussing colonialism, but as with other themes which interest ordinary folk, it might be trivial only from the viewpoint of what Passerini has called 'historiographical ethnocentrism'.

6 Italian Colonialism, Italian Character: Sex, Friendship and National Character

Colonialism has attracted scholars from an array of disciplines and ideological standpoints, and among this hybrid group a broad consensus seems to have been reached: *nothing* can be said for colonialism. As Nicholas Thomas recently put it, colonialism is generally regarded as 'pervasively efficacious: natives were extirpated, the impact was fatal, the colonized were dominated and assimilated'. As Thomas further notes, however, the impact of the colonisers was not nearly as pervasive and totalitarian as assumed by modern discourse.[1] For historians the implications of these limitations are important. Conquest, exploitation and resistance do not cover all that needs to be known about the colonial past, particularly if one is interested in the colonised and their experiences 'from below'. The predominant discourse does not account for the fact that in many cases, dominated peoples could find the various offerings from their colonial rulers attractive, without necessarily accepting the legitimacy of their subjugation. Other layers of history exist outside the power struggle between coloniser and the colonised, and these need to be accounted if we are to have a variegated understanding of the colonial condition.

The Greeks who lived under Italian rule resented their domination, and they much preferred being ruled by their own. The islanders were also mindful, from beginning to end, that Italian domination was sustained by the threat of brutal sanctions. Yet the following pages will show that for the colonised, the experience was also a time for self-appraisal and even self-realisation. Considerable scope existed for accepting the virtues and offerings of the dominant group; to learn, appreciate, and even be beguiled. The 'history of everyday life' approach, which has forced a general revision of Nazi Germany and Fascist Italy, reminds us that social experiences of phenomena like fascism and colonialism were complex, and that the victims of oppression not only had an existence outside the purview of the regime, but also felt entitled to accommodate agreeable aspects of the regime.

On the island of Rhodes and its tributaries, the Italians are remembered as having brought progress, from high employment and civic order to road construction and modern towns, and the islanders have freely exchanged this nostalgic view to one another and to unthreatening outsiders. The Italian Occupation can produce nostalgia as well as disturbing recollections of oppression, both fond memories and bitter feelings for their colonisers. The following pages will assess the significance of these many positive memories of social interaction. Dodecanesians were very interested in what the Italians were like 'as people' (san ánthropi), especially how the occupiers 'presented themselves' (pos ferthíkane), and how they compared to the Turks, Germans and British. In weighing up the benefits and drawbacks of foreign rule, the interviewees considered social relations between occupiers and occupied an important criterion, and therefore the 'character' of the dominant group was deemed relevant. Interviewees found that explaining the 'character' of the dominant group a useful way of evoking the character of the occupation in general.

THE MYTH OF ITALIAN 'HUMANITY'

The notion of 'character' has been important to both occupiers and occupied. This is particularly true in postwar Italy, where collective memory of colonial rule has been employed to sustain widely cherished notions of national character.[2] In the Dodecanese, local impressions of the Italians 'as people' corresponded to a popular international myth which held that the Italians were more 'humane' than other European national cultures. When it came to the treatment of colonial subjects in Africa, or occupied peoples and POWs during the Second World War, the Italians were widely reputed as more compassionate and civil. Whilst 'national character' is a rather dubious conceptual category, many respectable scholars have identified behaviour characteristic to certain peoples at certain moments in time. In attempting to explain why Italian officers risked their own lives to protect Jews during the war, Hannah Arendt raised the 'automatic general humanity' of the Italian people as an important factor.[3] As Jonathan Steinberg suggests, Italy's exceptional record in harbouring Jews is related to the propensity of

Italians not to allow 'secondary virtues', like civic duty or patriotism, to take precedence over basic human morality. Indeed, as Steinberg points out, protecting Jews became a mark of honour among Italian officers. In the dying stages of the war, as Fascist Italy verged on collapse, her 'diplomats and soldiers [seemed] even less willing to cooperate in the extermination of the Jews than before'.[4]

Cultural explanations have also been offered to account for the relatively successful social interaction between ordinary Italians and colonial subjects, especially when compared to their British and French counterparts. As Alberto Sbacchi has plausibly suggested, the Fascists introduced apartheid-styled legislation in East Africa to counter the proclivity of colonial personnel to fraternise with the indigenous peoples. The Fascists sought to instil in Italians a sense of racial and social superiority which was evidently lacking. Sbacchi claims that cordial relations with the Ethiopians were possible because the Italians had 'almost *instinctively* avoided despising or abusing the Ethiopians' (my italics).[5] In his study of colonial Somalia, Robert L. Hess gave similar reasons for why 'Italians are respected and liked in independent Somalia, as in Ethiopia, although colonialism as a whole is condemned'.[6] Luigi Preti also offered, albeit in passing, a cultural explanation for Italian behaviour in the colonies:

> In short, the native populations of the empire could expect economic benefits and protection under the law, protected perhaps by the innate humanitarianism of the Italian people....[7]

Some historians, however, such as Giorgio Rochat and Angelo Del Boca, have shown how the myth of 'brava gente' has served to conceal the many atrocities committed in the African colonies. Rochat notes that Italian colonialism has enjoyed a posthumous reputation as being non-racist and exceptionally humane, which is normally associated with the allegedly good character of the Italian people. This myth, he emphatically asserts, 'é radicalmente falsa'.[8] The concentration camps in Cyrenaica, the savagery of the conquest of Ethiopia, which included gas warfare, and the massacre at Lepkept in 1936, all go far towards discrediting the myth of exceptional humanity. But a counter-myth of Italians as exceptionally brutal will not do either. As Steinberg points out, easy generalisations about national character do not explain why the same Fascist state which introduced racial laws would later save so many Jews. Rather, Italian behaviour is best explained as arising 'from a complex matrix of institutions, traditions, habits, customs, unspoken assumptions... leadership, order and chaos'; one might equally say the same for their behaviour in the colonies.[9] If racism was the hallmark of Italian colonialism, then one would need to explain the 'familiarità' which developed among so many Italians and East Africans. The Irish novelist Gerald Hanley, who took great interest in comparing British and Italian colonialism in Somalia, claimed the latter were more willing to socialise with the colonised. The British, Hanley claimed, never made the Somalis feel socially acceptable, 'and their resentment was all in the more painful area of the most important territory, human relationships'. But towards the Italians, the Somalis held a different attitude; they 'liked the Italians, when all was taken into account; most people did when they got to know them'.[10]

In the Dodecanese, the Italian occupiers were remembered as 'good' and 'civilised' people ('ítan kalí' or 'politisméni'), who treated the islanders with courtesy and respect. Overall, the oral testimonies describe relations between Greeks and Italians as being amicable and civil. Genuine friendships were forged, intermarriage was common, and, as will be shown below, such relationships were possible because locals perceived a correspondence of values between occupied and occupiers. The Italians were seen to share similar views regarding marriage, family and honour, as well as cultural tastes, including music, singing and even romantic love. The popular phrase, 'una faccia, una razza' (literally 'one face, one race'), often heard in its Greek rendition as 'mía fátsa, mía rátsa', did not merely suggest similar 'racial' appearance, but evoked a sense of likeness. As will be shown later, the interviewees conveyed their appreciation by comparing Italians with other foreign occupiers, namely the Turks, Germans and British.

All colonial powers, including Italy, projected their *imperium* in various symbolic forms, such as in grand public ceremony and architecture. Claims to mastery were also evinced in everyday social contexts, where the colonisers asserted their haughtiness and mastery by treating 'natives' like children or lesser beings. The colonisers deemed it important to instil into the colonised the belief that the colonisers were a superior race worthy of their dominion, and this involved avoiding forms of social interaction which might reveal their human weaknesses. Social exchange and intimacy, which might have reduced the image of the coloniser from 'superhuman' to mere 'human', were discouraged or forbidden.[11] Yet as Frantz Fanon decried, the colonised were often hungry for respect and felt humiliated by their social subordination.[12] While the colonised sometimes did begin to believe they were inferior, more often they resented the coloniser's conceited claims to higher social or racial status. As will be shown below, such feelings were developed in the Dodecanese in reaction to the apparent 'coldness' of British administrators between 1945 and 1947.[13]

In his useful study on power relations, James C. Scott likens the interaction between dominant and subordinate groups to theatrical role-playing. Thus in face-to-face confrontations, the former would act in a way which consistently upheld their image of mastery, while the latter would 'render a credible performance of deference and humility'. Scott calls this open discourse between the dominant and the dominated as 'public transcript', which was quite different to what each group said 'off-stage' among themselves.[14] In the Italian Dodecanese, however, occupier and occupied would often put their 'public transcripts' aside and interact on the same social plain. This peculiarity is exploited in the popular Italian film *Mediterraneo* (1991), which considers the experiences of Italian soldiers marooned on an Aegean island during the Second World War. In this light comedy, the Italians are reluctant to play the role of fearsome invader, though they initially make some pathetic attempts to play their expected role. The local people are confident that Italians are naturally warm and friendly, and carry on with their business unperturbed. Though Greece and Italy are supposedly at war, the protagonists prefer to socialise, eat, play and even sleep together. Of course, the *familiarità* between Greeks and Italians is greatly exaggerated in the film, for the intention is to exploit a popular national myth for comic effect. Nevertheless, *Mediterraneo* is no less accurate a representation of social relations among Italy's Aegean possessions than that provided by Greek historians, who insist the 'enslaved' islanders were always zealously hostile towards their Fascist 'tyrants'.[15] Certainly, oral sources do not sustain this nationalist interpretation. Interviewees claimed it was common to find individual Italians interacting with locals on an equal level; they often revealed their 'human' side, shared their sorrow in being separated from their families, and showed photographs of their wives and children. Indeed, their failure to uphold an image of social superiority actually enhanced, rather than diminished, their reputation as colonisers. Despite the brutalities committed during the invasion and pacification of Ethiopia, 'the average Italian's generosity and kindness', claims Sbacchi, effectively won 'over the Ethiopians to the Italians'.[16] The same holds true in the

Dodecanese, where the Italians 'as people' were popular because the average Italian was regarded as 'good' and 'civilised'.

'ROMANTIC FOOLS': SEX RELATIONS AND INTER-MARRIAGE

When the colonisers projected their social superiority, one of their least convincing pretences was their ability to control their sexual needs. The British in India, for instance, expected colonial personnel to abstain from sexual relations with 'natives', at least in public, in order to promote an image of extreme discipline. Their inevitable failure to uphold this image exposed them to ridicule.[17] In contrast, the Italian colonisers seemed least capable of concealing their sexual needs. In his novel *The Consul at Sunset*, Gerald Hanley draws comparisons with the British to evoke the uniqueness of the Italian colonisers, who 'laughed more and sang more, were honest about their need for women, were friendly and did not mind sitting down in one's house for a cup of tea'.[18] This stereotypical image of Italians, however, also made them vulnerable to caricature. During the Second World War, the Italian soldiery were reputed among allies and enemies for their 'unmilitary concern with comfort and their lack of sacrificial impulse'.[19] This negative image spread to the Dodecanese, where Italian failure to defend the heavily fortified island of Leros, the so-called 'Malta of the Aegean', in 1943, astonished many local patriots. For Kostas Tourtoulis, the Italians were better suited to chasing women than martial combat. Tourtoulis felt the loss of Leros was due to this disposition:

> They were 'romantic fools' (glikogynaikádes), they did not know how to fight. If the Greeks were defending Leros, with all its armaments, the Germans would never have had a chance. Never! Never![20]

Male islanders would often joke about Italian masculinity, insinuating a propensity for cowardice. Yet such jokes concealed a feeling of insecurity among Dodecanesian men, for these 'romantic fools' posed a real threat to their monopoly on local women. The Italians represented formidable competition, for they were well-paid, well-dressed and were renowned for their courting skills. According to Ioannis Alahiotis, the suave occupiers posed a threat to the chastity of Dodecanesian women:

If a German officer came to your door, the first thing he'd do is knock on your door.... When he entered, he would only look at you. An Italian, on the other hand, would knock and then enter your home, and the first thing he would do is look at your daughters and your wife. *Then* he would look at you.[21]

More than often, however, the interviewees presented romantic foolery as an endearing quality. Local women in particular regarded Italian behaviour as something that their own menfolk would have done well to adopt. A 'romantic fool' was considered someone who knew how to please a woman, who cared for her needs, and went to great lengths to woo her. Italians were popularly regarded as 'meraklídes', which roughly translates as 'men of taste'. A 'meraklís' (singular) knew how to dress, how to dance and how to court a woman. The occupiers were remembered as well-groomed, well-shaven, neatly attired and very courteous. As Anna of Simi pointed out with a puckish smile, 'If they [the Italians] saw a girl and she was beautiful....well...they'd make themselves known....they were "romantic fools", they showed off in front of women....'[22]

Unfortunately, women interviewees preferred to keep their comments on Italian males 'off the record' because they feared their personal integrity might be questioned. Each reference to the Italian romantic foolery, however, when related either 'off' or 'on' the record, was given as a mischievous concession. Some of these women boasted that they were 'chased' (kinigísan) and were 'asked for' (mas zitoúsan) by Italians, but each of these women claimed they steadfastly rebuffed all advances. Local women were evidently flattered by all the attention, and they were obviously enchanted by Italian courting techniques. As Sevasti Kortesi of Kalymnos conveyed in her oral testimony, women deeply appreciated romantic gestures, which Italian men seem to carry on in marriage:

They were well dressed, *meraklídes*, and what song!...beautiful! There was much singing. Once we went up to Goúrnes [a neighbourhood on the island of Kalymnos] with a group of friends to listen to this Italian who sang...in his house was a woman, she had married this Italian. She loved him. His name was Mario, he was an officer, and they were married, and when things got bad he sent her to Italy for safety. But he sang to her so beautifully....[23]

Women interviewees regarded Italians as men who were predisposed to romance. Their own menfolk evidently did not share such qualities, perhaps because Dodecanesian males thought it unnecessary. Since arranged marriages were still the norm, especially among village communities, males hardly saw the need to adopt courting techniques. Nor apparently did married men take much care in their appearance or shower attention on their wives, otherwise Italian 'romantic foolery' would not have struck such a positive cord among womenfolk.

At the same time, most interviewees, male and female, claimed Italian intentions towards local women were always honourable. Formal courting required parental consent and was always supervised. Interviewees believed Italians also expected local women to remain chaste, and claimed that unchaste women were taken away and sent to the brothels. Moral integrity was something of which interviewees were wary when broaching this subject. Hence their emphasis on Italian honour, which was meant to allay any suspicions regarding the chastity of Dodecanesian women. Kalliope Harapas of Kos Town explained that the only women who were 'dishonoured' were those who actively sought to be dishonoured. Occupiers and occupied seemed to share the same moral values:

> As people they [the Italians] presented themselves very well. They did not touch any of our girls.... I remember walking freely in the street as a young girl, without ever being touched or chatted to by an Italian. If you wanted it [attention], you got it, and they would enter your house. If you did not, they would not force themselves on you. This I swear in the name of God and Man.... In short, they were a civilised people....[24]

Interviewees provided an image of sexual relations in which there was little suggestion of exploitation by the dominant group, especially as romantic liaisons were expected to lead to marriage. Parish records of the 1920s show that Italian grooms were prepared to wed in a Greek Orthodox church, and be baptised as Orthodox Christians (though clerics complained that these converts were rarely seen attending church services).[25] The colonial regime later insisted that such marriages be conducted within the Roman Catholic Church, and that Greek brides receive a Catholic education in local seminaries. This requirement, however, did not stop intermarriage. The most commonly heard phrase in the Dodecanese is 'many, many [women] were taken' (polés, polés pírane), which means many Italian grooms 'took' local brides. Anna of Simi's description is a typical representation of intermarriage in the Italian Dodecanese:

> Italian marriages?...lots. Back then, these foreigners had such a great need to marry our own girls. Oh yes. And they took them with them [back to Italy]. Now there are no differences.... They were, they were girls of good families too, not of bad families...some were poor, but I knew some, like a friend whose brother wanted to take her to America but she said 'I don't want to go to America, I want to marry him [an Italian].' There were poor families too.... If you are poor you have few choices.... I had five daughters, how was I going to give each a house [in their dowry], how could I meet these expenses? So if an Italian came along...well....[laughs].[26]

Local historians have never mentioned these marital unions; officially they would no doubt be thought of as shameful since Italians were Catholic and foreigners. The more patriotically minded islanders regarded intermarriage as collaboration, yet they would also admit to the virtues of these unions. Here again, the *morfoméni* would produce disemic responses on the topic. When asked how many mixed marriages took place in Kalymnos, Loizos Loizou instinctively asserted that there were none, though he contradicted himself later in his testimony, using the catchphrase 'many, many [women] were taken'.[27] The possibility of patriotic moral sanctions did not seem to hinder the frequency of intermarriage. On the contrary, some interviewees showed great pride in the fact that Italian men were prepared to marry local women. For Sophia Paskalis of Kos, this made them far better occupiers than the Germans, who during the war preferred to keep their distance. 'The Italians "took" many girls from here', she asserted. 'To marry, of course! Many [local girls] took Italians and got married.' In comparison, the Germans were as asexual as mules:

> The Germans were shit. The Italians were not so bad, they were good people. And any of our women who married them lived well. They were *meraklídes*. The Germans were mules. The Italians, our religion is somewhat similar, not as different as the Germans. It was the Germans, they were, they were [mules]....[28]

Once again, social memory is shown to provide subtextual commentary on social life. Paskalis's denunciation of Germans as 'mules', which was also no doubt related to German plundering of scarce food supplies, can be understood as a reflection of her dissatisfaction with traditional Greek betrothal customs. As with Anna of Simi, Paskalis noted that poor girls were often left unmarried because their families could not afford to provide dowries. Dodecanesians generally followed a matrilineal inheritance system, and contending males or families would negotiate dowries before agreeing on marriage.[29] This would often determine whether a young girl was 'taken' or left unmarried (anípantri). Interviewees, particularly women, conceded that these traditional customs were exceedingly unfair and backward, and the cause of much misery. What distinguished the Italians was their preparedness to marry women without any concern for dowry. They were admired because of their willingness to 'take' brides from poor families, though they also 'took' brides from other social classes. This break with custom, to marry for love rather than property, was widely viewed as socially progressive, a break from out-dated and barbaric custom. Here the colonial power is seen to have interceded and rectified a problem which the islanders could not do themselves.

It is difficult to tell when companionate marriages started to become popular in the Aegean, but the oral sources suggest that unarranged unions were becoming increasingly acceptable during the occupation. Serenading and eloping were not uncommon rituals in this period, and the exclusion of women from social functions was increasingly seen as a rustic or 'Turkish' trait, a sign of backwardness.[30] Kastrounis claimed he was shocked to find in the late 1930s that Kastellorizian men continued to hide their prepubescent daughters from male visitors, while Anastasios Karanastasis measured social progress in late nineteenth- and early twentieth-century Kos by the increasingly active participation of women in wedding celebrations. He claimed that among the more socially progressive villages, one would find women singing and dancing with their male partners.[31]

Even an ardent nationalist like Giorgos Kastrounis of Rhodes admitted in his interview that the Italians had a positive influence in changing dated marriage practices. Since Italians were supposed to be national enemies, however, *morfoméni* interviewees were generally ambivalent about the issue. Kastrounis initially insinuated that Italian males were left with the 'scraps', that is, all the poor and ugly women whom no one else wanted, but he then went on to admit the Italians proved to be good husbands and fathers:

I can tell you the following: They could only get the ones which were never going to get married [laughs]. If there was a girl who was a bit ugly, or if she was the poorest girl of the village, no one would take her...they [the Italians] took the girls with no hope. In those days, customs were strictly observed. Dowries were serious...you could not marry anyone you liked...and if a girl lost her virtue, was defamed, no one wanted to marry her. These girls were swept up by the Italians. They swept them up.... I can say that in Athens, where the Italians stayed for only a few months during the war, many more were swept up. You understand. More than in the Dodecanese! In every street there were always one or two [girls] who were not going to find a husband.

Those they took with them back to Italy lived well. They are 'kalogynaikádes' [another rendition of 'romantic fools']. They lived well, they took them home with them. We hear later that they raised families, educated their children. They worship their wives. They are 'kalogynaikádes'.[32]

Like Loizos Loizou, Kastrounis initially asserted that very few local women intermarried. That more intermarriage took place in wartime Athens than in thirty years of Italian Occupation on Rhodes is given as a measure of Rhodian patriotism and morality. Yet *morfoméni* and common folk alike were flattered that a members of a European, 'civilised' nation like Italy were willing to 'take' local brides. They also felt reassured that these 'civilised' people would treat their brides well. Most locals have maintained the impression that women who followed their husbands back to Italy were loved and pampered, and that these couples lived happily ever after. Giorgos Sakellaridis asserted with patriotic pride that whilst the Italians proved to be good, attentive husbands, their brides remained faithful to country of birth:

There were some social relations with the Italians, as seen in the mixed marriages which took place. There were very few of course, very few. I'll tell you this though; these men [Italians] came from good families, well-mannered men...this is quite well known...these marriages with public servants, with policemen...as a rule, the women were treated rather well. The Italians, are, of course, 'romantic fools'. Yes. They looked after them [women]. They come back here from Italy now and then...and these women are still Greek, of course.[33]

Common folk were much less ambiguous about intermarriage. The general opinion among interviewees was that these brides remained very happy (íne efharistiménes) and that 'they lived very well' (pernáne kalá). Stamatis Athanasiadis of Rhodes stressed quite clearly that intermarriage was a progressive development for Rhodian society:

> All the girls here got married. The Italians married them. Here for a girl to get married she had to have a dowry. She needed to have a house. It had to have furniture inside. Many families did not have the means to do this. So they grabbed a good man, got married, and then, after the war, they took them to Italy with them. And they all live well, they're all very happy.[34]

The absence of post-occupation reprisals, in contrast, say, to France after the German Occupation, suggested that intermarriage was not a controversial issue. Ioannis Alahiotis remembered that during 1945 he and some fellow villagers jeered at brides from another village, who were on their way to joining their husbands in Italy, but he recounted this as an embarrassing confession. He admitted that their jeering was 'barbaric', and he noted that many of these women would have otherwise remained unmarried.[35] Whatever the possible unpatriotic implications of these marriages, most Dodecanesians were convinced of their propriety. In cases of conflict between patriotic and social moral values, the latter would take precedence among common folk. As for illicit unions and rape, the oral archive provides no insight whatever. It would be very surprising if none did take place, especially during the war, but interviewees were not prepared to jeopardise the good name of their region. If we are to believe them, sexual relations in the Dodecanese did not take place outside of marriage.

There was another feature of these unions which served to bring occupiers and occupied closer. In her testimony, Kalliori Dimitriadis complained that the wealthy families of Kos forbade their children from marrying below their status in order to keep their property and social integrity intact.[36] In the Italian Dodecanese, intermarriage served to subvert the colonial power structure because it was a social leveller. Many of the occupiers now had kinfolk among the occupied, and would soon have children in common. As will be shown in the next section, other forms of social relations, such as friendships, were conducted outside the power structure, which in turn served to reduce social distances between the occupiers and occupied.

ITALIAN CIVILITY AND FRIENDSHIPS

The islanders often characterised the Italians as 'soft people' (malakí ánthropi), which meant warm, affable and kind. While foreign occupiers were normally expected to be 'hard' (sklirí) or ruthless people, the Italians were thought of as 'soft', that is, unusually charitable, friendly and merciful. The interviewees remembered having lived under both 'soft' and 'hard' occupiers, and they definitely preferred the former, partly because they left greater scope for resistance. During protests, women felt bold enough to hit, kick and throw rocks at Italian soldiers because they expected mild retribution. (Doing the same to German troops was considered inconceivable.) In his testimony, Mikhail Mihalandos of Simi recalled how he accidentally injured an Italian officer during a stone-throwing clash with a rival children's gang. He gave the following anecdote to convey the 'softness' of the Italians:

> There was upper Simi and the lower, that is, Hora and Gialo. We had separate gangs and we fought each other. We also hit others who might get in the way. One day, on the way up to Hora came two *carabinieri*, one was called Baroni, a big man, tall....
>
> We saw some kids running, so we started throwing rocks at them. And as my rock flew down – and it was a big rock too, we would fill our shirts with them – the *carabiniere* was hit right here [points to his forehead]...so we scattered like rats, quicker than rats...so they couldn't see us. The next day he wore a big bandage, and he couldn't wear his hat. He went to the pharmacy to stitch it up....They could never catch us....There were hundreds of kids up in Hora, so who would they interrogate first? [laughs]...that was what you called a 'rock war'.
>
> They weren't very tough, you know. I threw a rock at a *carabiniere*...and broke his brains [laughs]. We were children. The next day they came around but nothing much happened. What I mean to say is that they were not people who were cruel or tough....the Germans were tough, but the Italians....[37]

Mihalandos's anecdote reminds us of the mutability of stereotypes. Being characterised as 'soft' could be interpreted as either ridicule or praise, depending on the story-teller's motives.[38] Mihalandos seemed at first to boast about how he injured an Italian officer, and how his failure to exact retribution was a sign of weakness. Yet in the same breath, this 'weakness' is also presented as a positive attribute, a good human quality. Like most Italians, he seemed to be 'civilised' and 'soft', not 'cruel' like the Germans.

The general consensus among the islanders was that 'softness' was a quality to be praised, an attribute of a civilised people. The popular image of the Italians as 'soft' people corresponds somewhat to Arendt's notion of Italian 'humanity', of a people with an instinctive disposition to be civil and humane. The oral sources are full of stories which tell of Italian humanity, ranging from the massive relief effort carried out after the earthquake in Kos Town in 1933, to more basic civil gestures such as officers doffing their hats to passing women. Dodecanesians felt they could coexist comfortably with these occupiers.

The interviewees used their personal experiences to illustrate their impressions of Italian 'humanity'. Acts of kindness from individual Italians, for instance, remained fixed in personal memories. Ioannis Alahiotis remembered falling seriously ill when he was about ten years old, the year the Italians had invaded (1912). Doctors in Kos Town were unable to treat the problem, and, on the suggestion of a family friend, his father sought the advice of a doctor in the Italian military. The doctor gave Alahiotis a thorough examination and concluded that an operation was necessary. He explained, however, that he could not attend to the problem personally because he had too many other responsibilities. Alahiotis then recalled his mother suddenly bursting into tears:

> He looked at my mother and comforted her, saying, <<coraggio, coraggio>>. In Italian and Greek it means the same thing. 'Have courage, have courage'. 'I will try something' (he said), 'I will come back tomorrow and if I can do anything, well and good.'
>
> He came back the next day and conducted a real operation.... They extracted a lot of pus – I get sick when I recall all this stuff. He then tried to tell us that his operation was not completely successful, that he tried to get all the bad stuff out...he said it would take months to heal, and that he would not be here for that long.... So they took me to Kalymnos where there was a doctor, an excellent surgeon called Zervos, and he saw my wound and the way it was treated. He said, 'who did this operation on him? You don't have such good surgeons on Kos.'
>
> 'It was an Italian doctor', my father said.
>
> 'Ahh, well, now I understand. I can make the boy well, but he will have to stay here for two months. He must be cared for constantly.'

Now I ask you, how much did we pay [the Italian]? Nothing! They were true men, true professional.... I heard later that he died, in Libya I think.[39]

Alahiotis couldn't resist using this piece of nostalgia against the poor state of medical care today. While local Greek doctors had a reputation for charging enormous fees, the Italian doctor, a supposed enemy of Hellenism, saved his life and did it for free. The doctor's instinctive attempt to comfort his distressed mother confirmed in his mind that the Italians were 'humans' (ánthropi) first and Italians second. For Alahiotis, an autodidact well-read in Greek patriotic history, this and many other experiences of Italian kindness taught him to be sceptical of 'official' versions of history and foreign occupations. This made him unique amongst literate interviewees. When he began his oral testimony, he explained he wanted to recount the 'good *and* the bad things' (na poumé ke ta kalá, ke ta kaká), forewarning that he was about to flout many highly cherished national myths. He pointed out one must always be able to distinguish 'people' from the nations they represent:

I could tell you frankly that there were among them [the Italians] good people, some were better than us; more true, more innocent. But [they were good] as people, not as rulers. Not as rulers... many who had jobs, who were in official positions were dogs. But when they retired, we could later approach them, and they were nice, accommodating. They came to see how they could help you. These kind of people existed. Nowadays if you want a civil servant to help you he must be bribed. Otherwise they will not help you. As people, they [the Italians] were fine. It is one thing to be a civilian and another to be in power. Even the Turks – today they are our enemies, but it is their government which is at fault. Not all Turkish people are bad. They of course have their barbaric types, their fanatics, and they are influenced by their leaders. But these situations exist in all countries. I will not say lies and claim ours [the Greeks] are pure.[40]

Most of the islanders were careful not to conflate ordinary Italians with Mussolini's regime. Even those who suffered directly from the regime's policies, such as Gabriel Kosaris and Sophia Paskalis, whose best family properties were expropriated for colonisation programmes, nevertheless maintained that Italians were kind and friendly.[41] Similarly, historian Alberto Sbacchi claims Ethiopians had also learned to make the same distinction, and this helped save many Italian personnel from retribution when colonial rule collapsed in 1943.[42]

When German troops had withdrawn from the Dodecanese in early 1945, few Dodecanesians felt the urge to exact vengeance on the Italian administrators. Rather, locals felt obliged to reciprocate the civility long shown towards them. Christoforos Fournaris claimed in his interview that he led the charge to reclaim public buildings in Kos Town, and did so in the name of Greece. The most important of these buildings was the *podestria* (*demarchía* in Greek), where Fournaris formally notified the *podestà* that his commission was now terminated:

> I climbed first into the *demarchía*. I found the *podestà*, who happened to be a very nice man. Luigi Pistone was his name. He was traumatised by all the noise and fuss.... He was frightened. I brought our choice for the new *démarchos*:
>
> 'I introduce the new *démarchos*, Mr Koutsouradis, could you make way for him please.' He [Pistone] was trembling, he was very frightened, he said, 'Yes, its all yours.'
>
> I then said, 'Well, give us the keys to the offices, the insignias, everything. And I will take you home.'
>
> He thanked me, gave me a big hug...I told him, 'Don't be frightened, you silly man'....Anyway, he voluntarily gave up...and so I took him down the stairs, with great respect, 'after you sir', and 'if you please'. I was very respectful.

Fournaris was keen to point out in his interview that the transition was conducted in a civilised manner. The courtesy shown towards the former *podestà* was meant to convey how locals were civilised and hence responsible enough to assume control of their own affairs. Unfortunately a group of thugs decided to attack Pistone as he left the building:

> There was this fellow, Tsakalis – one of 'ours' [sighs] – who wanted to show how 'patriotic' he was...he hit him with a piece of wood. But he [Pistone] was a good man and a good Christian! I gave him a hanky so he could clean the blood. I said to them [Tsakalis and company], 'Who should I first hit? You should be ashamed of yourselves.' I got him as far as his home. He begged me to stay with him. 'Stay with me.' I was obliged to stay and look after him for a while....[43]

Tsakalis's actions, which were considered unnecessarily barbaric, reflected badly on the community's reputation. In any case, as Fournaris pointed out, Pistone was a 'good man', one who had enjoyed a good rapport with many of the local inhabitants. Fournaris seemed intent on *fare una bella figura*, to conduct the transition in a proper and civilised manner. In most cases, interviewees would assert that most Dodecanesians did not retaliate against their former occupiers as 'barbarians' might, while Tsakalis's clumsy attempts to express his patriotism merely exposed his moral failings.

Most of the islanders would also disapprove of the rough behaviour of Greek troops who arrived a few days later, whose treatment of Italian prisoners was considered unnecessarily harsh. Soldiers went through a ritual of smashing and defacing Italian monuments, throwing office furniture into the streets, and beating Italian administrative personnel and un-armed soldiers. The chaos frightened many of the locals. Archondoula Kanaris recalled how a desperate young Italian soldier approached her during the mayhem and begged for sanctuary. Recalling the turmoil brought tears to her eyes:

When the war ended, then the Greeks came. They had three days to do as they pleased, that is 'our' boys. The airplanes dropped bombs, they made noise, they tried to wreck the cinema, and anywhere they saw Italians, they'd hit them, using their weapons....Eh, there where I was standing, near the cinema, I saw all these bad things happening – they threw all this lovely furniture out the window.

There where I was standing, I saw a soldier. He shouted, <<Mamma, mamma, aiutami>>. 'Mother, help me', he said. He cried like a young boy. <<Signora, aiutami>>. I remember this boy like it was today, and I weep. What could I do? We had our shop near there. I told him to come with me. I hid him under a bunk, and I told him, 'Don't come out'. He cried. <<Mamma mia, signora, aiutami>>. They were going to hit him.

A Greek soldier came looking for him. He said, did you see an Italian soldier around here? My husband came around to find out what was happening. I told him they wanted this young boy and that they wanted to kill him. I hid him....

Later that day I went back to the shop and took him out of the shop. We took him to the place where they were holding the other Italian prisoners. They [the prisoners] were happy to see him alive.

Did this boy do anything wrong? He said <<Non dimenticare niente (*sic*)>>. 'I will never forget you', he said to me. <<Grazie, mille grazie>>, they shouted, all of them [prisoners]. He was a mere child. I will never forget this. The crying I did.... [44]

Kanaris had worked for many years in her husband's café and was on amicable terms with many Italian customers. The specific situation of the young man prompted an instinctively humane reaction. Decades of friendly relations had taught Italians and islanders to view each other more 'as people' (san ánthropi) than as national foes. This was born out in numerous war stories from the German occupation, in which locals risked their own lives in sheltering pro-Badoglio officers, or smuggling them to Turkey.[45] Less sympathy was shown towards the Jews of Rhodes and Kos, whom the Germans would dispatch to the death camps. Many interviewees remembered how Jewish families were assembled into the piazzas before deportation, but each interviewee conveyed a detached feeling of pity rather than moral outrage. Greeks, Turks and Jews had lived peacefully together in Rhodes and Kos for centuries, but their social worlds had remained segregated. Intermarriage was rare, and social relations were minimal, save, as one interviewee put it, for the exchange of a polite ' "Good day", that is all' (mia kaliméra, aftó ítane).[46]

In contrast, relations between individual Greeks and Italians have been characterised in oral tradition as warm and interactive. Despite official nationalist disapproval of social relations with 'the enemy', male interviewees, including many *morfoméni*, were prepared to discuss their friendships in some detail. As the oral sources indicate, the islanders were touched, indeed flattered, that their occupiers were prepared to treat them as equals. For instance, they liked the fact that Italians would sometimes share their personal concerns with them. When Italy itself became a battleground in 1943, many Italians based in the Dodecanese began to worry about the safety of their loved ones. Mikhail Mihalandos recalled an encounter with an Italian friend who happened to be wandering around the main harbour of Simi, pensively awaiting news about his family:

I went to work in the *Ronda*, now it's the *Eli*,...it was a hotel...it was built near the harbour...it is called the *Eli* now....I worked in the kitchen like many other Simians, and the cook, he was Giovanni from Milan, and he was a good man...he came to Simi, but he seemed a worried, depressed man. I said,

'What is wrong, Giovanni?'. He said, 'I don't know what is happening with my family.' He had a wife and two children, and he wondered what had happened to them. He told me to stay in Simi because they were bombing Rhodes, he said 'Stay here'....they were good people, good as civilians...there was another Italian here, some soldiers...at the customs house...these were good people.[47]

The fact that their respective countries were at war didn't greatly affect their personal relationships, especially as 'Giovanni' seemed to be a normal person, who, like Mihalandos, worried deeply about his family and wanted to share his concerns. Hence these occupiers, this ruling 'people', were also normal people, and drew a mixture of admiration and sympathy among the occupied Greeks. As with the other interviewees, Mihalandos believed Greeks and Italians were *una faccia, una razza*, two cultures which not only looked alike, but shared many other traits as well. This feeling was particularly conveyed in memories of inter-ethnic friendships.

These friendships, which were largely a male phenomenon, were sometimes explained by interviewees on the basis of shared social interests. Gabriel Kosaris fondly remembered one particular officer who, like him, loved the French language and playing musical instruments:

> There was an Italian fellow who loved to speak in French, and he always tried to find me when he came to the village. He wanted to practise his French because he did not know the language well. He wanted '*conversation*'. There was another thing. He liked to play the mandolin. I used to play in front of audiences. I played a very difficult number, the 'French Spirit' (*sic*). Very difficult. I used to play this with him. Because this Italian – well most of them – played musical instruments....
>
> ....He was an officer, but he was also a philhellene! In fact they reprimanded him once. I said to myself, if this was not a spy, he must have Hellenic roots. That was how much he loved us. He learned to speak and write in Greek...he would still write to me until about five years ago. He said of the Greeks when he went back to Italy, 'What kind of people did we try to conquer?.'
>
> Well, he played the mandolin very well. And he would come up and we would play music a lot. If I picked up a mandolin now I don't know if I could make music, but back then I was a master.[48]

Conscious that such friendships might be interpreted as collaboration, *morfoméni* and autodidacts like Kosaris would assert that their Italian friends were either secret philhellenes or anti-fascists. Kosaris implied that politics was not a factor in these relationships, and that in any case, Greeks and Italians were so much alike that they should never have been pitted against each other.

Indeed, nationalism seemed too solemn a subject to be associated with social relationships, which were usually characterised by fun and laughter. Though a *morfoménos* and ardent nationalist, Basil Galettis's oral testimony was full of references to bantering, jokes, and what he called 'good company' (kalés parées). The formal political realities were temporarily disregarded, as Galettis remembered teasing his Italian friends without fear of recrimination. The point of contention in the following anecdote is the official prohibition on blue-and-white colour clothing, but Galettis's purpose in retelling this story was to show how friendship took precedence over politics and nationalism:

I was over-seeing some workers in the cemetery. I woke up one afternoon after my *siesta* and went over to check on the workers. But to get there I had to pass by the school. There in the schoolyard I saw the principal walking around – of this man I have to tell the following; he was a good man and we played billiards together – then this sailor came up to us and said, 'Did you know that Hitler has invaded Austria, and that Mussolini has sent troops to the north [of Italy]?'

The principal said to me, 'What am I to do, I'm more Austrian than Italian.' [laughs]

Then I went up to the graveyard with the principal, and he noticed some of the men were wearing blue.

'They can't wear these colours. This is forbidden.'

I said, 'Leave these fellows alone.'

'No, they must change.'

I decided to scold him. 'Why? I have a neck-tie at home sent to me from Australia, but I can't wear it because it is blue-and-white. Your tie is blue, isn't it?'

'My blue is different.'

'What do you mean, it's different?'

'No, no....'

'Look, what ever you do, you can't eliminate blue, for the sea is blue, and the waves make white [foam], and at night the sky is

blue and the stars are white.'
'I will report you and have you thrown into gaol...'
Then I said, 'Yes, but "*I'm more Austrian than Italian*".'
Then he said, 'Well, *paesano*, we won't worry about it.' We
laughed a lot.[49]

In this encounter, shared humour defused a situation which might
have led to conflict. The Italian momentarily felt duty-bound to
punish the culprits, which would have had friends revert to using
their formal 'public transcripts'. However, Galettis's humorous
comment reminded the Italian of their friendship, and as if to
re-confirm their sense of likeness and congeniality, Galettis was re-
affirmed as a '*paesano*'.

These friendships could also be a forum in which Italians and
Greeks shared seditious ideas and sentiments. Galettis remembered
another Italian friend stationed on Kastellorizo, who told him many
anti-Fascist jokes:

They were good company, the Italians. They told me, 'Don't say
anything against Italy, and against Mussolini, because, if they
report you, we'll have to put you in.'
Then I said, 'Listen, friend, don't worry.'
'Can I tell you something which is anti-Fascist?'
I said, 'What do you want to tell me?'
'A woman goes to the doctor and says, "My husband is
incapable of doing anything [sex]."'
[Doctor] 'When you go home, sing to him when he wakes up.
Sing "Avanti, avanti, sano fascismo, contro il comunismo."'
She goes to her husband. He wakes up. She sings this to him.
One day, two days, three days pass, and nothing happens. She
goes back to the doctor. 'Oh doctor, I did what you told me to
do but nothing happened.'
'That is strange! With this song Fascism brought Italy back to
life in 1922, how could it not bring your husband to life?' [laughter]
This story was told to me by a *maresciallo*. He told me in
confidence. He would not betray me if I did not betray him.
[more laughter][50]

The Italians had gained a reputation for being good-humoured, and
this included Mario Lago himself, who would share his wit when
mingling with civilians. Gabriel Kosaris remembered another good-
humoured Italian official in Kos Town named 'Farina', who struck up

a rapport with crowds protesting against food shortages some time before the German invasion. He defused the tension by making a pun on his name, which literally means 'flour':

> Then we got hungry, and so people would go outside his office and shout, <<Vogliamo, Farina>>, 'We want Farina, we want to eat.' And you know what he did? He came out on his balcony and said, <<Eccomi>>, 'Here I am, eat me up.' <<Mangiatemi>>. Everyone laughed.....[laughs][51]

Formal distinctions between occupier and occupied were rendered meaningless within contexts of friendship. Epaminondas Diamandaras worked as a young boy in his grandfather's café in Alinda, Leros, where most of his clientele were Italian soldiers. He remembered how Italians would often come to the café, and how he was on friendly terms with many of them. Diamandaras recalled one incident in which his grandfather was forced to punish a drunken soldier:

> Once I remember there was a man in the café called 'o begrís' [the drunkard], and I remember he always wanted his glass filled to the top. He'd say 'I don't want a *colleto*, *collaro* [he wanted it filled], up to the top.' This did not suit me, to fill his glass. It would cost me more. Once he was very drunk, and I didn't fill his glass, so he started chasing me around the café. He wanted to grab me and hit me. My grandfather saw us – I was still very young – my grandfather grabbed him and started to slap him in the face until he came to his senses. My grandfather said, 'Don't come into my café again.' The others in the shop then began to scold the *begrís* as well.... [52]

The other Italians in the café did not regard the proprietor's actions as an affront to Italian authority. Instead, they agreed that the *begrís* deserved to be punished and brought to his senses. That he was punished by the Greek proprietor, one of the occupied, was immaterial. For the Greeks, and so it seemed for the Italians, friendship negated all other forms of social division, and affirmed a feeling of commensal solidarity. Friendship represented a kind of 'antistructure' in which Greeks and Italians felt free to exchange their concerns, feeling and ideas without fear of official sanctions.[53] These relationships confirmed in local minds that Greeks and Italians were *una faccia, una razza*, people with similar feelings, tastes and values.

'SOUTHERNERS' AND 'FASCISTS'

Despite the power of Greek national history and ideology, which brands all foreign occupiers of Greek soil as villains, the Dodecanese islanders continue to maintain that Italians were 'humane'. Even remote villages and isolated islets, which had little contact with the occupiers, came to accept the stereotype as a truism. It stands to reason, however, that this stereotype did not always accord with reality. Many Italians encountered in everyday life did not fit the standard image; some were no doubt rude, uncouth, brutal and imperious. Indeed interviewees were keen to show that relations were not always good, and they accounted for un-stereotypical Italians by devising separate categories which allowed them to retain more differentiated and credible memories.

Italian colonists, for instance, many of whom were brought from Italy's impoverished south, were regarded by locals as 'backward' and 'un-European'. The islanders had little previous knowledge about these people, as there had been little economic, cultural or historical contact between the Dodecanese and southern Italy. The islanders had nevertheless adopted the prejudices of their occupiers, for these 'backward' types were disparagingly described by interviewees as 'southerners'. To be sure, some islanders harboured resentment against them, especially locals who had been displaced by land expropriation policies, but more often the interviewees were concerned about the apparent cultural 'backwardness' of these colonists. In Kos Town, locals were shocked when colonists were seen eating raw whitebait in the marketplace. Eating raw meat or fish was regarded as primitive, something not expected of 'civilised' Europeans. As Kalliroi Dimitriadis recalled, these people seemed so uncultivated that they must have come 'from the mountains' (ápo ta vouná):

> I don't know from where they brought these people, eh... 'from the mountains'. They would grab a whitebait and just swallow it whole! We would look at them and get sick. My insides would start to turn upside down as I watched them. They ate these raw! Raw! I don't know how they could do it.[54]

Such was the impression made that nearly all interviewees from Kos Town invoked the 'whitebait' story.[55] In his oral testimony, Christoforos Fournaris tried to explain why the colonists were so backward and so unlike most Italians:

They also built colonies. They brought citizens, they brought people here from southern Italy...from Bari, Brindisi and Calabria, they built many homes for them....

They would come into town to shop, but they appeared to be in a terrible state. I mean in cultural ways, they were very backward. They were Italians from the south; Italians themselves look down on them! From what I have learned from the Italian [television] channel, there is a kind of racism there. This exists today....

They were this [low class]..., they looked it,...eh, nice people, but this all looked very strange to us, that is, what I have to tell you,....

There was a fish shop here in the harbour...I saw this with my own eyes. They would buy whitebait and they would eat it like that [raw]...and I thought to myself, 'are they *that* hungry', poor wretches [laughs]. I remember this quite clearly.... [56]

On Leros, 'un-Italian' types were singled out among imported labourers, who were also seemed to be from the Mezzogiorno. For Giorgos Valsamis, their cultural 'depravation' had to do with their low standard of education, and he further claimed that these 'backward' Italians regarded the people of Leros as under-class rivals:

I'll tell you, educated Italians were good people. The others were a little fanatic. The workers, they were a bit rough,...but there were many educated Italians, as well as Fascists, who were nasty.... Generally speaking the 'enemies' came from the lower orders...they were anti-Greek.... workers brought in from the ports of Italy...but they competed amongst each other to show who was more patriotic.

This was the standard set by Mussolini...as soon as Mussolini fell they changed completely...and of course when they did change sides, the Greek people of Leros decided to give them sanctuary, feed them, looked after them, and so forth...we showed that we were very humane.... [57]

The most unpopular Italians were the Fascists. Like Haile Selassie, who in 1961, in a spirit of *rapprochement*, proclaimed that Italians and Fascists were different altogether, Dodecanesians formulated a separate character typology to account for those who donned the *camicia nera*. Governor Cesare de Vecchi (1936–1941) was remembered as the quintessential Fascist. In attempting to convey the oppressive nature of De Vecchi's governorship, Denis Mack

Smith claimed the *Quadrumviro* was so nasty that 'even the Duce was moved to anger at his incompetence and inhumanity'.[58] Dodecanesians would regard these comments as an exaggerated characterisation of the period, though they did feel De Vecchi's 'Fascist' rule was uncivilised and hardly what they expected of Europeans. The more oppressive conditions of De Vecchi's governance had locals associate these conditions with Fascism, and hence they would remember this period as the time 'when Fascism came' (ótan írthen o fasismós). Kostas Tourtoulis, a café owner in Leros in the late 1930s, remembered what happened to troublemakers under the Fascists:

> If they knew that your café was anti-Italian, they would turn the café into a wreck. From the time we heard of news of war in Albania [1941], we never left our homes at night. We hid safely inside. They'd kill you! The Fascists especially, who wore the black shirt, with a black hat, they were truly 'Fascists'. If they caught you saying, 'Hey Alex', or anything else [in Greek], they would hit you with a rifle butt. They were always armed.[59]

Most Dodecanesians had a limited understanding of Fascism as a political movement and ideology, though some interviewees drew parallels with the Metaxas dictatorship and that of the Greek Colonels. Broadly speaking, 'Fascism' was popularly associated with oppression and not with Italian civility and humanity. The De Vecchi period did not draw nostalgic memories. Interviewees talked of incarceration for speaking Greek in public, of being smacked in the face by black-shirted Fascists for wearing a blue-and-white coloured tie, or for failing to doff one's hat as De Vecchi's cavalcade rode by.[60] The Fascists seemed determined to affirm Italian mastery and power, and did so in rather brutal ways. Even for *morfoméni* like Giorgos Sakellaridis, Fascist style was not 'Italian':

> It is true of the Italians that they are a civilised people. In fact, Fascism was accepted and fought for by only a minority of Italians. Many Italians had democratic feelings, and many of these 'democrats' were sent here.... Mussolini characterised these men as unworthy.... <<*Italiani cola cola*>>(*sic*) he called them.
> That is why they were easy people to get on with.... And they were very good people. They were anti- Fascist.... Many of them have come back here since the war to see the place, to meet again with old friends....[61]

In creating a separate 'Fascist' category, however, Dodecanesians affirmed their fondness for Italians in general. Those who wore the *camicia nera* were regarded as wholly different people; they were the thugs and vagrants, the village idiots of Italy. Unlike normal 'Italians', Fascists did not have manners or a sense for *fare una bella figura*. Fascist pretension and ostentation became a source of ridicule for Italian anti-Fascists and Dodecanesians alike. Jokes abound. One of the most popular subjects was De Vecchi's well-publicised status of *Quadrumviro*. De Vecchi made an official visit to a school in Lindos, Rhodes, to see how much progress had been made in Italian language skills. During the inspection, one child was asked to say something of De Vecchi and his place in Italian history. The child replied: 'He is one of the *quadropede* [four-legged ones] of the Fascist Revolution.'[62] De Vecchi had become a figure of fun, and as Athanasiadis explained, most people believed he had delusions of grandeur (fantasía), as exemplified by his ridiculously long name:

> I was riding around on my bicycle, on my way to the village. As I heard his car horn being blown from far away, I'd press the brakes hard, get off my bike, and stand still until De Vecchi came up, and do this [the Fascist salute], and then I'd get on with it. [Laughter] He was a 'crazy-house'...do you know how many names he had? Do you know?.... 'Cesare Maria de Vecchi di Val Cismon', 'Cesare Maria de Vecchi di Val Cismon'....[Laughter]
>
> De Vecchi, when he would come out of his doorway – he had a driver, you know – anyhow, the driver would blow his horn from far away, and the people would be notified that De Vecchi's car was near. And we had to, as he came near, we would do this [the Fascist salute], and if you did not, they'd grab you here [by the collar], and they'd drag you in [to gaol]. The salute was a kind of greeting...De Vecchi was crazy...the people did not like him. He was mean; a bad dog...we had to endure bad times with him.[63]

Locals greatly resented De Vecchi's policy of forced assimilation, and as shown in Chapter 3, they regarded his rough methods as counter-productive. Unlike Mario Lago, who sought to win hearts, De Vecchi, spoiled any chance of assimilation by fostering popular indignation and discontent. As the following anecdote told by Giorgos Kastrounis shows, locals were bemused by De Vecchi's insistence on meaningless ceremony:

We would get orders sent to the village, that De Vecchi was touring the villages. An Italian policeman would come [to the village], and he'd say, 'Quickly, get everyone into the village square, because De Vecchi is coming.' Okay. It is about seven or eight in the morning, okay. We'd stop, we'd assemble in the main square in an orderly way. But when would he come?...at one o'clock in the afternoon...or two in the afternoon, or three.

You understand! All the villages would stand in a line for him....[64]

While De Vecchi was associated with 'Fascism', his more popular predecessor Lago was associated with things 'Italian'. The latter was regarded as a benevolent, warm-hearted man, and at the same time, more politically skilled, diplomatic and persuasive. To many politically minded islanders, this made him more dangerous than de Vecchi. Lago, claimed Ioannis Alahiotis, could disarm anyone 'with a smile'. When asked to describe De Vecchi, Alahiotis prefaced his answer by describing the responsibilities of governorship and why Lago fitted the bill. Lago was a better 'politician' because he sought to secure respect and popular consent, and after attaining this consent, Lago could do as he pleased. His finesse and charm showed how 'Italian' he was:

We had governors, and they passed laws as well...they needed someone who could rule civilians, not just the military...a man called Mario Lago came. He had, as it appeared – well, they say his wife was a member of the royal family, and for this reason they had appointed him to this big job, and he had titles. He was a senator. He had some political experience, so they sent him here. He came here [to Kos] many times; he was tall, with a big red moustache, he was gregarious, and when he passed by, whether you were Jew or Turk, he would greet you with a warm smile, with 'good feeling' (me hará). His wife did the same....

Now, as a ruler – he was an educated man – he tried to introduce Italian [language] slowly, slowly. This the people accepted readily. 'Now he wants to educate us, hooray,' we'd said. Everyone saw him with a 'good eye' (me kalómáti).

Mario Lago...to me he was a more dangerous man [than De Vecchi] because he was a very clever man, a good diplomat, a good manipulator (katafertzís), yes. He could convince you that black is white [laughs]; we even said we were lucky to have him, and yet he was our enemy....[65]

De Vecchi was Lago's antithesis. Lago sought to get his way with 'kindness' (me to kaló) and 'slowly, slowly' (sigá, sigá), like a 'diplomat', a term which in this context denotes 'clever manipulator'. De Vecchi, on the other hand, failed because he used threats and violence. The islanders certainly regarded Fascism as a 'parenthesis' or an aberration of Italian rule in the Dodecanese. They saw De Vecchi as an unworthy representative of an otherwise civilised people, and the Fascist Party as a bandwagon or haven for Italian ruffians and layabouts. Only Italy's marginal types were presumed to have joined the Fascist party, and as Sakellaridis eloquently explained, De Vecchi and Fascism changed the character of the occupation:

> Initially, Mussolini would send people he did not like to the Dodecanese. Therefore we had educated people here, good people. Upper class, well intentioned. So the people here looked upon them with great sympathy.... When, however, Mussolini started to think about empire, then things changed. The people he sent initially, in 1922, 1923, 1924, he started to recall, and in their place he sent his own [Fascists]. They were brutes, ugly people. Mussolini wanted to make the Dodecanese a... a vantage point from which he could implement his plans... and things changed.
>
> Many smarter Italians would tell us that De Vecchi was not sent here by Mussolini because he was good, but because he wanted to get rid of him. Because he made a mess of any position entrusted to him, like education....[66]

When describing the transition from 'Italian' to 'Fascist' rule, interviewees claimed that inter-ethnic relations had deteriorated. The popular phrase 'we were doing well' (prín ta pigéname kalá) conveyed how Lago's regime seemed to promote social harmony between occupiers and occupied, but, as the interviewees would point out, then came the Fascists and 'things were spoiled' (hálasan ta prámata). The occupiers, who were once characterised as 'civil' and amiable, now began to treat the occupied as social inferiors. The good relationship which had prevailed under Mario Lago was seen to have been 'spoiled'.

OTHER 'EUROPEANS': GERMANS AND BRITISH

By claiming the Fascists had spoiled occupier–occupied relations, interviewees showed how far they appreciated the relationship. This appreciation was also conveyed through comparisons made between Italians and other occupiers. This section will consider, albeit briefly, Dodecanesian perceptions of the Germans and British 'as people', and how the interviewees employed these comparisons to illuminate their perceptions of 'humane' Italians.

The Wehrmacht earned a rather fearsome reputation during the Second World War, a reputation which had preceded it before assuming control of the Dodecanese in May 1943.[67] The islanders were nevertheless shocked by the ferocity which marked its arrival. When it came to ruthlessness, even the Fascists were no match for Germans. Marigo Katris remembered the way in which pro-Badoglio officers based on Astypalea were massacred:

> they took those poor Italians and drowned them, they drowned them, they put them in boats and then a plane came down and dropped a bomb on them...we had many fears, many fears...we saw hunger, great sadness....[68]

Dodecanesians were so frightened by the Wehrmacht that they dismissed any thought of open protest or armed resistance. As Katris pointed out, 'we were afraid of them, we were afraid of Germans, but with the Italians we lived quite well'. The new occupiers had made their position regarding sedition quite clear; severe retribution followed any transgression of German authority, and they did not hesitate setting early examples. Kalliroi Dimitriadis claimed she could not forget the sight of a pregnant woman, accused of sending radio messages to the Allies, hanging from a tree in a Kos Town piazza. Her body was deliberately left hanging for days.[69] Giorgos Giorgalos of Asklepion, Rhodes, remembers being chosen for execution when he and others from his village refused to divulge the name of a spy. Only a twist of fate saved them:

> I knew an Italian, and he was a spy. He used to send messages to the English. One day, without warning, they [the Germans] gathered twenty of us in this main square...to kill us. We had our hands up. They wanted us to tell them where the spy was. We knew where he was, but we were scared to tell them. You know, if you told them, you were implicated too, you know what I mean. So the Germans came to kill, but our luck had it that a German woman came along...she was a friend of this Italian...and she got us off the hook....

....it was a cruel life, the Germans would even kill women.
And if they took your mule away, you couldn't say a word in
protest.[70]

Comparisons between Italians and Germans made the latter seem
exceptionally fearsome. The general impression was that Italians were
not inclined to kill, whereas Germans seemed to think nothing of it.[71]
The islanders had no illusions as to whether the Germans would carry
out their threats of retribution. This was exemplified by the local
maxim, 'Kill one German, and the Germans kill ten
[Greeks]' (skótones éna Germano, aftí skótonan déka).[72] As
Fournaris showed in his testimony, the new occupiers were seen as
merciless:

The 'German-arades' were not cruel people.[73] But they were very
disciplined. If you disobeyed their rules, they punished with great
severity. To set an example, during the first few days of their
arrival, two men started a fight, one was a shepherd, a bit crazy,
the other was another villager. They hanged them both – this was
a cruel thing! To see a hanging for the first time in your life is an
unforgettable thing. One day I happened to be at church. I was
helping the priest inside the altar. The priest said to me, 'They
hanged the shepherd Kapiri from Antimachia.'
My blood curdled.... I left the church of St Paraskevi, I went
outside, and I see in the marketplace, hanging off a large fig tree,
the shepherd.... They had a sign hanging off him, saying that he
had committed an offence in wartime.... Then they were about
to hang the other man. This man had already looked half dead
from his imprisonment, beatings and hunger...they [the
Germans] played a death march, just like in the movies...they
asked him if he had last words. He cried, 'My children!'[74]

That the occupiers were prepared to execute two civilians for merely
quarrelling testified to the severity of German authority. Order was
maintained with extreme measures. There was no room for pity or
clemency.

Yet the Germans were not regarded as 'uncivilised' as say the
Turks. As there was no armed resistance movement among the
islands, there was no 'barbarisation' of war, or war against civilians
in the Dodecanese, except against the Jewish community.[75] Oral
sources from the Dodecanese depict the Germans as harsh but fair,
zealous in the application of rules, but harbouring no animosity

against the Greek 'race'. The Germans were regarded as dispassionate, arbitrary and impartial. For patriot Giorgos Kastrounis, there was some consolation in the fact that the Greeks had been defeated by worthy adversaries who were not anti-Greek:

> With 'the German', we had no real historical relations, they were only here to enforce their laws. [The German] is a hard fighter, a hard master, and he did not want anyone to bother him, to break his laws, his plans.... They were tougher, more threatening.... The Italians were softer, less threatening. We were not scared of the Italians...the Germans looked upon 'the Greek' as a Greek. He did not hate 'the Greek'.... Only if you got in his way did he...during the war, the Germans did not stop us from teaching Greek....[76]

The islanders often described the typical German soldier in superhuman terms; he was typecast as a machine, a robot devoid of human frailties and weaknesses. He was tall, highly disciplined and courageous, with a propensity to kill anyone when given the order, even women and children. Such was their discipline that Germans seemed almost impervious to local women. In the Dodecanese, German troops were forbidden from engaging in any sexual relations with local womenfolk, and as Antonis Stergalas sought to point out, the Germans applied this rule very strictly:

> As for honour, well, they would not touch any of our women. They were indeed honourable. They never touched one. One soldier followed a girl in Antimachia. She was about to draw water from a well which was a little further out [from the village]. As soon as she went to draw water, the German grabbed her from behind. She screamed very loudly, and was heard by, eh, an officer, who came around. The officer killed him on the spot! Do you believe it!...
> The Italians could not even spare a male cat during wartime.... But he [the German officer] killed him cold to set an example. This happened in Antimachia.[77]

In avoiding sexual relations, the Germans were thought to be respecting the honour of local womenfolk, but as Mark Mazower has shown, the Wehrmacht believed that contacts with local women threatened 'security, physical health and racial purity; to direct feelings towards them that were more properly kept for German women was thought to threaten the soldier's will to act with the necessary harshness towards the enemy'.[78] Much as in Occupied France, where Germans 'were enjoined to present a correct but firm appearance', in the Dodecanese the Germans were thought of as well-behaved and honourable men.[79] Any resentment harboured against the Germans was related to competition for scarce resources, especially food. Sevasti Kortesi described the Germans as 'disgusting people' because they had taken food she had stored in her home, though she also added that they were honourable. 'They did not touch our women', she claimed, 'only those [women] who wanted it.'[80]

The British, whom locals referred to as 'the English' (i Egglézi), were also frequently compared to the Italians in the oral sources. General impressions of the British 'as people' were formed during the period of temporary British administration between 1945 and 1947, and though the administration shipped in desperately needed food supplies, and had transported many refugees to and from the Middle East, the British 'as people' were not very popular.

Memories of 'the English' have no doubt been influenced by anti-British sentiments since the war, especially among left-wing Greeks, who believe Britain had precipitated the Greek Civil War and had a hand in the Turkish invasion of Cyprus in 1974.[81] Yet politically conservative interviewees also gave negative representations of the British. 'We considered the English presence here as if it were another occupation', argued Christoforos Fournaris, 'because they wanted to impose their own laws, as they did earlier in Cyprus.' Though British administration was promised to end once the fate of the islands had been determined by the United Nations, many locals feared British administration might become permanent. Pantelis Tripolitis explained in his testimony that patriotic Dodecanesians were preparing for a political struggle:

When they came, they established the British Military Administration [BMA]. They established port control, their own police, many of whom were Cypriots, and some of our boys who returned from the Middle East, they served as police too. Then they printed their own currency, with BMA on it . . . and their own stamps. They tried to establish an autonomous Dodecanese, but they found no local support. We would not have it . . . . With their [British] appetite for staying, the Dodecanesians got upset. In 1945–6, the people were very enthusiastic for unification . . . . Then we had a plebiscite...we marched on their headquarters, with placards, with flags, 'We want Greece'...we established a secret movement...this happened in every island. There was not one wall which did not have our graffiti on it. This was all designed to keep the Hellenic flame alight....[82]

The British were seen to be frustrating local aspirations for unification with Greece, as well as refusing to involve locals in the postwar administration. These issues served to ferment animosity among local patriots for 'the English', who were increasingly regarded as new enemies.

Frustrated political aspirations fostered the construction of a negative stereotype of the British 'as people'. 'The English' are popularly characterised in oral tradition as patronising, dismissive and rude, and most interviewees described the new 'occupiers' as 'cold people' (kríi ánthropi), which could mean aloof, distant and unfriendly. The most commonly heard catchphrase was 'the English were cold people' (i Egglézi ítan kríi ánthropi). The following anecdotes show how British unpopularity was related to their perceived lack of 'human' qualities, which set a contrast to the stereotypical Italian.

Giorgos Kastrounis expected the British would treat the Greek population with respect, given that Britain and Greece were wartime allies. He admitted the British brought greatly needed food relief to Kastellorizo, where he spent most of the war, but be resented what seemed to be their 'sahib' mentality. In the following anecdote, Kastrounis remembered how hungry children appeared to be treated like vagrants:

> They were cold people. They treated us as they would Indians or Africans. I remember one day, sipping coffee in the harbour, when I saw two officers sitting at a table, eating biscuits. One of them had dropped a biscuit on the ground, and a little boy ran over to grab it. So do you know what one of them did? He stepped on his hand, and started to crush his hand. And they were laughing!... I ask you, why, if the biscuit is on the ground, would you step on his hand? Only very cold people could do such a thing. The boy was hungry![83]

The British were commissioned to administer the Dodecanese Islands until their future was settled by the United Nations, and the maintenance of law and order, in the face of increasing political unrest, did require the British to apply a firm hand. Yet it is likely that many British personnel did bring a 'sahib' mentality to the administration, which caused much resentment amongst locals. Locals felt the British regarded them as mere subject peoples, if not inferior beings. Any superiority complex held by the occupiers was not lost on the occupied, who deeply resented its implications.

Kalliroi Dimitriadis tried to convey the notion of British 'coldness' by focusing on their apparent ingratitude. She recalled how she and her sister assisted a number of British soldiers stranded among the Dodecanese Islands after the abortive Allied invasion in early 1943. She claimed they also helped Italian soldiers escape, giving them boats in order to get to the Turkish coast. While these Italians would send them letters of thanks long after the war had ended, she claimed they received nothing from the British:

> Do you know how many English and Italians we got across to Turkey, my sister and I? How many we got across [to Turkey]? The Italians still send us letters, thanking us. Even today! But the English...nothing! Not one letter of thanks. What ungrateful people! What cold people![84]

Locals believed the national 'character' of the occupiers determined the nature of the occupation; thus the fearsome and austere Germans made their occupation a terrifying experience, while the apparent 'coldness' and imperiousness of 'the English' explained the tension and animosity which dominated the period of British administration. In both cases, German and British rule involved a strict social demarcation between occupiers and occupied. *Familiarità* with the occupied was not encouraged, and as the oral testimonies suggest, ordinary German or British personnel did not seem willing to interact on their own accord. What distinguished the Italians was their propensity to interact and promote *familiarità*, which the islanders duly appreciated.

CONCLUSION

In using 'character' to explain the nature of foreign rule, the interviewees point us towards a neglected factor in power relations in colonial contexts. Social alienation was an intrinsic feature, for as

Fanon claimed, colonial exploitation included the process of instilling a feeling of inferiority among the colonised, which served to make colonialism a humiliating and wounding experience.[85] With their proclivity to interact with the colonised, the Italians 'as people' served to mitigate the alienating effects of foreign rule on the occupied. Inter-ethnic friendships and intermarriage, for instance, served to bridge differences between occupiers and occupied, and these relationships produced the popular impression that Greeks and Italians were *una faccia, una razza*. Despite the bellicose rhetoric of the Fascist regime, and its attempts to forcibly assimilate the islanders, Dodecanesians found it comforting to know that Italians 'as people' seemed to be more 'human' than 'Italian'.

Epilogue: After the 'Redemption'

After the islands were formally ceded to Greece in 1947, the memory of Italian rule quickly assumed an important role in the lives of ordinary Dodecanesians. Though they identified with Greece as their nation, and accepted Greek rule as legitimate, they also felt that for some time after unification they were experiencing a new 'occupation', and they conveyed this feeling by describing the Greek state as 'other'. Among the interviewees, this was conveyed in expressions such as 'life under the Greeks', and 'when the Greeks came' ('me toús Ellines', and, 'ótan írthan i Ellines'). Whilst they had changed from being subalterns to citizens, the oral sources sometimes gave the impression that Dodecanesians had remained victims of an oppressive, extraneous power. The interviewees were well aware that voicing criticism of Greek rule was morally and politically dangerous, and that it could be construed as unpatriotic, yet the islanders believed there was scope for subtle criticism, and this took the form of nostalgic memories for the Italian period.

Nostalgia for 'foreign rule' was certainly not to be expected after unification. Historians have viewed Greece's irredentist programme as a process of national redemption, for as the various regions were incorporated into modern Greece (Thessaly in 1881, Crete, Macedonia and Epiros 1912–13, eastern Thrace 1920), each was seen to be returning to their mother's embrace. One of the most peculiar features of regional history in Greece is that there is very little history written on any territory after 'redemption'. For the Dodecanese, readers will find almost nothing on such important themes as mass emigration in the 1950s and 1960s, the impact of unification on the local economy, the land redistribution programme, the impact of the military junta (1967–74), and the ramifications of mass tourism from the late 1970s. The assumption is that national unification allowed Dodecanesians to live happily ever after.

On the contrary, unification did not improve living conditions among the islands, at least not in the short term. In 1947 Greece was in the midst of a civil war, from which she was to emerge both devastated and bankrupt. The decades which followed were years of economic and political instability, culminating in the military junta of the Colonels. Until the massive increase in tourism from the late 1970s, the islanders seemed unable to break out of 'the black life'. Whilst the prospect of unification before 1947 had raised expectations of better times to come, such hopes were not really fulfilled. Moreover, unification with Greece immersed the islanders in the vicious factionalism of Greek politics, and introduced new sources of intra-communal division. Dodecanesians had to declare themselves as 'monarchists', or supporters of Karamanlis, of Giorgos Papandreou or Papadopoulos. Party allegiance determined whether one could secure a public service job, receive fair treatment in the courts, or attain any licence or permit. These new divisions gave scope for settling old scores or creating new conflicts, as rivals defamed each other as Communists or 'Junta-ists' (Hountikós).

Whilst political allegiances were eventually accepted as a fact of life, many Dodecanesians viewed this new source of community segmentation with considerable distaste. Gabriel Kosaris believed he could stay above all this by posturing as a lover of democracy. In his testimony he boasted that he was a 'democrat', yet complained that he found it almost impossible to stay above the political rivalries. In 1947 the diocese of Kos sought to redress the shortage of priests and made a general call for volunteers. Kosaris was an ideal candidate for the priesthood for he was literate, worldly, having lived in France in the 1920s, well read in the scriptures, and a church chanter. But the higher clergy felt his politics were highly suspect:

> We went through much ordeal, we went through so much pain so that we might become part of Greece. Once they came, they made us feel depressed....Very much! 1947, 1948. They [the Greek authorities] called me in. They said they were going to fix my head. Why? 'Because you love Communism.' I never was a Communist, I was always a democrat. I grew up in a country, France, where democracy was in the people's blood. So I could not digest these new things. It was another kind of slavery. You had to be one of theirs, a right-winger, to the right, of the right. They expected you to betray someone else and say 'He is a Communist', understand.
>
> I got into trouble again....I told them, 'It would have been better if you never came, if this is what you are all about'....I loved things 'democratic'. There is no need for the one man making all decisions. When I tried to become a priest after the war, the bishop was very right-wing, God rest his soul, Emmanuel

his name was. They went and told him that Kosaris,... 'Kosaris, well, he is a "Plastirian",[1] a democrat.' I told him, 'Keep your job, and good day to you.' I continued to be a chanter. Later, he relented, and he called me up again. He said, 'Believe what you believe'... so they let me become a priest....[2]

Kalliroi Dimitriadis explained how her husband was victimised by authorities because someone had wrongly denounced him as a Communist. He also thought he could stay above the political mire by claiming he was a 'democrat',[3] but most of the islanders had come to realise that they had to declare their loyalties to the ruling regime, regardless of whether Karamanlis, G. Papandreou or the Colonels were in power. They resented being questioned and harassed by officials from the mainland, and the new intra-community divisions which 'politics' had created. Whilst *morfoméni* did discuss high politics among themselves during the Italian Occupation, it was only after unification that political loyalties became a real source of community division.

Similar reasoning explains the silence associated with the failure of the Greek state to improve living conditions in the Dodecanese. The state did attempt to ameliorate agricultural problems and the social inequalities by, for example, pursuing a comprehensive redistribution of arable land. But demand for local products, like tomatoes, citrus fruits and almonds fluctuated markedly in the postwar period, and poor marketing and labour shortages assisted in the continual decline of local agriculture. Further, while sponge fishing remained the islands' chief export commodity, yields dropped from a pre-war average of 120 tonnes to 47 tonnes in 1962.[4] A strong indication of persistent hardship was emigration. Between 1951 and 1971, the population figures of the Dodecanese remained static, as birth rates were negated by departures. In that period, numbers in Tilos had dropped from 1052 to 309, Simi 4003 to 2497, Nisyros 2327 to 1289, and Karpathos from 7069 to 5433.[5] Large numbers also left Kos, Kalymnos and Rhodes for Germany, Canada, the United States and particularly Australia.

Emigration was fostered by necessity rather than choice. 'We suffered here', claims Mehmet Meerzam, 'under the Greeks! There was no work':

That is why everyone left. Some to Australia, some to Canada. Here, half of Kos was emptied. The people were leaving to improve their lives... there were no jobs. There were jobs here again, there was growth again, after the junta (1974).[6]

In Australia or Canada they could find work, eat properly, and 'live like humans'. In *Mermaid Singing*, Australian author Charmian Clift provided an evocative portrait of life in Kalymnos in the 1950s, and showed why the islanders were forced to part with their beloved islands. Her Kalymnos was a place of limited prospects, of scarcity and hopelessness. 'In nothing', she claimed, 'is the cruel poverty of this island revealed more clearly than in the diet of its inhabitants':

America and Australia are spoken of in terms of food. A migrant writes from a works project in New South Wales to say that they eat four times a day, and this startling information is carried all over town and discussed for days. 'No work, no food!' is an expression heard as frequently as the half-despairing, half-ironic, 'Ah, it passes the time!' from the listless coffee-house gamblers who have no work and no escape.[7]

The distance between monumental and social time is evidently great, with history seemingly coming to an end in 1947, and yet ordinary folk continued to experience 'histories' of their own kind. This study has sought to account for this glaring discrepancy, to juxtapose official and vernacular memories, and to assess what these co-existing, and often tangled, traditions can say about a particular culture. If anything, the apparently naïve testimonies of ordinary Dodecanesians, which say good things about a state run by Mussolini, represent a stark reminder of the incomplete ascendancy of the nation-state, in this case Greece, for every time they claim that they 'lived well' (pernoúsame kalá) under the Italians, they question the ideological structure, though not the legitimacy, of such a seemingly powerful official culture.

Appendix: Interviewees' Details

Name	Birth	Island	Occupation*
1. Antonis Stergalas	1916	Kos	farmer, barber
2. Panormitis Menouhos	1922	Kalymnos	mariner
3. Nikolaos Poulas	1897?	Kalymnos	shepherd
4. Epaninondas Diamandaras	1928	Leros	café waiter, student
5. Kostas Tourtoulis	1912	Leros	café owner
6. Philipos Sofos	1911	Rhodes	farmer
7. Giorgos Giorgalos	1926	Rhodes	farmer
8. Sophia Paskalis	1916	Kos	housewife
9. Ioannis Petalas	1922	Kos	builder
10. Kalliroi Dimitriadis	1917	Kos	housewife
11. Loizos Loizou	1916	Kalymnos	baker
12. Ioannis Alahiotis	1903	Kos	miller
13. Giorgos Papanikolaou	1907	Kos	teacher, tax farmer
14. Giorgos Sakellaridis	1914	Rhodes, Nysiros, Kalymnos	civil servant
15. Giorgos Valsamis	1916	Leros	student
16. Paraskevi Angopian	1910	Kos	housewife
17. Basil Galettis	1908	Kastellorizo	clerk
18. Mikhail Hatsithemelis	1916	Kalymnos	tailor, farmer
19. Christoforos Fournaris	1909	Kos	clerk
20. Stamatis Athanasiadis	1908	Rhodes	farmer, barber
21. Giorgos Kastrounis	1910	Rhodes, Kastellorizo	teacher
22. Manolis Kiapokas	1928	Kos	teacher
23. Kalliope Harapas	1920	Kos	housekeeper
24. Mehmet Meerzam	1914	Kos	farmer
25. Argyro Papadopoulos	1906?	Leros, Kos	housekeeper
26. Giorgos Koulianos	1905	Rhodes, Leros, Kalymnos, Kos	teacher
27. Lefteris of Leros	1923	Leros	shopkeeper
28. Archondoula Kanaris	1915	Kos	café owner
29. Mikhail Hatsinikolaou	1926	Kos	farmer
30. Sevasti Kortesi	1905	Kalymnos	housewife
31. Marigo Katris	1901	Astypalea	housewife
32. Theofilis Kazouris	1903	Kalymnos	farmer

33. Nikolaos Kazonis	1906	Kalymnos	shepherd
34. Vania Bitsikas	1920?	Kastellorizo	student
35. Dimitrios Samios	1914?	Kalymnos	seaman
36. Mikhail Mihalandos	1915	Simi	café owner
37. Anna of Simi	1914?	Simi	housewife
38. Pantelis Tripolitis	1929	Kos	student
39. Giorgos Petalas	1915?	Rhodes	carpenter
40. Gabriel Kosaris	1906	Kos	farmer
41. Zaharia of Asklepio	1923?	Rhodes	farmer
42. Kostas of Gennadi	1915?	Rhodes	teacher
43. Maria Atzemis	1928	Kastellorizo	housewife
44. Evdokia Jackomas	1922	Kastellorizo	housewife
45. Mihalis Koungras	1927	Kastellorizo	student
46. Venedictos Livisianis	1912	Kastellorizo	barber

N.B. The great majority of interviews were conducted in the Dodecanese in 1990, between July and November. Nearly all the interviews were recorded on sixty-minute length cassette tapes. Only three of the interviewees requested pseudonyms. These were Lefteris of Leros, Anna of Simi and Zaharia of Asklepio. The last four interviews were conducted between February and May 1995, in Sydney with Nicholas G. Pappas.

*Working occupations of interviewees during the Italian period.

Notes

INTRODUCTION

1 Luisa Passerini, 'Oral Memory of Fascism', in David Forgacs (ed.), *Rethinking Italian Fascism: Capitalism, Populism and Culture* (London, 1986), pp. 185–96; Detlev J.P. Peukert, *Inside Nazi Germany: Conformity, Opposition and Racism in Everyday Life* (Harmondsworth, 1987); Richard Cobb, *French and Germans, Germans and French: A Personal Interpretation of France under Two Occupations, 1914–1918/ 1940–1944* (Hanover, Conn., 1983).
2 For the diplomatic history of the Dodecanese, Renzo Sertoli Salis, *Le isole italiane dell'Egeo dall'occupazione alla sovranità* (Rome, 1939) has not been superseded. See also Stephen L. Speronis, 'The Dodecanese Islands: A Study of European Diplomacy, Italian Imperialism and Greek Nationalism, 1911–1947', Unpublished PhD thesis, University of Michigan, 1956.
3 Alekos Markoglou, *Koakó panórama 1900–1948* (Kos, 1992), p. 35.
4 Passerini, 'Oral Memory of Fascism', op. cit, p. 186.
5 Passerini, *Fascism in Popular Memory: The Cultural Experience of the Turin Working Class* (Cambridge, 1987), pp. 4–7.
6 J-L. Miège, *L'imperialisme Colonial italien de 1870 à nos jours* (Paris, 1968), pp. 193–4. The Dodecanese was essentially treated as a colony, and is referred to as such throughout this study. I also make no distinction between 'foreign occupation' and 'colonial rule'. An good discussion of the status of the Dodecanese in the Italian imperial system can be found in Mia Fuller, 'Colonizing Constructions: Italian Architecture, Urban Planning, and the Creation of Modern Society in the Colonies, 1869–1943', PhD thesis, University of California, Berkeley, 1994, pp. 110ff.
7 Tekeste Negash, *Italian Colonialism in Eritrea, 1882–1941: Policies, Praxis and Impact* (Uppsala, 1978); Angelo Del Boca (ed.), *Le Guerre coloniale del fascismo* (Rome and Bari, 1991). There are some studies on the colonial wars, especially the conquest of Ethiopia, such as Del Boca, *Italiani in Africa orientale: la conquista dell'impero* (Bari, 1979) and Roberto Battaglia, *La prima guerra d'Africa* (Rome, 1958). See also Luigi Goglia, *Storia fotografica dell'impero fascista, 1935–1941* (Rome, 1985).
8 Denis Mack Smith, *Mussolini's Roman Empire* (London and New York, 1976); Alberto Sbacchi, *Ethiopia under Mussolini: Fascism and the Colonial Experience* (London, 1985); Claudio Segrè, *Fourth Shore: The Italian Colonization of Libya* (Chicago, 1974); *Italo Balbo: A Fascist Life* (Berkeley, California, 1987).
9 Haile M. Larebo, *The Building of an Empire: Italian Land Policy and Practice in Ethiopia, 1935–1941* (Oxford, 1994), p. vi.
10 Annalisa Pasero, 'Madamismo, Meticciato and the Prestige of the Race in Italian East Africa', *The Italianist*, 11 (1991), p. 182.

11 Cf. Irma Taddia, 'Il Silenzio dei Colonizzati e il Lavoro dello Storico: Oralità e Scrittura nell'Africa Italiana', in Del Boca (ed.), *Le Guerre coloniale del fascismo*, p. 512.

12 E.g. Peukert, op. cit; Ulrich Herbert, 'Good Times, Bad Times: Memories of the Third Reich', in Richard Bessel (ed.), *Life in the Third Reich* (Oxford, 1987), pp. 97–110.

13 Geoff Eley, 'Labor History, Social History, *Alltagsgeschichte*: Experience, Culture, and the Politics of the Everyday – a New Direction for German Social History?', *Journal of Modern History*, 61 (1989), pp. 315 and 323. See also Ian Kershaw, *The Nazi Dictatorship: Problems and Perspectives of Interpretation* (London, 1989), p. 152.

14 Michael Herzfeld, *Anthropology Through the Looking-Glass: Critical Ethnography in the Margins of Europe* (Cambridge, 1987), pp. 41–3.

15 The cultural and social history of modern Greece is a relatively new field. Excellent studies include; Richard Clogg, 'Elite and Popular Culture in Greece under Turkish Rule', in John T.A. Koumoulides (ed.), *Hellenic Perspectives: Essays in the History of Greece* (London, 1980), pp. 107–43; Nicos Mouzelis, *Modern Greece: Facets of Underdevelopment* (London, 1978); John Koliopoulos, *Brigands with a Cause: Brigandage and Irredentism in Modern Greece, 1821–1912* (Oxford, 1987); Mark Mazower, *Inside Hitler's Greece: The Experience of Occupation, 1941–1944* (New Haven, Conn., 1993). The useful survey by Alexander Kitroeff, 'Continuity and Change in Contemporary Greek Historiography', *European History Quarterly*, 19 (1989), pp. 269–98, esp. pp. 294–6, shows the extent to which social history in modern Greece is 'underdeveloped'.

16 Among the most influential works are Ernestine Friedl, *Vasilika: A Village in Modern Greece* (New York, 1962) and J.K. Campbell, *Honour, Family, and Patronage: A Study of Institutions and Moral Values in a Greek Mountain Community* (Oxford, 1964). This study has been greatly influenced by Michael Herzfeld, whose works include: 'The Horns of the Mediterraneanist Dilemma', *American Ethnologist*, 11 (1984), pp. 439–54; *The Poetics of Manhood: Contest and Identity in a Cretan Mountain Village* (Princeton, New Jersey, 1991); and *Anthropology Through the Looking-Glass*. See also Anna Collard, 'Investigating "Social Memory" in a Greek Context', in Elizabeth Tonkin, Maryon McDonald and Malcolm Chapman (eds), *History and Ethnicity* (London and New York, 1989), pp. 89–103. A more recent example is Yiannis Papadakis, 'The Politics of Memory and Forgetting in Cyprus', *Journal of Mediterranean Studies*, 3 (1993), pp. 139–54.

17 Detailed information on the interviewees is provided in the Appendix.

18 Quoted from Kenneth Thompson, *Emile Durkheim* (London and New York, 1982), p. 14.

19 Passerini, *Fascism in Popular Memory*, pp. 1–2.

20 James Fentress and Chris Wickham, *Social Memory* (Oxford, 1992), p. 10.

21 Ronald Fraser, *Blood of Spain: An Oral History of the Spanish Civil War* (New York, 1986), pp. 31–2.

22 Christodoulos Papachristodoulou, *Istoria tis Ródou ápo tous proistorikoús chrónous éos tin ensomátosi tis Dodekanísou* (Athens, 1971); Vasilis S. Hatsivasiliou, *Istoría tis Nísou Ko: Archéa, Meseonikí, Neóteri* (Kos, 1990).

23 A good introduction to the nature of Greek nationalism and the importance of history and memory is Roger Just, 'Triumph of the Ethnos', in Tonkin, McDonald and Chapman (eds), op. cit, pp. 71– 88.

24 The development of folklore studies in Greece is dealt with by Herzfeld, *Ours Once More: Folklore, Ideology, and the Making of Modern Greece* (Austin, Texas, 1982).

25 See G. Koukoulis, *H Kálymna tis Istorías* (Athens, 1980).

26 See Hercules Millas, 'History Textbooks in Greece and Turkey', *History Workshop Journal*, 31 (1991), pp. 21–33. Sample textbooks are K. Sakkadakis, *Ellinikí istoría ton neotéron chrónon* (Athens, 1972) and G. Kafentzis, *Istoría ton neótron chrónon* (Athens, 1976).

THE DODECANESE IN 1912

1 Fentress and Wickham, op. cit, p. 88.

2 Sotiris Agapitidis, 'Plithismiakés Exelíxis sta Dodekánisa', *Dodekanisiaka Chronika*, IA' (1986), p. 18.

3 Skevos Zervos, *La Question du Dodecanese et ses Documents Diplomatiques* (Athens, 1926), p. 12. Also included among the 'Privileged Islands' was Ikaria, an island west of Samos.

4 See e.g. Emmanual A. Kariotis 'Simpliromatikés selídes ton agónon gia ti diásosi ke epikírosi tou kathéstotos tis Mahtoú Dodekanísou', *Dodekanisiaka Chronika*, T' (1977) p. 32.

5 E.g. Ermanno Armao, *Annuario Amministrativo e Statistico per l'Anno 1922* (Rome, 1922), p. 4.

6 *Dodecanese* (London: Admiralty. Naval Intelligence Division, 1943) (Geographical Handbook Series), hereafter referred to as *Dodecanese* (GHS), p. 6; Giorgio Roletto, *Rodi. La Funzione Imperiale Mediterraneo Orientale* (Milan, 1939), p. 43–4.

7 *Dodecanese* (GHS), pp. 6–9.

8 *Dodecanese* (GHS), p. 11. Myres reports that in 1936, Karpathos had no rainfall from May to December (p. 15). See also Roletto, op. cit, pp. 45–7, for temperature charts. Annual metereological reports during the Italian occupation are provided in *Rassegna Economica delle Colonie* (Rome).

9 Agapitidis, 'Plithismiakés Exelíxis sta Dodekánisa', pp. 12 and 18. See also Roletto, op. cit, p. 53; and Z. Stephanopoli, *Les îles de l'Egée, leurs privilèges* (Paris, 1913), pp. 147–9.

10 The island of Rhodes and its capital normally go by the same name, as is the case with Kos. To avoid confusion, the capitals will be referred to as 'Rhodes Town' and 'Kos Town' respectively.

11 Agapitidis, 'Plithismiakés Exelíxis sta Dodekánisa', p. 18.

12 Fernand Braudel, *The Mediterranean and the Mediterranean World in the Age of Philip II*, Vol. 1 (London, 1972), p. 154.

13 Ibid., p. 158.

14 Petros Kladakis, 'To pronomiakó kathestós en Sími, *Simaika*, B (1974), pp. 5–6.

15 B. Randolph, *The Present State of the Islands in the Archipelago (or Arches) Sea, of Constantinople, and the Gulf of Smyrna; With the Islands of Candia and Rhodes* (Oxford, 1687), p. 28. See also, B. Slot, 'I Sími ópos tin perigráfoun taxidiótes ke geográfi, *Simaika*, B, (1974), pp. 115–64; and N.G. Mavris, 'I xéni ke geográfi diá tin Nísiron', *Nisyriaka* (1963), pp. 7–17.

16 Randolph, op. cit, p. 28.

17 G.M. Sakellaridis, 'Autodiíkisi sta chrónia tis Sklaviás', *Kalymniaka Chronika*, E' (1986), p. 61; Stephanopoli, op. cit, pp. 142–4.

18 Ibid., p. 46.

19 Mihail Skandalidis, 'Simvolí sta onomatologiká Hálki Dodekanísou', *Dodekanisiaka Chronika*, IA' (1986), p. 54.

20 Miltiadis Logothetis, 'Plirofories giá tin ikonomía ke kinonía tis Dodekanísou sta téli tou 19ou eóna', *Dodekanisiaka Chronika*, IA' (1986), p. 115.

21 Explanations for the survival of small vessel transport is given by Braudel, op. cit, p. 109.

22 G. M. Sakellaridis, 'Autodiíkisi sta chrónia tis Sklaviás', p. 67.

23 Armao, op. cit, p. 144.

24 As the monasteries also required a steady source of building materials, six workshops were specifically engaged in brick making. See Logothetis, 'Plirofories giá tin ikonomía ke kinonía tis Dodekanísou', p. 117.

25 Nikolaos Tomadakis, 'O apoikismós Karpathíon is Mikrasían ke sto Aïdíni', *Kapathiake Melete*, 1 (1979), pp. 24–32.

26 Antonis Anastasis 'I Koinótis Emporíou ke i metanástefsis', *Nisyriaka*, 1 (1963), pp. 126–7.

27 A short survey of the Karpathian diapora is given in K. and Y. Bolzano, *Karpathos* (Salzburg, 1981), p. 6.

28 Manolis Isihos, *To panórama tis Lérou* (Leros, 1989), p. 143.

29 *Dodecanese* (GHS), p. 43.

30 Roger Owen, *The Middle East in the World Economy, 1800–1914* (London, 1981), p. 241.

31 G. Drakidis, *Léfkoma ton Dodekanisíon* (Athens, 1913), p. 89; Logothetis, 'Plirofories giá tin ikonomía ke kinonía tis Dodekanísou', p. 116.

32 *Dodecanese* (GHS), p. 109.

33 Paul Vouras, 'The Development of the Resources of the island of Rhodes under Turkish rule, 1522–1911', *Balkan Studies*, 14 (1963), pp. 40–3.

34 Virgil, *Georgics*, II. 106; Suetonius, *Vitae Tiberius*, 11.

35 Victor Guérin, *Ile de Rhodes* (Paris, 1880), trans. by M. Papaioannou, (Athens, 1989), p. 51.

36 Ibid., pp. 51–2, 77f. Sources from the 1880s confirm continuing stagnation in Rhodian agriculture. See Miltiadis Logothetis, 'To empório stis Nóties Sporádes (Dodekánisa) káta ta teleftéa chrónia tis Tourkokratías', *Dodekanisiaka Chronika,*   (1983), p. 145; and 'Plirofories giá tin ikonomía ke kinonía tis Dodekanísou', p. 105. See also Heracles Karanastasis, *I pedía stin Ko – Apo tin Tourkokratía os símera (1522–1979)* (Athens, 1979), p. 55.

37 'Tsiflikia' is the Greek rendition of the Turkish word *çiflik*. See Heracles Karanastasis, *To chronikó mias oikogénias* (Athens, 1977), p. 74.

38 Paul Vouras, op. cit, p. 40; *Dodecanese* (GHS), p. 54.
39 Cf. Jill Dubisch, 'The Ethnography of the Islands: Tinos', in Muriel Dimen and Ernestine Friedl (eds), *Regional Variation in Modern Greece and Cyprus: Toward a perspective on the ethnography of Greece*, Annals of the New York Academy of Sciences, 268 (1976), p. 318; Susannah Hoffman, 'The Ethnography of the Islands: Thera', in Dimen and Friedl (eds), op. cit, p. 330.
40 Gabriel Kosaris, OT, 3 November 1990.
41 *Dodecanese* (GHS), p. 57.
42 Nikolaos Zarakas, *Istoría ton lesperídon tis Ko ton chrónon tis Doulías* (Athens, 1983), p. 41-2.
43 Hatsivasiliou, *Istoría tis Nísou Ko*, p. 399.
44 Mikhail Hatsinikolaou, OT, 12 August 1990; Gabriel Kosaris, OT, 3 November 1990.
45 Guérin, op. cit, pp. 77ff
46 Karanastasis, *I Pedía tis Ko*, p. 36.
47 Randolph, op. cit, pp. 29, 56-7.
48 Jules Verne, *The Archipelago on Fire* (London, 1888), p. 155.
49 John Pemble, *The Mediterranean Passion: Victorians and Edwardians in the South* (Oxford, 1987), p. 31.
50 The Koan village of Antimachia experienced a similar transition. See Hercules Karanastasis, *Laografiká tis Kos* (Athena, 1980), p. 11.
51 The surnames of many of these wealthier families ended with the suffix '-ides' (e.g. Ioannides, Nicolaidis), which was characteristic of Greek communities from Anatolia, especially of the Pontus or Trebizond region.
52 *Dodecanese* (GHS), p. 87; Karanastasis, *Istoría mias Ikogénias*, p. 62.
53 Isihos, op. cit, p. 50.
54 Manolis Papaioannou, *Diagóras Olimpionikís – O Ródios gimnastikós síllogos <<Diagóras>>* (Athens, 1983), p. 52.
55 The secondary school in Rhodes Town was called 'the Venetoklíon' after its benefactor Venetoklis, while one of the girls' schools was named 'the Kazoulíon' after Nikolaos Kazoulis.
56 A vivid description of peasant life is given in Karanastasis, *Istoría mias Ikogénias*, pp. 74-5.
57 Guérin, op. cit, p. 92.
58 Nikolaos Poulas, OT, 11 August 1990.
59 G.T. Bergiotis, 'H igemonikí ke farmakeftikí períthalfis sti Sími', *Simaika*, (1984), p. 38. A similar service was offered in Kalymnos. See Armao, op. cit, p. 142.
60 Basil Galettis, OT, 9 October 1989.
61 H. Russell Bernard, 'Kalymnos: The Island of the Sponge Fishermen', in Dimen and Friedl (eds), op. cit, p. 305.
62 William Travis, *Bus Stop Symi* (Newton Abbot, Devon, 1970), pp. 103-4.
63 Logothetis, 'Plirofories giá tin ikonomía ke kinonía tis Dodekanísou', p. 113.
64 Armao, op. cit, pp. 74 and 218.
65 Ibid., pp. 159 and 244.
66 Ibid. The number of Turks living in Kastellorizo in 1886 numbered about fifty.

67 Sevasti Kortesi, OT, 22 August 1990.
68 Guérin, op. cit, p. 84.
69 Guérin, op. cit, p. 85; Karanastasis, *Laografía tis Ko*, pp. 154–66.
70 Guérin, op. cit, pp. 99ff.
71 See Hizikia M. Franco, *Les Martyrs Juifs des Rhodes et de Cos* (Katanga, Zaire, 1952).
72 Logothetis, 'Plirofories giá tin ikonomía ke kinonía tis Dodekanísou', pp. 99–101.
73 Giorgos Koukoulis, 'I simvolí tis Kalímnou stous agónes gia ta Pronómia', *Kalymniaka Chronika*, (1984), p. 27; Theologos Bikinos, 'Ta pronómia ke i autonomía ton Sporádon Nisón tou Egéou stin Othomanikí Autokratoría', *Dodekanisiaka Chronika*, I ' (1989), pp. 261–68. The Ottomans occupied these islands in 1867 after their refusal to accept an increase of their tribute (Mahtoú) by 10 per cent. The violation of their autonomy was taken up by Lord Stanley in the House of Commons, and by Jules Ferry in the Chamber of Deputies in Paris (Bikinos, op. cit, p. 263).
74 M.E. Yapp, *The Making of the Modern Near East, 1792–1923* (London, 1987), p. 36.
75 Bernard Lewis, *The Emergence of Modern Turkey* (Oxford, 1961), ch. IV, esp. pp. 120–8; Yapp, op. cit, p. 96.
76 Ibid., p. 10.
77 Sevastos I. Hatsisevastos, *Astikón dikéon is Notíous Sporádas epi Tourkokratías ke Italokratías* (Athens, 1977), pp. 99ff. A useful discussion of the millet system is given by Cesare Marongiu Buonaiuti, *La politica religiosa del Fascismo nel Dodecanneso* (Naples, 1979), pp. 11–16.
78 An idealistic, though very informative, portrait of Greek local government during the Ottoman period is given by D.A. Zakythinos, *The Making of Modern Greece: From Byzantium to Independence* (Oxford, 1976), pp. 56–69.
79 Greek forces had control of the Dodecanese when the peace settlements were taking place in 1832. The provisional Greek government, however, traded the Dodecanese for the more strategically valuable island of Euboea. See *Dodecanese* (GHS), p. 36.
80 Feroz Ahmad, 'Unionist Relations with the Greek, Armenian, and Jewish Communities of the Ottoman Empire, 1908–1914', in B. Braude and B. Lewis (eds), *Christians and Jews in the Ottoman Empire*, Vol. I, *The Central Lands* (New York, 1982), p. 412.
81 Kariotis, op. cit, p. 41.
82 Papachristodoulou, *Istoría tis Ródou*, p. 33; Details of the conquest are given in G. Georgiadis, *Rodiakón Istorikón léfkoma epi ti katálipsi tis Nísou Ródou* (Athens, 1912).
83 K. Tsalahouris, 'To Kastellórizo stis paramonés tis epanastáseos tis 1is' Martíou 1913', *Dodekanisiaka Chronika*, IA' (1986), pp. 189–90.
84 Theologos Bikinos, 'Ellinikí ke diethnís politikí sto Egéo ápo to 1911 eós to 1914', *Karpathiake Melete*, 4 (1987), p. 400: P. Kastrounis, 'I istoría tou Dodekanisiakoú Agónos épi tin Egipton (1912–1925)', *Dodekanisiaka Chronika*, ' (1974), p. 238–9.
85 P. Kastrounis, op. cit, p. 243.

86 Richard Bosworth, *Italy, the Least of the Great Powers: Italian Foreign Policy before the First World War* (Cambridge, 1979), p. 306.
87 These petitions are collected in Skevos Zervos, *The Dodecanese (White Book): Resolutions and Documents concerning the Dodecanese* (London, 1919?). Some of the petitions show much bravado. The people of Nisyros warned, 'We hold the European Powers responsible for the painful consequences should our desires remain unrealised.' (p. 15)
88 Papachristodoulou, *Istoría tis Ródou*, p. 539.
89 See Renée Hirschon, *Heirs of the Great Catastrophe: The Social Life of Asia Minor Refugees in Pireaus* (Oxford, 1989), p. 29; and Herzfeld, *A Place in History: Social and Monumental Time in a Cretan Town* (Princeton, 1991), p. 64.
90 Ambivalence towards Ottoman rule in social memory was also conveyed by people interviewed in Evritania in Central Greece. See Anna Collard 'Investigating Social Memory in a Greek Context', op. cit, pp. 95–8. In the Dodecanese the confusion is evident in the G.M. Sakellaridis's article on Kalymnian privileges, which is entitled 'Autonomy in the Age of Slavery' (Autodiíkisi sta chrónia tis Sklaviás).

ITALY'S AEGEAN POSSESSION

1 Britain was particularly concerned that her route to India might be threatened. See M. Kent, 'Great Britain and the End of the Ottoman Empire, 1900–23', in M. Kent (ed.), *The Great Powers and the End of the Ottoman Empire* (London, 1984), pp. 184–5.
2 Bosworth, *Italy, the Least of the Great Powers*. See also the same author's *Italy and the Approach of the First World War* (London, 1983).
3 Bosworth, *Italy, the Least of the Great Powers*, p. 318.
4 See Bosworth, 'Britain and Italy's Acquisition of the Dodecanese, 1912–1915', *Historical Journal*, 13 (1970), pp. 683–705.
5 Bosworth, *Italy and the Approach of the First World War*, p. 113; the intricacies of San Giuliano's dealings with the Dodecanese are described in greater detail in Bosworth's 'Britain and Italy's Acquisition of the Dodecanese, 1912–1915', pp. 683–705; and in *Italy, the Least of the Great Powers*, pp. 299–336.
6 *Italy, the Least of the Great Powers*, p. 299.
7 This useful distinction is made by Martin Clark in *Modern Italy 1871–1995*, 2nd edn (London, 1996), p. 154.
8 Despite being a member of the Triple Alliance, Italy looked to Britain as her patron in international affairs. See Bosworth, *Italy, the Least of the Great Powers*, p. 3.
9 The governors of the Dodecanese between May 1912 and September 1920 were: Ameglio (May 1912–October 1913), Francesco Marchi (November 1913–April 1914), Giovanni Croce (April 1914–May 1917), Vittorio Elia (May 1917–December 1919) and Achille Porta (December 1919–August 1920). These were followed by civil governors; Felice Maissa (September 1920–August 1921), Alessandro de Bosdari (August 1921–November 1922),

Mario Lago (November 1922–November 1936), Cesare de Vecchi (1936–40),
(Ettore Bastico 1940–41), G. Campione (1941–43) and G. Faralli (1943–45).
10 Sertoli Salis, op. cit, p. 15.
11 Ibid., p. 458.
12 Kostas A. Sakellaridis, 'Apo tin Istoría tis Dimogerontías Nísyrou méchri
ta próta chrónia tis Italikís katohís', B. 'O Dímarchos Geórgios Kammás
(Períodos 1916–1920)', *Nisyriaka*, Vol. 10 (1987), p. 314.
13 P. Kipriotis, 'I drási ton dimogerontón tis Ellinikís Orthodóxou
Koinótitos Ródou káta ta próta éti tis Italikís Katohís 1912–1914',
Dodekanisiaka Chronika, (1983), p. 104.
14 *The Times*, 3 November 1913 and *Le Temps*, 3 February 1913. See
Speronis, op. cit, pp. 95 and 115.
15 Hatsivasiliou, *Istoría tis Nísou Ko*, p. 459.
16 Bosworth, 'Italy and the End of the Ottoman Empire', in M. Kent (ed.),
op. cit, p. 64.
17 Papachristodoulou, *Istoría tis Ródou*, pp. 544–9. See also, Hatsivasiliou,
Istoría tis Nísou Ko, p. 458.
18 The new administration did attempt, with limited success, to raise
local taxes, to assert some authority over local judicial systems, and
to abrogate various traditional rights. Pantelis Kastrounis, 'I Istoría
tou Dodekanisiakoú Agónos epi tin Egitpton', *Dodekanisiaka Chronika*,
(1978), pp. 250–1; Ippokratis Frangopoulos, *I Dodekánisos ípo
Italokratían* (Athens, 1958), p. 34.
19 *Dodecanese* (GHS), p. 60.
20 The population dropped from 9000 to 4020 people, while in the same
period numbers in Kasos were reduced by one-fifth. See Agapitidis,
'Plithismiakés exelíxis sta Dodekánisa', p. 12.
21 Nikolaos S. Pizanias, *H Kálymnos, ápo ploutologikís dimografikís idía de
dimosionomikís apópseos* (Athens, 1935) pp. 33–5.
22 Kosta Sakellaridis, op. cit, p. 314.
23 In that same period, the population of Halki fell from 3215 to 1300. See
Agapitidis, 'Plithismiakés exelíxis sta Dodekánisa', p. 12.
24 A.J.P. Taylor, *The Struggle for Mastery in Europe, 1848–1918* (Oxford,
1955), p. 561. n.1; M.S. Anderson, *The Eastern Question, 1774–1923*
(London, 1966), pp. 343–4.
25 Bosworth, 'Britain, Italy and the Dodecanese', p. 704.
26 Skevos Zervos, *The 'White Book'*, p. 46.
27 Apostolos Mitropolitis Rodou, *Apomnimonévmata, íti chronografikís
istoría tis Ekklisiastikís Eparchías Ródou epí Italo-Germano-Agglokratías
(1912–1947)* (Athens, 1947), p. 74.
28 Much detail on the plebiscite is given by I.G. Stefanídis, *Rodós – I nimfi
tou Ilíou* (Athens, 1971), pp. 420–6; *APO*, p. 132.
29 Stamatis Athanasiadis, OT, 28 October 1990.
30 See, G. Georgiadis, *To Emateró Páscha tou 1919* (Athens, 1919).
31 See N. Petalis-Diomidis, *Greece at the Paris Peace Conferences (1919)*
(Salonika, 1978), p. 202.
32 Emmanouil Melas, 'O Venizévlos ke ta Dodekánisa', *Dodekanisiaka
Chronika*, Τ' (1979), p. 319; APO, pp. 81–3; Marongiu Buonaiuti, op.
cit, pp. 37–8.

33 C.J. Lowe and F. Marzari, *Italian Foreign Policy, 1870–1940* (London and Boston, 1975), pp. 186–7; Alan Cassels, *Mussolini's Early Diplomacy* (Princeton, 1970), p. 22.
34 Hatsivasiliou, *Istoría tis Nísou Ko*, pp. 432–3.
35 Another important factor was deteriorating relations between Britain and Greece towards the end of the Greco-Turkish war. See Cassels, op. cit, pp. 38–9.
36 Marongiu Buonaiuti, op. cit, pp. 35 ff.
37 Quoted in A.J.P. Taylor, *English History 1914–1945* (Oxford, 1965), p. 214.
38 Cassels, *Mussolini's Early Diplomacy*, pp. 222–3.
39 This maxim is used by Bosworth in 'Britain, Italy and the Dodecanese', esp. p. 690.
40 Papachristodoulou, *Istoría tis Ródou*, p. 550.
41 A 'tower of skulls' was another characterisation of Ottoman and Near Eastern rule. See Yapp, op. cit, p. 39.
42 A good survey of interwar colonial ideas is found in Raymond Betts, *Uncertain Dimensions: Western Overseas Empires in the Twentieth Century* (Minneapolis, 1985), pp. 76–113.
43 Cf. W.S. Blunt, *The Italian Horror and How to End It* (London, 1911), p. 5.
44 C.D. Booth and Isabelle Bridge Booth, *Italy's Aegean Possessions* (London, 1928), pp. 277 and 291.
45 Segrè, *Italo Balbo*, pp. 291–2.
46 *MR*, 5 April 1933.
47 Vittorio Alhadeff, *L'ordimento giuridico di Rodi e delle altri Isole Italiane dell' Egeo* (Milan, 1927), p. 121.
48 Ibid., p. 123.
49 Alhadeff, op. cit, p. 135.
50 Gennaro Mondaini, *La Legislazione Coloniale Italiana nel suo sviluppo Storico e nel suo stato attuale (1881–1940)* (Milan, 1941), p. 831.
51 Alhadeff, op. cit, pp. 130–4.
52 Ibid., p. 134.
53 Tommaso Gandini, *I Carabineri Reali nel Mediterraneo Orientale e Particolarmente nelle Isole Italiane dell' Egeo* (Rome, 1934), p. 62.
54 See Chapter 5.
55 *AKPL*. Miscellaneous Papers, 34–9, A/3, Legione Territoriale dei Carabinieri Reali di Bari, 29 June 1935.
56 Vittorio Buti, 'La Funzione di Rodi e delle Isole dell'Egeo', *Rassegna Italiana*, August–September (1934), p. 207.
57 Roletto, op. cit, p. 108.
58 Amedeo Giannini, 'Le Isole Italiane Dell'Egeo (Acquisto, Natura Giuridica, Funzione),' *Oriente Moderno*, July (1932), p. 323.
59 Cf. Hatsivasiliou, *Istoría tis Nísou Ko*, p. 470.
60 Mihail I. Samárkos, *Léros, I Málta tou Egéou (Chronikó 1912–1948)* (Athens, 1974), pp. 136–7.
61 Booth and Booth, op. cit, p. 277.
62 Lefteris, OT, 18 October 1990; Tourtoulis, OT, 5 November 1990.
63 MacGregor Knox, *Mussolini Unleashed, 1939–1941: Politics and Strategy in Fascist Italy's Last War* (Cambridge, 1982), p. 174.

64 G.M. Fessopoulos, *Alítrotos Ellinismós – I Dodekánisos mas* (Athens, 1935), p. 47.
65 Mondaini, op. cit, p. 856; G.M. Sakellaridis, 'Antonio Ritelli', *Kalymniaka Chronika,* T' (1986), p. 151.
66 Roletto, op. cit, p. 69; M. Mikhailidis-Nouarou, *Giá na gnorísoume tin Dodekániso* (Athens, 1946), p. 24.
67 Hatsivasiliou, *Istoría tis Nísou Ko*, p. 556.
68 Fessopoulos, op. cit, pp. 50–1.
69 *DHA*, Italian Collection, no. 1874, 12 May 1930.
70 Santi Nava, 'Una realtà dell'avvaloramento economico di Rodi', *Gerarchia* 1 (1933), pp. 33–7.
71 E.g. *Rassegna Economica Delle Colonie*, Vols 5–6 (May–June 1935), p. xlvi; Vols 7–8 (July–August 1935), p. 817.
72 See Sbacchi, op. cit, p. 75.
73 Alfredo Lenzi, 'Lo sviluppo economico di Rodi', *La Rassegna Italiana*, February (1932), p. 469.
74 Mack Smith, *Mussolini's Roman Empire*, p. 108.
75 Segrè, *Italo Balbo*, p. 291.
76 Betts, op. cit, p. 4.
77 Ibid., p. 78.
78 Buti, 'La funzione di Rodi', p. 214.
79 *AAI,* p. 852.
80 Alfredo Lenzi, 'Le frutta di Rodi', *Rassegna Economica delle Colonia*, April (1934), p. 355.
81 *AAI*, p.840.
82 Papachristodoulou, *Istoría tis Ródou*, p. 558.
83 Sotiris Agapitidis, *I Katástasis ton Dodekánison* (Athens, 1945), p. 65.
84 Hatsivasiliou, *Istoría tis Nísou Ko*, p. 435.
85 E.g. Cesare Cesari, *Colonie e Possedimenti Coloniali* (Rome, 1930), p. 6.
86 Fernando Gori, *Egeo Fascista* (Rome, 1938), p. 22.
87 Gori, op. cit, p. 82.
88 Gori, op. cit, p. 127.
89 Gori, op. cit, pp. 127–130; Giuseppe Stefanini and Ardito Desio, *Le Colonie, Rodi e le Isole Italiane dell' Egeo* (Turin, 1928).
90 *DHA*. Italian Collection, no. 1021, 19 January 1931; no. 27357, 13 November 1930; no. 15737, 14 January 1939; no. 20478, 19 May 1939.
91 *AAI*, p 1015.
92 *AAI*, p. 1017; *Rodi – Guida del Turistica* (Milan and Rome, 1928), pp. 111–12.
93 *MR*, 19 February 1933.
94 *AAI*, p. 1015.
95 Papachristodoulou, *Istoría tis Ródou*, p. 561.
96 The Patriarchate of Constantinople recognised the Church of Greece rather belatedly in 1852. See Charles D. Frazee, *The Orthodox Church and Independent Greece, 1821–1852* (Cambridge, 1969).
97 Marongiu Buonaiuti, op. cit, p. 39.
98 Quoted in Constantinos Halkias, 'Germanós Monioúdis H. Monodiádis, Mitropolítis Karpáthou kai Kásou, *Karpathiake Melete*', Vol. I (1978), p. 252.

99   *APO*, pp. 56–7 and 129.
100 Marongiu Buonaiuti, op. cit, p. 44
101 See also *APO*, p. 127.
102 Marongiu Buonaiuti, op. cit, pp. 33–4.
103 *AD*, 15 May 1924.
104 Orthodox–Catholic relations has been a source of division among Greek clergymen for centuries. See e.g. Steven Runciman, *The Great Church in Captivity* (Cambridge, 1968), p. 237.
105 Marongiu Buonaiuti, op. cit, pp. 74–5.
106 Kostas Tourtoulis, OT, 5 November 1990: Samarkos, op. cit, p. 76.
107 Themelina Kapella, 'O agónas ton gynaikón sto 1935 ke o petropólemos', *Kalymniaka Chronika*, T' (1986), pp. 87–102.
108 *DNI*, p. 41.
109 *DHA*, Italian Collection, no. 1055, De Vecchi to Count Galeazzo Ciano, Ministry of Foreign Affairs, 20 January 1937. See also Marongiu Buonaiuti, op. cit, p. 97.
110 Cf. ibid., p. 95.
111 Ibid., p. 110.
112 *MR*, 1 January 1926. C.f. *DNI*, p. 41.
113 *DNI*, p.41.
114 Quoted in Gori, op. cit, p.107.
115 Mikhailidis-Nouarou, op. cit, p. 32. Mikhail Hatsinikolaou, OT, 12 August 1990.
116 Theofilis Kazouris, OT, 10 August 1990.
117 Kostas Tourtoulis, OT, 5 November 1990.
118 John Ehrman, *Grand Strategy*, Vol. V, *August 1943 – September 1944* (London, 1956), p. 93.
119 Winston S. Churchill, *The Second World War*, Vol. V, *Closing the Ring* (London, 1952), pp. 180 and 193.
120 The battle raged between November 12 and 16. A detailed account of the battle is given by Samarkos, op. cit, pp. 136 ff; and Ehrman, op. cit, p. 102.
121 Apostolos Mitropolitou Karpathou-Kasou, *Tó chronikón tís Italokratías tis Ródou* (Athens, 1973), p. 136, n. 27.
122 G.M. Tsoukalas, *Dodekánisos – Ethnikí antístasi, 1940–1945* (Athens, 1989).
123 Hatsivasiliou, *Istoría tis Nísou Ko*, pp. 634–5.
124 For a comprehensive and evocative study of Greece under German occupation, see Mark Mazower, *Inside Hitler's Greece*.
125 Papachristodoulou, *Istoría tis Ródou*, p. 581. An account of the destruction of the Dodecanesian Jewry is given by Hizikia M. Franco, op. cit, and Martin Gilbert, *The Holocaust: A History of the Jews of Europe during the Second World War* (New York, 1985), pp. 706–10.
126 Hatsivasiliou, *Istoría tis Nísou Ko*, p. 569.
127 Papachristodoulou, *Istoría tis Ródou*, p. 584.
128 A disclaimer of this commonly held view is given by Hatsivasiliou, *Istoría tis Nísou Ko*, p. 625.
129 *L'Italia a Rodi*, Istituto Poliografico Dello Stato (Rome, 1946), p. 37.

PROTEST AND PROTO-NATIONALISM

1 Henri Rousso, *The Vichy Syndrome: History and Memory in France since 1944* (Cambridge, Mass., 1991); John Bodnar, *Remaking America: Public Memory, Commemoration, and Patriotism in the Twentieth Century* (Princeton, New Jersey, 1992); Richard Bosworth, *Explaining Auschwitz and Hiroshima: History Writing and the Second World War* (London and New York, 1993); Robert Gildea, *The Past in French History* (New Haven, Conn., 1994).

2 Bodnar, op. cit, p. 14.

3 Philipos Sofos, OT, 22 August 1990.

4 Mikhail Hatsinikolaou, OT, 8 August 1990.

5 One very popular quote, which is wrongly attributed to Winston Churchill, makes reference to Greece's success on the Albanian front in 1941: 'Till now we used to say that Greeks fight like heroes, henceforth we shall say heroes fight like Greeks.' South African Prime Minister Jan Smuts was the real source. (Cited in Irene Economou, *The Two Faces of Greece: A civilisation of 7000 years* (Athens, 1988), p. 132).

6 Herzfeld, *Anthropology Through the Looking-Glass*, p. 123.

7 Evdokia Jackoumas, OT, 14 March 1995.

8 For a detailed investigation of this microhistory, see Nicholas Doumanis and Nicholas G. Pappas, 'Grand History in Small Places', *Journal of Modern Greek Studies* (forthcoming).

9 Mikhail Mihalandos, OT, 3 February 1992.

10 Between 1912 and 1936, Simi's population had dropped from 22 450 to 8182; see Agapitidis, 'Plithimismiakés Exelíxis tis Dodekanísou', p. 12.

11 *DI*, 1 March 1934; Mikhail Mihalandos, OT, 3 February 1992.

12 Richard Clogg, *A Concise History of Greece* (Cambridge, 1992), p. 15.

13 *DI*, 15 May 1936.

14 *DI*, 1 August 1936.

15 E.g. Temma Kaplan, *Red City, Blue Period: Social Movements in Picasso's Barcelona* (Berkeley, California, 1992), pp. 79–125; Adrian Shubert, *A Social History of Modern Spain* (London, 1990), pp. 195–6; Timothy Tackett, 'Women and Men in Counterrevolution: The Sommières Riot of 1791', *Journal of Modern History*, 59 (1987), pp. 680–704; E.P. Thompson, *Customs in Common* (Harmondsworth, 1991), pp. 305–36.

16 Herzfeld, *Anthropology Through the Looking-Glass*, p. 36.

17 *DI*, 1 March 1934.

18 Ippokratis Frangopoulos, *Istoría tis Kalymnou apó tin archeótita méchri símera*, Vol. 2 (Athens, 1952), pp. 104–5.

19 Ibid., pp. 106f.

20 *DI*, 25 March 1933. On the exile of Kalymnian leaders, see Zacharia N. Tsirpanlis, 'Stin Kálymno tou 1935', *Kalymniaka Chronika, Z'* (1988), pp. 153–89.

21 Cf. Thomas Gallant, 'Peasant Ideology and Excommunication for Crime in a Colonial Context: The Ionian Islands (Greece), 1817–1864', *Journal of Social History*, 23 (1990), pp. 487, 500–1.

22 Frangopoulos, *Istoría tis Kalymnou*, p. 116.
23 Ibid., p. 119.
24 *DI*, 1 November 1935.
25 N. Kechagias-Nethonas, *Dodekanísou i anéntachti* (Athens, 1985), p. 35.
26 Fessopoulos, op. cit., p. 31.
27 Ibid. The arrest took place on 16 January 1936.
28 Mikhail Hatsithemelis, OT, 27 July 1990.
29 Mikhail Hatsithemelis, OT, 27 July 1990.
30 His ordeal while under arrest was mentioned in J.N. Casavis, *Italian Atrocities in the Grecian Dodecanese* (New York, 1936), p. 10.
31 Frangopoulos, *Istoría tis Kalymnou*, p. 123.
32 Quoted in Kapella, op. cit., p. 93.
33 Ibid., p. 93.
34 *DI*, 1 November 1935; Fessopoulos, op. cit., p. 33.
35 'Diakos, Kolokotronis, Miaoulis, and Kanaris' are celebrated heroes of the Greek War of Independence.
36 Ioannis Zervos, 'Trís méres agónas', *Kalymniaka Chronika*, E' (1985), pp. 298.
37 *AD*, 1 April 1936.
38 Quoted in Kapella, op. cit., p. 96.
39 *MR*, 11 April 1935.
40 *AKPL*, Miscellaneous papers, *Richiesta e Citazione Diretta*, 3 July 1935; *Tribunale di Apello di Rodi (Egeo), Decreto di Citazione*, 17 September 1935.
41 *DI*, 1 January 1936.
42 The Diocese of Kos and Nisyros had not had a sitting bishop since 1922. See Hatsivasiliou, *Istoría tis Nísou Ko*, p. 511.
43 Frangopoulos, *Istoría tis Kalymnou*, p. 123.
44 *DI*, 16 October 1935.
45 Giorgos S. Sakellarios, *I Ethniko-Thriskeftikí Antístasis tis Kalymnou tou étos 1935* (Athens, 1977), p. 93.
46 The most notable of these works is Sakellarios, op. cit., which mainly celebrates the male heroes of Kalymnos. See also articles in *Kalymniaka Chronika*, T' (1986), especially Ioannis Manglis, 'O Italós katachtitís', pp. 211–15. See also Tsoukalas, op. cit., pp. 171–9, and Ioannis Zervos, *Istoriká Simiómata* (Athens, 1960).
47 Sakellarios, op. cit., pp. 158–9.
48 *AKLP*. Miscellaneous Papers. Report from Podestà of Kalymnos, De Bisognio to Governatore, 9 April 1935; Vittorio Caradaci, *Legione Territoriale dei Carabinieri Reali di Bari*, 'Situazione del comune di Calino', 29 June 1935.
49 Giorgos Sakellaridis, OT, 27 September 1990. A similar view is found in a fictional work by Niki Billiri, *I Kálymnos mas* (Athens, 1982), p. 77.
50 Loizos Loizou, OT, 10 August 1990. For another example of males minimising the role played by women in popular protests, see Tackett, op. cit, p. 692.
51 *AKLP*. Miscellaneous Papers. Report from Podestà of Kalymnos, De Bisognio to Governatore, 9 April 1935.
52 Birilli, op. cit., p. 77.

53 See, Kapella, op. cit.

54 See H. Russell Bernard, 'Kalymnos: The Island of the Sponge Fishermen', in Dimen and Friedl (eds), op. cit., pp. 306–7. An important recent study is David Sutton, 'Images of History: The Uses of the Past on a Greek Island', PhD thesis, University of Chicago, 1994.

55 Panormitis Menouhos, OT, 11 August 1990; See Bernard, op. cit., p. 306.

56 Loizos Loizou, OT, 10 August 1990.

57 Cf. Tackett, op. cit., p. 702.

58 The 'David and Goliath' analogy has often been made in Kalymnian writings. See e.g. Sakellarios, op. cit., p. 48.

59 Ibid., p. 119.

60 Mikhail Hatsithemelis, OT, 27 July 1990.

61 Sevasti Kortesi, OT, 22 August 1990.

62 Ibid.; Loizos Loizou, OT, 10 August 1990.

63 Mikhail Hatsithemelis, OT, 27 July 1990.

64 Nikolaos Poulas, OT, 11 August 1990.

65 Mikhail Hatsithemelis, OT, 27 July 1990.

66 Kapella, op. cit, p. 95.

67 Ibid., p. 99.

68 Herzfeld, *Anthropology Through the Looking-Glass*, pp. 36–8.

69 Pantelis Efthimios, 'Mia foní ápo to 1913', *Dodekanisiaka Chronika*, A' (1972), p. 133.

70 *AD*, 15 February 1924; 15 May 1924; 1 November 1931; 1 March 1935.

71 See Sakellariou, op. cit, pp. 129 and 131; Kapella, op. cit, p. 102; Giorgos Sakellaridis, OT, 27 September 1990.

72 Ioannis Alahiotis, OT, 1 August 1990.

73 In 1910 the population density of Kalymnos was 156 per sq. km, which was three times the Dodecanesian average. Population density had fallen to 95 per sq. km by 1945. See Agapitidis, 'Plithismiakés Exelíxis tis Dodekanisou', p. 18.

74 Kostas Tourtoulis, OT, 5 November 1990.

75 E.J. Hobsbawm, *Nations and Nationalism since 1780: Programme, Myth, Reality* (Cambridge, 1990), p. 46; Patricia Crone, *Pre-Industrial Societies* (Oxford, 1989), pp. 186f.

76 Miroslav Hroch, 'From National Movement to the Fully-formed Nation: the Nation-building Process in Europe', *New Left Review*, 198 (1993), p. 12. See also Benedict Anderson, *Imagined Communities* (London, 1992), p. 144; and Peter Vandergeest, 'Constructing Thailand: Regulation, Everyday Resistance, and Citizenship', *Comparative Studies in Society and History*, 35 (1993), pp. 133–58.

77 D.I. Rusinow, *Italy's Austrian Heritage 1919–1946* (Oxford, 1969), pp. 199–207.

78 *MR*, 23 July 1937.

79 E.g. Ioannis Alahiotis, OT, 1 August 1990; Giorgos Kastrounis, OT, 27 October 1990.

80 Frangopoulos, *Istoría tis Kalymnou*, p. 90.

81 *DHA*, Italian Collection, no. 342, tel. 2150, 21 April 1927; Hatsivasiliou, *Istoría tis Nísou Ko*, p. 496.

82 This was the impression received by Booth and Booth, op. cit, p. 260.

83 Gabriel Kosaris, OT, 8 August 1990.
84 Ioannis Alahiotis, OT, 1 August 1990.
85 Christoforos Fournaris, OT, 12 August 1990.
86 Alexandros S. Karanikolas, *To ekpaideftikón próvlima tis Dodekanísou* (Athens, 1945), p. 10.
87 Mikhail Hatsinikolaou, OT, 12 August 1990. Similar personal accounts are given by Kalliope Harapas, OT, 3 August 1990 and Manolis Kiapokas, 8 August 1990.
88 Mondaini, op. cit, p. 885.
89 Gabriel Kosaris, OT, 8 August 1990; Kalliroi Dimitriadis, OT, 21 April 1992; Antonis Stergalas, OT, 4 September 1990.
90 *CIP*, p. 82. n. 6.
91 Mikhail Hatsinikolaou, OT, 12 August 1990.
92 Kalliope Harapas, OT, 3 August 1990.
93 Mikhail Hatsinikolaou, OT, 12 August 1990.
94 E. Bakiris, *Ródos: To Ethnikó Zítima, 1912–1947* (Rhodes, 1989), p. 64.
95 Gabriel Kosaris, OT, 8 August 1990.
96 Frangopoulos, *Istoría tis Kalymnou*, p. 103.
97 Nikolaos Kehagias-Nethonas, *O Protosíngelos tis Ródou* (Athens and Ioannina, 1987), p. 58.
98 Zaharia of Asklepio, OT, 22 August 1990.
99 Mikhailidis-Nouarou, op. cit, p. 32.
100 Ibid., p. 34.
101 *CIP*, p. 82.
102 Markoglou, op. cit, p. 170.
103 E.g. E. Bakiris, 'Esoterikí Ierapostolí tis ekklisías Ródou sta chrónia tis Italokratías', *Dodekanisiaká Chroniká, Z'* (1978), p. 64; Kehagias-Nethonas, *O Protosíngelos tis Ródou*, p. 57.
104 The myth produced arguably the best known children's poem in modern Greek culture, 'Feggaráki mou Lampró'.
105 One of the obvious problems with this myth is accounting for the ascendancy of Greeks in the Ottoman bureaucracy in the eighteenth and nineteenth centuries, and the persistence of Greek local government and schools. (See Helen Angelomatis-Tsougarakis, *The Eve of the Greek Revival: British Travellers' Perceptions of Early Nineteenth-Century Greece* (London and New York, 1990), pp. 122–3.) Common folk are often quite resistant to revisionist interpretations. After my interview with Antonis Stergalas, I pointed out to his friends that Greek Dodecanesian learning had flourished in the last decades of Ottoman rule. One of Stergalas's friends became visibly agitated, and asserted: 'No, no, this is not true. Rubbish. I don't care what they write, I still believe in the child gatherings (Jannisary levy) and the "secret school!" '
106 Gabriel Kosaris, OT, 8 August 1990.
107 The 'secret school' of national mythology is also distinguished by the accent on the last 'o' (scholió), which was also the convention used by interviewees.

THE POETICS OF PATRIOTISM

1 Miroslav Hroch, *Social Preconditions of National Revival in Europe: A Comparative Analysis of the Social Composition of Patriotic Groups among the Smaller European Nations* (Cambridge, 1985), p. 23. See also his 'From National Movement to the Fully-formed Nation', pp. 3–20.

2 H.D.F. Kitto, *In the Mountains of Greece* (London, 1933), p. 30

3 Roger Owen, op. cit, p. 287. The implications of Ottoman modernisation for the Greek *millet* has been recently appraised by Gerasimos Augustinos in *The Greeks in Asia Minor: Confession, Community and Ethnicity in the Nineteenth Century* (Kent, Ohio, 1992), pp. 91–107.

4 Christos Sp. Soldatos, *I Ekpaideftikí ke Pneumatikí Kínisi tou Ellinismoú tis M. Asías (1800–1922)*, Vol. II (Athens, 1989); Augustinos, op. cit, ch. 6, pp. 145–85.

5 A convenient survey of the number of schools and students in the Dodecanese is provided in Armao, op. cit.

6 Heracles Karanastasis, *Anamnísis ekpedeftikoú: chronikó* (Athens, 1982), p. 46.

7 Ibid., p. 77.

8 Ibid., pp. 78–9.

9 John Peristiany, 'Introduction to a Cypriot Mountain Village', John Peristiany, (ed.), *Contributions to Mediterranean Sociology: Mediterranean Rural Communities and Social Change* (Athens, 1968), p. 82.

10 Booth and Booth, op. cit, pp. 141–3; Zarakas, op. cit, pp. 119ff.

11 In his study of the social structure of the Cycladic island of Ios in the 1960s, anthropologist Richard Currier noted education and occupation as criteria of social stratification. The peasants referred to professionals (teachers, clerks, inspectors, doctors) and the landed elites as 'the aristocrats', or as 'they who know words' (aftí pou xéroun grámmata). See 'Social Interaction and Social Structure in a Greek Island Village', in Dimen and Friedl (eds), op. cit, pp. 310–11.

12 Herzfeld, *Anthropology Through the Looking-Glass*, pp. 33ff.

13 Karanastasis, *Anamnísis ekpedeftikoú*, p. 11.

14 Christoforos Fournaris, OT, 6 August 1990.

15 *CIP*, p. 12.

16 Karanastasis, *Anamnísis ekpedeftikoú*, p. 55.

17 Karanastasis, *To gió tis mamís* (Athens, 1978), p. 26.

18 Nikolaos Poulas, OT, 12 August 1990.

19 Ioannis Zervos, *Istoriká Simiómata*, p. 35.

20 Prime examples of this tradition include Ioannis Zervos, *Istorikà Simiómata*; G.S. Sakellariou, op. cit; I. Frangopoulos, *I Dodekánisos ipó Italokratías*; and Mihail Skardasis, *Ta Kalymniaká* (Athens, 1979), p. 26.

21 In Modern Greece, oral traditions have been categorised as 'folklore' (laografía), and are not to be confused with the 'serious' history written by *morfoméni*. 'Folklore' as a discipline has nevertheless played an important role in supporting national ideology. See Michael Herzfeld, *Ours Once More*.

22 All important Kalymnian authors have preferred the formal title, including Ioannis Zervos, Frangopoulos, Drakidou and Sakellariou.
23 Emmanuel Th. Papamihail, *The* (*sic*) *Greece and the Greek Dodecanese* (Lisbon, 1943), p. 89.
24 Giorgos Koulianos, OT, 19 October 1990.
25 Ioannis Alahiotis, OT, 1 August 1990.
26 Manolis Kiapokas, OT, 8 August 1990.
27 Zirounis, *Katafroneméni Iríni* (Athens, 197?), p. 15.
28 Hatsivasiliou, *Istoría tis Nísou Ko*, p. 426.
29 (Athens, 1913), p. 5.
30 An extract from a poem written by G. Gerakis in Athens in 1940, which is reprinted in Gerakis, *Apo ti Zoí tis Kalymnou* (Athens, 1965), p. 149.
31 Passionate exhortations of patriotism remain a feature of local scholarship. See for instance Christodoulos Papachristodoulou, 'I Dodekánisos ítan pánta Ellinikí', *Dodekanisiaka Chronika, Z'* (1978), pp. 36–47: and E. Protopsaltis, 'Ta elefthéria tis Dodekanísou', *Dodekanisiaka Chronika, Z'* (1978), pp. 25–35.
32 Casavis's works include *Ta Ellinika Dodekanisa* (New York, 1941); and *The Religion of the Dodecanese and its Persecution by Italy* (New York, 1937). 'Casavis' is also written as 'Gazavis' and 'Kazavi'. Zervos's numerous works include *Rhodes and the Dodecanese* (London, 1920); *Ikonografómeni i Dodekánisos* (Athens, 1930); and *Rhodes: Capitale Du Dodecanese* (Paris, 1920).
33 See Skevos Zervos, *The 'White Book'*, p. 23.
34 Tsalahouri, op. cit, pp. 187–214; E. Kariotis, 'I prótes politikés energíes ton Egeopelagitón is tas Athínas ke ton Kalymníon is tin Kálymnon ke Petroúpolin to 1912', *Dodekanisiaka Chronika,* ' (1977), pp. 152–81.
35 *I Rodiakí*, 19 September 1933.
36 Ibid., 10 May 1963.
37 Ibid., 29 March 1951.
38 Ibid., 20 November 1950.
39 Kipriotis, 'I drási ton demogerónton', pp. 95–136.
40 Isihos, op. cit, p. 80.
41 *DHA*. Rhodes Demarchía Papers, *Proceedings of the Rhodian Demogerontia*, 18 November 1912.
42 Ibid., 7 May 1912.
43 Ibid., 9 September 1912.
44 Ibid., 28 September 1912; Skevos Zervos, *'The White Book'*, p. 18.
45 *DHA*. Rhodes Demarchía Papers, *Proceedings of the Rhodian Demogerontia*, 12 February 1913; 16 February 1913.
46 Christoforos Fournaris, OT, 6 August 1990.
47 Hatsivasiliou, *Istoría tis Nísou Ko*, p. 455.
48 Ibid., p. 451
49 Concentration on great figures of the past also reflects the conservative nature of local historiography. As with most of his Dodecanesian colleagues, Hatsivasiliou betrays a fetish for archival documents and a fascination for high politics. The first decade of Italian rule is unique in that it provides enough source material to piece together a 'serious' history, which includes a political narrative with historical events and

personalities. This conservatism is further exemplified in the common practice of reproducing documents, which are not always given supporting commentary because they are meant to 'speak for themselves'. To convey Ioannidis's commitment to Hellenism, Hatsivasiliou provides meticulous reproductions of his official correspondence and political statements. (See *Istoría tis Nísou Ko*, pp. 431–45.)

50 *AKPL*, Miscellaneous Papers. A/2, Tribunale di Apello di Rodi (Egeo), 17 September 1935.
51 See Bakiris, *Rhodes: The National Question.*
52 *CIP*, p. 66. n. 2.
53 Papaioannou is the subject of a hagiographical work by Kehagias-Nethonas, *O Protosíngelos tis Ródou.*
54 Though we only have a transcript of this speech, its content and style bears much resemblance to his personal memoirs. Ibid., p. 51.
55 Kostas of Gennadi, OT, 25 October 1991.
56 Ioannis Gounaris, 'Skópimes anamnísis tis zoís mou', *Kalymniaka Chronika*, Z', (1988), p. 375; Kostas of Gennadi OT, 25 October 1991.
57 Gounaris, op. cit, p. 372.
58 Denis Mack Smith, *Mussolini's Roman Empire*, p. 119.
59 John F. Sweets, *Choices in Vichy France: The French Under Nazi Occupation* (New York, 1986), pp. 44ff.
60 Gounaris, op. cit, p. 373.
61 Giorgos Kastrounis, OT, 25 October 1990.
62 Qualifications for primary school teaching varied from island to island, though all islands expected their teachers to have had some years of secondary schooling. See Bakiris, *Ródos – Ethnikó Zítima*, p. 47.
63 Passerini considers cultural identities and self-representations in *Fascism in Popular Memory*, Part I, pp. 17–63.
64 Greeks commonly referred to Istanbul, or Constantinople, as simply 'the City' (i Póli). The Greeks of Constantinople were hence called 'Polítes' (sing. 'Polítis').
65 Kosaris, OT, 8 August 1990.
66 Giorgos Koulianos, OT, 19 October 1990.
67 Ibid.
68 Ibid.
69 Ibid.
70 Ioannis Alahiotis, OT, 1 August 1990.
71 Giorgos Kastrounis, OT, 25 October 1990.
72 S.A. and A.S. Karanikolas, *Parimíes ke frásis ápo tin Sími* (Athens, 1980), p. 219.
73 On Pantelis Kastrounis, see his 'I Istoría tou Dodekanisiakoú Agónos epi tin Egitpon (1912–1925)', which is reprinted in *Dodekanisiaka Chronika*, (1975), pp. 222–314.
74 Giorgos Kastrounis, OT, 25 October 1990.
75 Ibid.
76 Ibid.
77 Ibid.
78 Ibid.

79 Giorgos Sakellaridis, OT, 27 September 1990.
80 Ibid.
81 Sakellaridis, 'Antonio Ritelli', p. 156.
82 Ibid., pp. 164–5.
83 Ibid, pp. 152–88. Included in this section are two patriotic orations on the Rock War, and the letters of a patriot who 'struggled' for the Dodecanese in Athens.
84 Sakellaridis's article can also be read as an essay on liberty. The anti-Fascist Ritelli seemed as much a victim of oppression as Sakellaridis, and their common ordeal under authoritarian rule seemed a binding experience.
85 Giorgos Papanikolaou, OT, 3 November 1990.
86 Ibid.
87 Ibid.
88 Ioannis Alahiotis, OT, 1 August 1990.
89 The circumstances surrounding the closure of the 'Diagoras' sporting club are given in Papaioannou, *Diagóras, Olimpionikís*, pp. 125–31.
90 Christoforos Fournaris, OT, 6 August 1990.

COLONIALISM AND MODERNITY

1 *MR*, 19 February 1933.
2 *MR*, 36 December 1936.
3 Some of the Duke's idea's on colonial governance had been formulated in his doctoral dissertation at the University of Palermo. See Sbacchi, *Ethiopia under Mussolini*, p. 55.
4 Segrè, *Fourth Shore*.
5 Betts, op. cit, ch. 3, pp. 76–113.
6 Mack Smith, *Mussolini's Roman Empire*, p. 123.
7 A recent example is Bahru Zewde, *A History of Modern Ethiopia, 1855–1974* (London, 1991), pp. 160–5. Zewde dismisses Italian administration with the following characterisation: 'There was a mania for creating committees and commissions, largely so that members might exonerate themselves from responsibility.' (p. 162)
8 Mack Smith, *Mussolini's Roman Empire*, p. 34.
9 Sbacchi, op. cit, p. 80; I.M. Lewis's discussion on Italian rule in his general text, *A Modern History of Somalia: Nation and State in the Horn of Africa* (London, 1980), pp. 92–101, 110–113, is unusual because it is balanced and dispassionate.
10 Segrè, *Italo Balbo*, pp. 331–2.
11 Of the Duke, Haile Selassie said he was <<... un *gentleman* a cui l'Etiopia deve gratitudine>>. See Edoardo Borra, *Amadeo di Savoia, terzo duca d'Aosta e vicere d'Etiopia* (Milan, 1985), p. 255.
12 Sbacchi, op. cit, p. 57–8.
13 Alessandro Triulzi, 'Review of books on Italian Colonialism and Ethiopia', *Journal of African History*, 23/3 (1982), p. 238.
14 Stamatis Athanasiadis, OT, 28 October 1990.

15 Prakash Tandon, *Punjabi Century 1857–1947* (Berkeley, California, 1968), p. 13.
16 Kalliope Harapas, OT, 3 August 1990.
17 Prakash Tandon, op. cit, p. 13.
18 Anna Collard, 'Investigating 'Social Memory' in a Greek Context', pp. 95–7. See also Herzfeld, *The Poetics of Manhood: Contest and Identity in a Greek Mountain Village* (Princeton, New Jersey, 1985).
19 Ioannis Alahiotis, OT, 1 August 1990.
20 Friedl, op. cit, p. 106.
21 Ibid., pp. 314–15.
22 Kosta Sakellaridis, op. cit, pp. 307–17.
23 The alleged 'factiousness' of the Greeks has also been used to convey positive notions of 'individualism'. See for example Friedl, op. cit, p. 106.
24 Cf. Michael Herzfeld, 'The Horns of the Mediterraneanist Dilemma', p. 441. Herzfeld complains in this paper that it is 'downright embarrassing to be told by Greeks . . . (that) the Greeks need a strong government, and therefore deserved the junta (the Colonels) . . .'. Herzfeld suggests that such comments perhaps echoed a dominant ideology at the time of the Colonels, but this does not quite explain why such sentiments could still be heard in the 1980s and 1990s.
25 *MR*, 4 October, and 23 November 1938.
26 *MR*, 5 October 1938.
27 *MR*, 4 March 1936; and 9 March 1938.
28 Kalliope Harapas, OT, 3 August 1990.
29 Lefteris of Leros, OT, 18 October 1990. Lefteris excused himself before mentioning the word 'beasts' (zóa), by which he meant either mules or donkeys. Lefteris was observing a standard form of etiquette practiced among Dodecanesian peasants. See Herzfeld, 'The Ethnographer in the Text', *Semiotica*, 46 (1983), pp. 159 ff.
30 Archondoula Kanaris, OT, 19 September 1990.
31 Archondoula Kanaris, OT, 19 September 1990; in Passerini's study among Turin workers, similar sentiments were expressed regarding Fascism and law and order, (e.g. see *Fascism in Popular Memory*, p. 130.)
32 'Introduction' to a special edition entitled, 'Memory and Counter-memory', *Representations*, 26 (1989), p. 4.
33 *The Past is a Foreign Country* (Cambridge, 1985), pp. 7 and 13.
34 Sevasti Kortesi, OT, 22 August 1992.
35 Kalliope Harapas, OT, 3 August 1990. By 1990, the *demarchia* had partly solved the traffic problem by turning most streets into 'one-way' thoroughfares.
36 Roletto, op. cit, pp. 67–8; *AAI*, p. 855.
37 *DNI*, p. 59.
38 Booth and Booth, op. cit, p. 261.
39 Philipos Sofos, OT, 22 August 1990.
40 Philipos Sofos, OT, 22 August 1990.
41 Jonathan Steinberg, *All or Nothing: The Axis and the Holocaust, 1941–43* (London, 1990), pp. 170–1.

42 D.K. Fieldhouse, *Colonialism 1870–1945: An Introduction* (London and New York, 1983), p. 27. See also William B. Cohen, *Rulers of Empire: The French Colonial Service in Africa* (Stanford, California, 1971), p. 107.

43 The popular concepts 'menefreghismo' and 'bustarella' are discussed by Steinberg in op. cit, p. 170.

44 An early, though inconclusive, attempt to explain the drawbacks of the Greek civil service is given by Demetrios Argyriades, 'The Ecology of Greek Administration: Some Factors Affecting the Development of the Greek Civil Service', in J.G. Peristiany (ed.), *Contributions to Mediterranean Sociology* (The Hague, 1968), pp. 339–49. See also William McNeill, *The Metamorphosis of Greece since World War II* (Chicago, 1978), p. 227; Herzfeld, *A Place in History*; and the same author's more recent *The Social Production of Indifference: Exploring the Symbolic Roots of Western Bureaucracy* (New York and Oxford, 1993). Parallels may be drawn with the Italian civil service, and what Steinberg calls the 'vices of Italian public life'. These include *furberia* (slyness) and *pressapochismo* (carelessness), (op. cit, p. 170).

45 Antonis Stergalas, OT, 4 September 1990.

46 Interviews with Kosaris, Alahiotis, Dimitriadis and Harapas.

47 Mehmet Meerzam, OT 3 August 1990.

48 Ioannis Alahiotis, OT, 1 August 1990.

49 See Mondaini, op. cit, pp. 872–84. See also Pavlos Theodoropoulos, *To ishíon en Dodekaníso díkeon* (Athens, 1981), pp. 131–2; Hatsivasiliou, *Istoría tis Nísou Ko*, p. 475.

50 Mikhail Hatsinikolaou, OT, 12 August 1990.

51 Lenzi, 'Lo sviluppo economico di Rodi', p. 471; 'Le frutta di Rodi', pp. 351–8; *AAI*, pp. 848–56.

52 Pantelis Tripolitis, OT, 1 November 1990. Reference to the one-and-a-half kilo onion is also made by Kalliope Harapas, OT, 3 August 1990, and Antonis Stergalas, OT, 4 September 1990.

53 Interviews with Stergalas, Dimitriadis and Harapas.

54 Ioannis Alahiotis, OT, 1 August 1990.

55 Archondoula Kanaris, OT, 19 September 1990.

56 Kalliroi Dimitriadis, OT, 21 April 1992.

57 *Diocese of Kos and Nisyros Archives*, Codex IG'; *MR*, 27 April 1933.

58 *MR*, 27 April 1933.

59 'Stamatis Kiapokas, 'O Megálos Sismós tis Ko (1933)', reprinted in *Ta Koaka*, Vol. ' (1989), pp. 299–302.

60 Karanastasis, *O Giós tis Mamís*, pp. 65–6: Evaggelos Vardamidis, *Istoría tis Nísou Megístis (Kastellorízou)* (Alexandria, Egypt, 1948), pp. 269ff.

61 Kalliroi Dimitriadis, OT, 21 April 1992.

62 Paraskevi Angopian, OT, 28 July 1990.

63 *MR*, 28 April 1933; Hatsivasiliou, *Istoría tis Nísou Ko*, p. 530.

64 Archondoula Kanaris, OT, 19 September 1990.

65 *AD*, 15 December 1935; Emmanouil Karpathios, *Ekklisía Ko Dodekanisou* (Athens, 1968), p. 474.

66 Archondoula Kanaris, OT, 19 September 1990.

67 *MR*, 25 April 1933.

68 Karpathios, op. cit, p. 476.

69 *MR*, 30 April; 2 May; 7 May 1933.

70 Hatsivasiliou, *Istoría tis Nísou Ko*, p. 547.

71 Ibid., p. 543.

72 *DHA*, Italian Collection, tel. no. 793/3, 9 November 1934.

73 Interviews with Dimitriadis, Harapas, Stergalas and I. Petalas.

74 Antonis Stergalas, OT, 4 September 1990.

75 Kalliope Harapas, OT, 3 August 1990.

76 *Mussolini's Roman Empire*, p. 81.

77 Angelo Del Boca, *The Ethiopian War 1935–1941* (Chicago, 1969), p. 232.

78 Lyautey showed the value of having European and Oriental quarters in a colonial city while building of Rabat. He claimed the juxtaposition of the two had its political, hygienic and aesthetic value, in that order. See Janet L. Abu-Laghod, *Rabat, Urban Apartheid in Morocco* (Princeton, New Jersey, 1980), p. 143.

79 Kalliroi Dimitriadis, OT, 21 April 1992.

80 Archondoula Kanaris, OT, 19 September 1990.

81 Antonis Stergalas, OT, 4 September 1990.

82 Ioannis Petalas, OT, 10 October 1990.

83 Argyro Papadopoulou, OT, 5 September 1990.

84 The symbolic power and the contested meanings of 'Europe' in Greek society have been discussed in many of the works Michael Herzfeld. See especially his *Anthropology Through the Looking-Glass.*

85 Lefteris of Leros, OT, 18 October 1990.

86 Rudolph M. Bell, *Fate and Honour, Family and Village: Demographic and Cultural Change in Rural Italy since 1800* (Chicago, 1979), pp. 151ff.

87 E.g. Buti, 'La funzione di Rodi', op. cit, pp. 207–14.

88 Philipos Sofos, OT, 22 August 1990.

89 Giorgos Sakellaridis, OT, 27 September 1990.

90 Ioannis Alahiotis, OT, 1 August 1990.

91 Kalliroi Dimitriadis, OT, 21 April 1992.

92 Kalliope Harapas, OT, 3 August 1990.

93 Agapitidis, 'Plithismiakés exelíxis sta Dodekánisa', p. 65.

94 Kalliope Harapas, OT, 3 August 1990; Ioannis Alahiotis, OT, 1 August 1990.

95 Betts, op. cit, p. 90.

96 *DNI*, p. 68.

97 Giorgos Giorgalos, OT, 23 August 1990.

98 Stamatis Athanasiadis, OT, 28 October 1990.

99 Stamatis Athanasiadis, OT, 28 October 1990.

100 Marigo Katris, OT, 7 August 1990.

101 Basil Galettis, OT, 9 October 1989.

102 Steinberg, op. cit, p. 179.

103 'Oréa prámata', the term most often employed by interviewees, corresponded most with *bella figura*. Surprisingly, the more precise Greek equivalent, 'figoúra', which is almost certainly borrowed from Italian, was not used by interviewees.

104 Diane Ghirardo, *Building New Communities: New Deal America and Fascist Italy* (Princeton, New Jersey, 1989), p. 9.

105 Mussolini finally opted for conservative architecture after the invasion of Ethiopia, where Italy's renewed enthusiasm for imperial adventures made the neo-classical style, with its association with Imperial Rome, seem more appropriate. For the competition between the Rationalists and the Monumentalists, see Ellen Shapiro, 'The Emergence of Italian Rationalism', *Architectural Design*, 51 (1981), pp. 5–9; Bruno Zevi, 'Gruppo 7: the Rise and Fall of Italian Architecture', op. cit, pp. 41–3; Denis Doordan, *Building Modern Italy: Italian Architecture 1914–1936* (Princeton, New Jersey, 1988); and Richard A. Etlin, *Modernism in Italian Architecture*, 1890–1940 (Cambridge, Mass., 1991), ch. 12, pp. 439–79.

106 The study of Italian architecture in the Dodecanese has been neglected by local historians because of its association with a foreign occupation. A rare, objective study is attempted by Antonis Antoniadis, 'I architektoniki ton Italón sta Dodekánisa', *O Dromos*, Vols 17–18, December (1983), p. 20.

107 Agapitidis, 'Plithismiakés exelíxis sta Dodekánisa' p. 66. ('. . . apetéli tin teleftéan diéxodon ton nisiotón allá ke to próton stádion tou afellinismoú ton níson'.)

108 Emmanuil Kariotis 'Ta Dimósia érga ton Italón is tin Dodekánison', *Dodekanisios*, A', 5 (1957), p. 56.

109 *Istoría tis Ródou*, p. 560

110 Antonis Stergalas, OT, 4 September 1990.

111 Ioannis Petalas, OT, 10 October 1990.

112 Philipos Sofos, OT, 22 August 1990.

113 Stamatis Athanasiadis, OT, 28 October 1990.

114 Kalliroi Dimitriadis, OT, 21 April 1992.

115 Kalliroi Dimitriadis, OT, 21 April 1992.

116 Mehmet Meerzam, OT, 3 August 1990.

117 Stamatis Athanasiadis, OT, 28 October 1990.

118 Of course, both regimes employed other strategies to nullify domestic opposition, particularly through the use of terror. Cf. Peukert, *Inside Nazi Germany*, ch. 11. For the effects of the 'atomisation' of German society and the withdrawal into private life, see ibid., ch. 13.

119 Herbert, op. cit, p. 102. See also Passerini's 'Work, Ideology and Working Class Attitudes to Fascism', in Paul Thompson and Natasha Burchardt (eds), *Our Common History: The Transformation of Europe* (New Jersey, 1982), p. 61.

120 Edward Banfield, *The Moral Basis of a Backward Society* (Glencoe, Illinois, 1958), p. 65.

121 The term 'la miseria' is a central theme of Banfield's dated classic, op. cit, pp. 63–7. A study of the plight of the peasantry of Kos is given in Zarakas, op. cit.

122 Carlo Levi, *Christ Stopped at Eboli* (London, 1963), p. 76.

123 Epaminondas Diamandaras, OT, 17 October 1990.

124 Lefteris of Leros, OT, 18 October 1990.

125 Cesare Vannutelli, 'The Living Standards of Italian Workers 1929–1939', in Roland Sarti (ed.), *The Ax Within: Italian Fascism in Action* (New York, 1974), p. 159.

126 Ioannis Petalas, OT, 10 October 1990.
127 See Ghirardo, op. cit, p. 98.
128 Agapitidis, 'Plithismiakés exelíxis sta Dodekánisa', p. 66.
129 Mehmet Meerzam, OT, 3 August 1990.
130 Ioannis Petalas, OT, 10 October 1990.
131 Stamatis Athanasiadis, OT, 28 October 1990.
132 Lefteris of Leros, OT, 18 November 1990.

ITALIAN COLONIALISM, ITALIAN CHARACTER

1 Nicholas Thomas, *Colonialism's Culture: Anthropology, Travel and Government* (Melbourne, 1994), p. 15.
2 A good discussion of the myth of Italians as 'brava gente' can be found in Mia Fuller, op. cit.
3 Steinberg, op. cit, p. 170.
4 Ibid., p. 180.
5 Sbacchi, op. cit, p. 170.
6 Robert L. Hess, *Italian Colonialism in Somalia* (Chicago, 1966), pp. 188–9.
7 Luigi Preti, 'Fascist Imperialism and Racism', in Roland Sarti (ed.), op. cit, p. 191.
8 Giorgio Rochat, *Il colonialismo italiano* (Turin, 1974), pp. 222–3.
9 Steinberg, op. cit, pp. 8–9.
10 Gerald Hanley, *Warriors and Strangers* (London, 1971), pp. 50 and 212–13. Hanley's impressions of Italian and British colonial rule are more extensively conveyed in his novel *The Consul at Sunset* (London, 1951).
11 James C. Scott, *Domination and the Arts of Resistance: Hidden Transcripts* (New Haven, Conn., 1990), pp. 12 and 45.
12 David Caute, *Fanon* (Fontana, 1970), p. 12. Cf. William Montgomery Watt, *Muslim–Christian Encounters: Perceptions and Misconceptions* (London, 1991), pp. 123–4.
13 Cf. Hanley, *The Consul at Sunset*, pp. 44–5.
14 Scott, op. cit, p. 11. Scott describes what the protagonists said among themselves 'off-stage' as the 'hidden transcript'.
15 Cf. Irma Taddia, 'Il Silenzio dei Colonizzati e il Lavoro dello Storico', pp. 511–12.
16 Cf. Sbacchi, op. cit, p. 169–70.
17 E.g. Sir Malcolm Darling, *Apprentice to Power: India 1904–1908* (London, 1966), p. 66.
18 Hanley, *The Consul at Sunset*, p. 44.
19 Paul Fussell, *Wartime: Understanding and Behaviour in the Second World War* (New York, 1989), p. 123. See also Mazower, *Inside Hitler's Greece*, p. 146.
20 Kostas Toutoulis, OT, 5 November 1990.
21 Ioannis Alahiotis, OT, 1 August 1990.
22 Anna of Simi, OT, 29 January 1992.
23 Sevasti Kortesi, OT, 22 August 1990.
24 Kalliope Harapas, OT, 3 August 1992.

25 *Diocese of Kos and Nisyros Archives*, Codex LA', n. 28
26 Anna of Simi, OT, 29 January 1992.
27 Loizos Loizou, OT, 10 August; 29 September 1990
28 Sophia Paskalis, OT, 6 September 1990.
29 For Aegean Island variations, see Bernard Vernier, 'Putting kin and kinship to good use: the circulation of goods, labour, and names on Karpathos (Greece)', in Hans Medick and David Warren Sabean (eds), *Interest and Emotion: Essays on the Study of Family and Kinship* (Cambridge, 1984), p. 69, n. 9.
30 Cf. Paul Sant Cassia with Constantina Bada, *The Making of the Modern Greek Family: Marriage and Exchange in Nineteenth Century Athens* (Cambridge, 1992), pp. 195–6.
31 Giorgos Kastrounis, OT, 25 October 1990; Anastásios M. Karanastavsis, *H zevgádes tis Ko – I zoí ke i asholíes tis* (Athens, 1952), p. 255.
32 Giorgos Kastrounis, OT, 25 October 1992.
33 Giorgos Sakellaridis, OT, 27 September 1992.
34 Stamatis Athansiadis, OT, 28 October 1990.
35 Ioannis Alahiotis, OT, 1 August 1990.
36 Kalliroi Dimitriadis, OT, 21 April 1992.
37 Mikhail Mihalandos, OT, 3 February 1992.
38 Michael Herzfeld, 'La Pratique des stéréotypes', *L'Homme*, 121 (1992), pp. 647–77.
39 Ioannis Alahiotis, OT, 1 August 1990.
40 Ibid.
41 Gabriel Kosaris, OT, 8 August 1990; Sophia Paskalis, OT, 6 September 1990.
42 Sbacchi, op. cit, p. 241.
43 Christoforos Fournaris, OT, 6 August 1990.
44 Archondoula Kanaris, OT, 19 September 1990.
45 E.g. Kalliroi Dimitriadis, OT, 21 April 1992; Stamatis Athansiadis, OT, 28 October 1990.
46 Pantelis Tripolitis, OT 3 November 1990. Despite these social prejudices, the Greek Orthodox population generally did not support German policy towards the Jews, and many actively assisted fugitive Jews. See Mazower, *Inside Hitler's Greece*, ch. 19, pp. 235–61. See also Steinberg, op. cit, p. 215.
47 Mikhail Mihalandos, OT, 3 February 1992.
48 Gabriel Kosaris, OT, 8 August 1990.
49 Basil Galettis, OT, 9 February 1990.
50 Basil Galettis, OT, 9 February 1990.
51 Gabriel Kosaris, OT, 8 August 1990.
52 Epaminondas Diamandaras, OT, 17 October 1990.
53 C.f. Euthymios Papataxiarchis, 'Friends of the Heart: Male Commensal Solidarity, Gender and Kinship in Modern Greece', in Peter Loizos and Euthymios Papataxiarchis (eds), *Contested Identities: Gender and Kinship in Modern Greece* (Princeton, New Jersey, 1991), p. 172. See also Herzfeld, *A Place in History*, p. 66.
54 Kalliroi Dimitriadis, OT, 21 April 1992.

55 E.g. Antonis Stergalas, OT, 4 August 1990; Pantelis Tripolitis, OT, 1 November 1992; Archondoula Kanaris, OT, 19 September 1990; Kalliope Harapas, OT, 3 August 1992.
56 Christoforos Fournaris, OT, 6 August 1990.
57 Giorgos Valsamis, OT, 17 October 1990.
58 *Mussolini's Roman Empire*, p. 119.
59 Kostas Toutoulis, OT, 5 November 1990.
60 E.g. Stamatis Athanasiadis, OT, 28 October 1990; Kostas Toutoulis, OT, 5 November 1990; Christoforos Fournaris, OT, 6 August 1990.
61 Giorgos Sakellaridis, OT, 27 September 1992.
62 <<Che ne sai, bimbo mio, di De Vecchi?>>, <<è un quadrupede [*sic*] delle grande Rivoluzione Fascista>>. Quoted in Karanastasis, *To ekpedeftikó próvlima tis Dodekanísou*, p. 14.
63 Stamatis Athanasiadis, OT, 28 October 1990
64 Giorgos Kastrounis, OT, 25 October 1990.
65 Ioannis Alahiotis, OT, 1 August 1990.
66 Giorgos Sakellaridis, OT, 27 September 1992.
67 Fussell, op. cit, pp. 121–3.
68 Marigo Katris, OT, 7 August 1990.
69 Kalliroi Dimitriadis, OT, 21 April 1992.
70 Giorgos Giorgalos, OT, 23 August 1990.
71 Paraskevi Angopian, OT, 28 July 1990; Archondoula Kanaris, OT, 19 September 1990.
72 E.g. Giorgos Giorgalos, OT, 23 August 1990; Kalliroi Dimitriadis, OT, 21 April 1992.
73 In demotic Greek, 'arádes' is an augmentative suffix.
74 Christoforos Fournaris, OT, 6 August 1990.
75 Mark Mazower has shown the extent to which Nazi racial ideology affected the Wehrmacht's behaviour in Greece. See his 'Military Violence and National Socialist Values: The *Wehrmacht* in Greece 1941–1944', *Past and Present*, 134 (1992), pp. 129–58; and *Inside Hitler's Greece*, chs 15–18. The fact that Greek Dodecanesians did not experience the mass violence and reprisals suffered on the Greek mainland and Crete was due to the absence of armed resistance activity. The Germans initially feared there were armed bands roaming the Rhodian interior (ibid., pp. 164–9), but no serious fighting ever took place during the German period.
76 Giorgos Kastrounis, OT, 25 October 1990.
77 Antonis Stergalas, OT, 4 September 1990. The belief that Germans were honourable because they respected local women was also recorded by Herzfeld. See 'The Horns of the Mediterraneanist Dilemma', p. 441.
78 Mazower, *Inside Hitler's Greece*, p. 146.
79 Sweets, op. cit., p. 192.
80 Sevasti Kortesi, OT, 22 August 1990.
81 This sentiment is noted in Herzfeld, *Anthropology Through the Looking-Glass*, p. 34.
82 Pantelis Tripolitis, OT, 1 November 1992.
83 Giorgos Kastrounis, OT, 25 October 1990.
84 Kalliroi Dimitriadis, OT, 21 April 1992.
85 Caute, op. cit, p. 20.

EPILOGUE: AFTER THE 'REDEMPTION'

1 Nikolaos Plastiras was a liberal anti-royalist who led the National Centre Progressive Union after the Civil War, and who advocated leniency towards the Communists. A useful short portrait is provided in Clogg's *A Concise History of Greece*, pp. 222–3.
2 Gabriel Kosaris, OT, 8 August 1990.
3 Kalliroi Dimitriadis, OT, 21 April 1992.
4 Roger E. Kasperson, *The Dodecanese: Unity and Diversity in Island Politics*, Department of Geography Research Paper No. 108 (Chicago, 1966), p. 82.
5 Agapitidis, 'Plithismiakés exelíxis sta Dodekánisa', p. 12.
6 Mehmet Meerzam, OT, 3 August 1990.
7 Charmian Clift, *Mermaid Singing* (Sydney, 1958), pp. 77–8.

Select Bibliography

Agapitidis, Sotiris, *I katástasi is tin Dodekánison* (Athens, 1945).
Agapitidis, Sotiris, 'Plithismiakés exelíxis sta Dodekánisa', *Dodekanisiaka Chronika*, IA' (1986), pp. 9–34.
Alhadeff, Vittorio, *L'ordinamento giuridico di Rodi e delle altri Isole Italiane dell'Egeo* (Milan, 1927).
Anderson, Benedict, *Imagined Communities: Reflections on the Origin and Spread of Nationalism*, 2nd edition (London, 1992).
Annuario dell'Africa Italiana ed Isole dell'Egeo (Rome, 1937–38).
Antoniadis, Antonis, 'I architektoniki ton Italón sta Dodekánisa', *O Dromos*, Vols 17–18, December (1983), pp. 20–30.
Apostolos Mitropolitou Karpathou-Kasou, *To Chronikón tis Italokratías tis Ródou* (Athens, 1973).
Armao, Ermanno, *Annuario Amministrativo e Statistico per l'Anno 1922* (Rome, 1922).
Augustinos, Gerasimos, *The Greeks in Asia Minor: Confession, Community and Ethnicity in the Nineteenth Century* (Kent, Ohio, 1992).
Bakiris, E.M., *Ródos: Ethnikó Zítima 1912–1945* (Rhodes, 1989).
Banfield, Edward, *The Moral Basis of a Backward Society* (Glencoe, Illinois, 1958).
Bertola, Arnaldo, 'L'ordinamento giuridico di Rodi', *L'Oltremare*, July, 5 (1931), pp. 282–6.
Betts, Raymond, *Uncertain Dimensions: Western Overseas Empires in the Twentieth Century* (Minneapolis, 1985).
Booth, C.D., and Booth, Isabelle Bridge, *Italy's Aegean Possessions* (London, 1928).
Borra, Edoardo, *Amadeo di Savoia, terzo duca d'Aosta e vicere d'Etiopia* (Milan, 1985).
Bosworth, Richard J.B., 'Britain and Italy's Acquisition of the Dodecanese, 1912–1915', *Historical Journal*, 13 (1970), pp. 683–705.
Bosworth, Richard J.B., *Italy and the Approach of the First World War* (London, 1983).
Bosworth, Richard J.B., *Explaining Auschwitz and Hiroshima: History Writing and the Second World War, 1945–1990* (London and New York, 1993).
Bosworth, Richard J.B., *Italy and the Wider World, 1860–1960* (London and New York, 1996).
Buti, Vittorio, 'La funzione di Rodi e delle Isole dell'Egeo', *Rassegna Italiana*, August–September (1934), pp. 207–14.
Buti, Vittorio, 'La legislazione sul lavoro nell'Egeo', *L'Oltremare*, December, 3 (1929), pp. 513–15.
Caradaci, Vittorio, *Legione Territoriale dei Carabinieri Reali di Bari*, 'Situazione del comune di Calino', 29 June 1935.
Casavis, J.N., *Rhodes and the Dodecanese* (London, 1920).
Casavis, J.N., *Rhodes: Capitale du Dodecanese* (Paris, 1920).
Casavis, J.N., *Italian Atrocities in the Grecian Dodecanese* (New York, 1936).

Cesari, Cesare, *Colonie e Possedimenti Coloniali* (Rome, 1930).

Clark, Martin, *Modern Italy, 1871–1995*, 2nd edn (London and New York, 1996).

Clift, Charmian, *Mermaid Singing* (Sydney, 1958).

Clogg, Richard, 'Elite and Popular Culture in Greece under Turkish Rule', in Koumoulides, John T.A. (ed.), *Hellenic Perspectives: Essays in the History of Greece* (London, 1980), pp. 107–43

Clogg, Richard, *A Concise History of Greece* (Cambridge, 1992).

Cobb, Richard, *French and Germans, Germans and French: A Personal Interpretation of France under Two Occupations, 1914–1918/1940–1944* (Hanover, Conn., 1983).

Collard, Anna, 'Investigating "Social Memory" in a Greek Context', in Tonkin, Elizabeth, McDonald, Maryon, and Chapman, Malcolm (eds), *History and Ethnicity* (London and New York, 1989), pp. 89–103.

Currier, Richard, 'Social Interaction and Social Structure in a Greek Island Village', in Dimen, Muriel, and Friedl, Ernestine (eds), *Regional Variation in Modern Greece and Cyprus: Toward a perspective on the ethnography of Greece*, Annals of the New York Academy of Sciences, 268 (1976), pp. 308–13.

Dainelli, Giotto, *Nell'Egeo* (Florence, 1923).

Davis, Natalie Zemon, and Starn, Randolph, 'Introduction' to 'Memory and Counter-memory', *Representations*, 26 Spring (1989), pp. 1–6.

De Grand, Alexander, *Italian Fascism: Its Origins and Development* (Lincoln, Nebraska, 1989).

Del Boca, Angelo, *Italiani in Africa orientale: la conquista dell'impero* (Bari, 1979).

Del Boca, Angelo, (ed.), *Le Guerre coloniale del fascismo* (Rome and Bari, 1991).

Dodecanese (London: Admiralty, Naval Intelligence Division, 1943) (Geographical Handbook Series).

I Dodekanisiakí (The Dodecanesian).

Dodekanisiakón Imerológion 1927 (Alexandria, 1927).

Doordan, Denis, *Building Modern Italy: Italian Architecture, 1914–1936* (New York, 1988).

Dubisch, Jill, 'The Ethnography of the Islands: Tinos', in Dimen, Muriel, and Friedl, Ernestine (eds), *Regional Variation in Modern Greece and Cyprus: Toward a perspective on the ethnography of Greece*, Annals of the New York Academy of Sciences, 268 (1976), pp. 328–40.

Etlin, Richard A., *Modernism in Italian Architecture, 1890–1940* (Cambridge, Mass., 1991).

Fentress, James, and Wickham, Chris, *Social Memory* (Oxford, 1992).

Fessopoulos, G.M., *Alítrotos Ellinismós: I Dodekánisos mas* (Athens, 1935).

Frangopoulos, Ippokratis, *I Dodekánisos ípo Italokratían* (Athens, 1958).

Frangopoulos, Ippokratis, *Istoría tis Kalymnou ápo tin archeótita mehri simera*, Vol. 2 (Athens, 1952).

Friedl, Ernestine, *Vasilika: A Village in Modern Greece* (New York, 1962).

Fuller, Mia, 'Colonizing Constructions: Italian Architecture, Urban Planning, and the Creation of Modern Society in the Colonies, 1869–1943', PhD thesis, University of California at Berkeley, 1994.

Gallant, Thomas, 'Peasant Ideology and Excommunication for Crime in a Colonial Context: The Ionian Islands (Greece), 1817–1864', *Journal of Social History*, 23 (1990), pp. 485–512.

Gandini, Tommaso, *I Carabinieri Reali nel Mediterraneo Orientale e Particolarmente nelle Isole Italiane dell'Egeo* (Rome, 1934).

Gayda, Virginio, 'L'economia del Dodecaneso', *L'Oltremare*, 2 April (1928), pp. 146–9.

Gellner, Ernest, *Nations and Nationalism* (Oxford, 1983).

Ghirardo, Diane, *Building New Communities: New Deal America and Fascist Italy* (Princeton, New Jersey, 1989).

Giannini, Amedeo, 'Le Isole Italiane Dell'Egeo (Acquisto, Natura Giuridica, Funzione)', *Oriente Moderno*, July (1932), pp. 313–25.

Goglia, Luigi, *Storia fotografica dell'impero fascista, 1935–1941* (Rome, 1985).

Gori, Fernando, *Egeo Fascista* (Rome, 1938).

Guérin, Victor, *Ile de Rhodes* (Paris, 1880), trans. by M. Papaioannou (Athens, 1989).

Hatzivasiliou, Vasilis, *Istoría tis Nísou Ko: Archéa, Meseonikíi, Neóteri* (Kos, 1990).

Herbert, Ulrich, 'Good Times, Bad Times: Memories of the Third Reich', in Bessel, Richard (ed.), *Life in the Third Reich* (Oxford, 1987).

Herzfeld, Michael, *Ours Once More: Folklore, Ideology, and the Making of Modern Greece* (Austin, Texas, 1982).

Herzfeld, Michael, 'The Horns of the Mediterraneanist Dilemma', *American Etinologist*, 11 (1984), pp. 439–54.

Herzfeld, Michael, *The Poetics of Manhood: Contest and Identity in a Cretan Mountain Village* (Princeton, New Jersey, 1991).

Herzfeld, Michael, *Anthropology Through the Looking-Glass: Critical Ethnography in the Margins of Europe* (Cambridge, 1987).

Herzfeld, Michael, *A Place in History: Social and Monumental Time in a Cretan Town* (Princeton, New Jersey, 1991).

Hess, Robert L., *Italian Colonialism in Somalia* (Chicago, 1966).

Hirschon, Renée, *Heirs of the Great Catastrophe: The Social Life of Asia Minor Refugees in Pireaus* (Oxford, 1989).

Hobsbawm, E.J., *Nations and Nationalism since 1780: Programme, Myth, Reality* (Cambridge, 1990).

Hoffman, Susannah, 'The Ethnography of the Islands: Thera', in Dimen, Muriel, and Friedl, Ernestine (eds), *Regional Variation in Modern Greece and Cyprus: Toward a perspective on the ethnography of Greece*, Annals of the New York Academy of Sciences, 268 (1976), pp. 314–27.

Hroch, Miroslav, *Social Preconditions of National Revival in Europe: A Comparative Analysis of the Social Composition of Patriotic Groups among the Smaller European Nations* (Cambridge, 1985).

Hroch, Miroslav, 'From National Movement to the Fully-formed Nation: the Nation-building process in Europe', *New Left Review*, 198 (1993), pp. 3–20.

Isihos, Manolis, *To panórama tis Lérou* (Leros, Greece, 1989).

L'Italia a Rodi, Istituto Poliografico dello Stato (Rome, 1944).

Just, Roger, 'Triumph of the Ethnos', in Tonkin, Elizabeth, McDonald, Maryon, and Chapman, Malcolm (eds), *History and Ethnicity* (London and New York, 1989), pp. 71–88.

Kapella, Themelina, 'O agónas ton gynaikón sto 1935 ke o petropólemos', *Kalymniaka Chronika,* T' (1986), pp. 87–102.

Kaplan, Temma, *Red City, Blue Period: Social Movements in Picasso's Barcelona* (Berkeley, California, 1992).

Karanastasis, Anastasis M., *I zevgádes tis Ko: I zoí ke i ascholíes ton* (Athens, 1952).

Karanastasis, Heracles, *To chronicó miás ikogénias* (Athens, 1977).

Karanastasis, Heracles, *To gió tis mamís* (Athens, 1978).

Karanastasis, Heracles, *I pedía stin Ko – Apo tin Tourkokratía os símera (1522–1979)* (Athens, 1979).

Karanastasis, Heracles, *Anamnísis ekpaideftikoú: chronikó* (Athens, 1982).

Karanikolas, Alexandros S., *To ekpaideftikón próvlima tis Dodekanísou* (Athens, 1945).

Karpathios, Emmanouil, *Ekklisía Ko Dodekanísou,* Vol. I (Athens, 1968).

Kasavis, Iakovos, *Ta Elliniká Dodekánisa* (New York, 1941).

Kasperson, Roger E., *The Dodecanese: Diversity and Unity in Island Politics,* Department of Geography Research Paper No. 108 (Chicago, 1966).

Kehagias-Nethonas, Nikolaos, *Dodekanisii anentachtoi* (Athens, 1985).

Kehagias-Nethonas, Nikolaos, *O Protosíngelos tis Rodou* (Athens and Ioannina, 1987).

Kipriotis, Fotis, *Dodekanisiakí ethnikí antístasi: Sta chrónia tis Italo-Germano-Agglokratías 1912–1948* (Rhodes, 1989).

Kitroeff, Alexander, 'Continuity and Change in Contemporary Greek Historiography', *European History Quarterly,* 19 (1989), pp. 269–98.

Kitto, H.D.F., *In the Mountains of Greece* (London, 1933).

Knox, MacGregor, *Mussolini Unleashed, 1939–1941: Politics and Strategy in Fascist Italy's Last War* (Cambridge, 1982).

Larebo, Haile, *The Building of an Empire: Italian Land Policy and Practice in Ethiopia, 1935–1941* (Oxford, 1994).

Lenzi, Alfredo, 'Lo sviluppo economico di Rodi', *La Rassegna Italiana,* May (1932), pp. 469–75.

Lenzi, Alfredo, 'Le frutta di Rodi', *Rassegna Economica delle Colonie,* May–June (1935), pp. 351–8.

Logothetis, Miltiadis, 'To empório stis Nóties Sporádes (Dodekánisa) kata ta teleftéa chrónia tis Tourkokratías', *Dodekanisiaka Chronika,* (1983), pp. 137–66.

Logothetis, Miltiadis, 'Pliroforíes gia tin ikonomía ke kinonía tis Dodekanísou sta téli tou 19ou eóna', *Dodekanisiaka Chronika,* IA' (1986), pp. 91–117.

Mack Smith, Denis, *Mussolini's Roman Empire* (London and New York, 1976).

Marongiu Buonaiuti, Cesare, *La politica religiosa del Fascismo nel Dodecanneso* (Naples, 1979).

Mazower, Mark, 'Military Violence and National Socialist Values: The *Wehrmacht* in Greece 1941–1944', *Past and Present,* 134 (1992), pp. 129–58.

Mazower, Mark, *Inside Hitler's Greece: The Experience of Occupation, 1941–1944* (New Haven, Conn., 1993).

McNeill, William H., *The Metamorphosis of Greece since World War II* (Chicago, 1978).

Il Messaggero di Rodi.

Miège, J-L., *L'imperialisme Colonial italien de 1870 à nos jours* (Paris, 1968).

Mihailidis-Nouarou, M., *Gia na gnorísoume ti Dodekániso* (Athens, 1946).

Mihailidis-Nouarou, M., *Istoría tis Nísou Karpáthou* (Athens, 1949).

Mihailidis-Nouarou, M., *Chronikón tis Nísou Karpáthou* (Pittsburgh, 1951).

Millas, Hercules, 'History Textbooks in Greece and Turkey', *History Workshop Journal*, 31 (1991), pp. 21–33.

Mondaini, Gennaro, *La Legislazione Coloniale Italiana nel suo sviluppo Storico e nel suo stato attuale (1881–1940)*, (Milan, 1941).

Mouzelis, Nicos, *Modern Greece: Facets of Underdevelopment* (London, 1978).

Nava, Santi, 'Una realtà dell'avvaloramento economico di Rodi', *Gerarchia* 1 (1933), pp. 33–7.

Negash, Tekeste, *Italian Colonialism in Eritrea, 1882–1941: Policies, Praxis and Impact* (Uppsala, 1978).

Ophuls, Marcel, *The Sorrow and the Pity: Chronicle of a French City under German Occupation* (St Albans, Herts, 1975).

Papachristodoulou, Christodoulos, *Istoría tis Ródou ápo tous proistorikoús chrónous éos tin ensomátosi tis Dodekanísou* (Athens, 1971).

Papamihail, Emmanuel T., *The (sic) Greece and the Greek Dodecanese* (Lisbon, 1943).

Papadakis, Yiannis, 'The Politics of Memory and Forgetting in Cyprus', *Journal of Mediterranean Studies*, 3 (1993), pp. 139–54.

Papataxiarchis, Euthymios, 'Friends of the Heart: Male Commensal Solidarity, Gender and Kinship in Modern Greece', in Loizos, Peter, and Papataxiarchis, Euthymios (eds), *Contested Identities: Gender and Kinship in Modern Greece* (Princeton, New Jersey, 1991), pp. 156–79.

Pappas, Nicholas G., *Castellorizo: An Illustrated History of the Island and its Conquerors* (Sydney, 1994).

Passerini, Luisa, 'Work, Ideology and Working Class Attitudes to Fascism', in Thompson, Paul, and Burchardt, Natasha (eds), *Our Common History: The Transformation of Europe* (New Jersey, 1982), pp. 54–77.

Passerini, Luisa, 'Oral Memory of Fascism', in Forgacs, David (ed.), *Rethinking Italian Fascism: Capitalism, Populism and Culture* (London, 1986), pp. 185–96.

Passerini, Luisa, *Fascism in Popular Memory: The Cultural Experience of the Turin Working Class* (Cambridge, 1987).

Peristiany, John, 'Introduction to a Cypriot Mountain Village', Peristiany, John (ed.), *Contributions to Mediterranean Sociology: Mediterranean Rural Communities and Social Change* (Athens, 1968), pp. 76–90.

Peukert, Detlev J.P., *Inside Nazi Germany: Conformity, Opposition and Racism in Everyday Life* (Harmondsworth, 1987).

Portelli, Alessandro, 'The Peculiarities of Oral History', *History Workshop Journal*, 12 (1981), pp. 96–107.

Preti, Luigi, 'Fascist Imperialism and Racism', in Sarti, Roland (ed.), *The Ax Within: Italian Fascism in Action* (New York, 1974), pp. 187–207.

Randolph, B., *The Present State of the Islands in the Archipelago (or Arches) Sea, of Constantinople, and the Gulf of Smyrna; With the Islands of Candia and Rhodes* (Oxford, 1687)

Rassegna Economica Delle Colonie, Vols 5–6 (May–June 1935) and Vols 7–8 (July–August 1935).

Rochat, Giorgio, *Il colonialismo italiano* (Turin, 1974).

Rodi: Guida del Turistica (Milan and Rome, 1928).

Roletto, Giorgio, *Rodi. La Funzione Imperiale nel Mediterraneo Orientale* (Milan, 1939).

Rousso, Henry, *The Vichy Syndrome: History and Memory in France since 1944* (Cambridge, Mass., 1991).

Rusinow, D.I., *Italy's Austrian Heritage, 1919–1946* (Oxford, 1969).

Russell Bernard, H., 'Kalymnos: The Island of the Sponge Fishermen', in Dimen, Muriel, and Friedl, Ernestine (eds), *Regional Variation in Modern Greece and Cyprus: Toward a perspective on the ethnography of Greece*, Annals of the New York Academy of Sciences, 268 (1976), pp. 291–307.

Sbacchi, Alberto, *Ethiopia under Mussolini: Fascism and the Colonial Experience* (London, 1985).

Sakellaridis, G.M., 'Autodiíkisi sta chrónia tis Sklaviás', *Kalymniaka Chroniká*, E' (1986), pp. 301–14.

Sakellaridis, G.M., 'Antonio Ritelli,' *Kalymniaka Chronika*,   T' (1986), pp. 151–69.

Sakellaridis, Kostas A., 'Apo tin Istoría tis Demogerontías Nisyrou méchri ta próta chrónia tis Italikín katohís', B. 'O Démarchos Geórgios Kammás (Períodos 1916–1920)', *Nisyriaka*, Vol. 10 (1987), pp. 300–25.

Sakellarios, Giorgos S., *I Ethniko-Thriskeftikí Antístasis tis Kalymnou to étos 1935* (Athens, 1977).

Samarkos, Mihail I., *Léros, I Málta tou Egéou (Chronikó 1912–1948)* (Athens, 1974).

Scott, James C., *Domination and the Arts of Resistance: Hidden Transcripts* (New Haven, Conn., 1990).

Segrè, Claudio, *Fourth Shore: The Italian Colonization of Libya* (Chicago, 1974).

Sertoli Salis, R., *Le isole italiane dell'Egeo dall'occupazione alla sovranità* (Rome, 1939).

Stefanini, Guiseppe, and Desio, Arditio, *Le Colonie, Rodi e le Isole Italiane dell'Egeo* (Turin, 1928).

Steinberg, Jonathan, *All or Nothing: The Axis and the Holocaust, 1941–43* (London, 1990).

Stephanopoli, Z., *Les îles de l'Egée* (Paris, 1913).

Sutton, David, 'The Uses of the Past on a Greek Island', PhD thesis, University of Chicago, 1994.

Sweets, John F., *Choices in Vichy France: The French Under Nazi Occupation* (New York, 1986).

Tackett, Timothy, 'Women and Men in Counterrevolution: The Sommières Riot of 1791', *Journal of Modern History* 59 (December, 1987), pp. 680–704.

Taddia, Irma, 'Il Silenzio dei Colonizzati e il Lavoro dello Storico: Oralità e Scittura nell'Africa Italiana', in Del Boca, Angelo (ed.), *Le Guerre coloniali del fascismo* (Rome and Bari, 1991), pp. 501–18.

Travis, William, *Bus Stop Symi* (Newton Abbot, Devon, 1970).

Tsalahouris, K., 'To Kastellórizo stis paramonés tis epanastáseos tis 1is Martíou 1913', *Dodekanisiaka Chronika*, IA' (1986), pp. 187–214.

Vardamidis, Evaggelos N., *Istoría tis Nísou Megístis (Kastellorízou)* (Alexandria, Egypt, 1948).

Vernier, Bernard, 'Putting kin and kinship to good use: the circulation of goods, labour, and names on Karpathos (Greece)', in Medick, Hans, and Sabean, David Warren (eds), *Interest and Emotion: Essays on the Study of Family and Kinship* (Cambridge, 1984), pp. 28–76.

Yapp, M.E., *The Making of the Modern Near East, 1792–1923* (London, 1987).

Zarakas, Nikolaos, *Istoría ton Iesperídon tis Ko ton chrónon tis Doulías* (Athens, 1983).

Zervos, Skevos, *Ikonografómeni i Dodekánisos* (Athens, 1930).

Zervos, Skevos, *The Dodecanese (White Book) – Resolutions and Documents concerning the Dodecanese* (London, 1919?).

Zervos, Skevos, *La Question du Dodecanese et ses Documents Diplomatiques* (Athens, 1926).

Zirounis, Giannis, *Katafroneméni iríni* (Athens, 197?).

Index

Africa, 5–6, 42, 45, 125–6, 136, 159, 164, 165
Africans in Dodecanese, 27–8
Agapitidis, Sotiris, 152
Alexandria, 19, 38, 102
Ameglio, Giovanni, 31, 36, 42
Anatolia, Asia Minor, 14–15, 18, 19, 23, 25, 31, 32, 37, 40, 46, 58, 106, 157
Aosta, Duke Amadeo of, 126–7, 222
Apostolos Kavakopoulos, Bishop of Kalymnos, Leros and Astypalea, 54, 68–9, 72
Apostolos Trifonos, Bishop of Rhodes, 39, 40, 53, 54, 108
archaeology, 36–7, 50–1, 138–9
architecture, 150–4, 226
Arendt, Hannah, 164, 176
Argai, Abebe, 127
assimilation, see Italian socialisation programmes
Astypalea, 15, 19, 29, 31, 45, 191
Athens, 38–9, 94, 102, 104, 112, 150, 157, 173
attendismo, 61, 109, 119–24
Australia, 9, 10, 37, 201

Badoglio, Pietro, 57
Balbo, Italo, 48–9, 126, 127
Balilla, 56, 108, 114
Banfield, Edward, 157, 226
bella figura, see Italian occupation
Bertola, Arnaldo, 53
Betts, Raymond, 48–9
Bloody Easter, Paradisi, Rhodes (1919), 39–40, 104
Booths, Isabelle and C.D., 42, 45, 135
Bosworth, Richard, 34, 41, 212
Bordeaux, 18
Braudel, Fernand, 16–17
Britain, 44, 45, 57, 166–8, 194–6

administration in the Dodecanese (1945–47) 42–9, 59, 128, 129
in international diplomacy, 34–6, 39–41
perceptions of British colonisers, 5, 126, 164, 165, 190, 194–6, 227

Cairo, 19
Canada, 200
Casavis, Iakovos, 102–3, 220
Chanak Crisis (1922), 40
Chios, 16
Churchill, Winston, 57, 215
Clemenceau, Georges, 40, 106
Clift, Charmian, 201
collaboration, see *attendismo*
collective memory, see memory
Colonels, Greek military junta (1967–74), 132, 187, 199, 200, 223
civic order, 44, 128–39, 141–4
local government, 25–6, 28–32, 63–5, 67, 82–3, 104–6, 112–13, 209, 223
benefaction, 22, 24, 95, 208
Constantinople (Istanbul), 19, 20, 24, 26, 221
Patriarch(-ate), 52–4, 60, 67, 72, 90, 109
Crete, 16, 20, 27, 106, 139, 198
Curzon, George Nathaniel, 41
Cyclades, 15, 18
Cyprus, 16, 42, 53, 194

Davis, Natalie Zemon, 134
Del Boca, Angelo, 5, 143–4, 165
De Vecchi, Cesare Maria, 43, 45, 51, 55–7, 62, 107–8, 119, 125, 126, 127, 175, 186–90
governorship, 80, 82, 84–9, 99
demarchia, see civic order
disemia, 38, 62, 123, 145, 149, 171–3

238